DANGEROUS ODDS

DANGEROUS ODDS

MARISA LANKESTER

Cappuccino Books

Library of Congress Control Number: 2014931839

ISBN 978-3-906196-00-8 (Hardcover)
ISBN 978-3-906196-01-5 (eBook)

Published by Cappuccino Books
Cappuccino Books by Viganò GmbH
Stansstaderstrasse 90, CH 6370 Stans, Switzerland
www.cappuccinobooks.com

Distributed by Midpoint Trade Books
www.midpointtrade.com
orders@midpointtrade.com

Interior design by Neuwirth and Associates, Inc.
Cover design by Daniel Donati, ZurichTokio
Cover images: Getty Images, iStockphoto, Adriano Viganò

Printed in the United States of America

10 9 8 7 6 5 4 3 2 1

DISCLAIMER BY THE AUTHOR

I have recreated the events depicted in my memoir from my memories, journals, photos, and extensive research. I have changed the names of certain individuals and places. Some identifying characteristics and details have been fictionalized.

ACKNOWLEDGMENTS

In September of 2007, Nicola Maffei offered me a no-strings-attached grant so I could write my memoir. This allowed me to take a leave of absence from the minimum-wage, manual-labor job at the factory where I was employed to start work on *Dangerous Odds*. I am profoundly grateful for his encouragement, support, friendship, and unshakable conviction that one day my story would be published.

A massive thanks to my daughter Justine, for reading every draft I cranked out, and to my family—especially my siblings, Peter, Heather, and Kathryn—for their encouragement.

In Zurich, a special thank-you to Lori Gadola, who was a second mother to my daughters while I was writing; Sylvie Domeniconi for bringing me coffee creamer from all over the world so that the thousands of cups I consumed working at my desk were all divine; Michele Donath for sharing the last year of madness with me; and Lotti Gut for her enthusiastic reaction to the almost-final draft, which made the last few weeks working on the manuscript a pleasure.

In London, many thanks to Neil Blair and Rebecca Cripps. In the States, I would like to thank Tony O'Neil for giving the manuscript a kick; John Paine for editing *Dangerous Odds;* and Maryann Palumbo for her faith in the project she so aptly named.

Lastly, I would like to offer my deepest gratitude to Adriano for being the backbone behind this project, for putting up with my nonsense, for our past and future adventures, and for making me believe in happily ever after.

For my daughters Justine and Jennifer

PROLOGUE

Santo Domingo, January 8, 1992

WHEN I LOOKED BACK later, I realized that the soldier pointing his gun at my head terrified me less than his confiscating my passport. Now I had no way to get off the island. *I should have left my passport at home,* I told myself. *I shouldn't have gone to work early.* I had plenty of time to indulge in pointless recriminations as I sat locked away in a filthy, rat-infested Dominican prison. In this concrete fortress, the heat was so oppressive that even the walls around me were sweating.

■

THE MORNING HAD BEGUN like any other in the city of Santo Domingo.

A furious chorus of car horns split the heavy tropical air, alerting me to the blackout even before I hit the massive traffic jam. Blackouts were a feature of everyday life on the island, a product of an unstable government presided over by the blind octogenarian president, Joaquín Balaguer. Poverty, widespread corruption, political "disappearances," and power outages were hallmarks of the era. An unlit traffic light dangled uselessly over the jammed intersection. It was too late to avoid the snarled traffic. Instead I shifted down into first gear, waiting my turn behind the other vehicles on Avenida Tiradentes.

Santo Domingo was a city of intoxicating contrasts—a place where extreme poverty rubbed shoulders with unimaginable wealth. I loved it from the moment I arrived, almost five years ago; though that was not the experience of countless other American expats, drawn by the lure of easy money, endless beaches, and tropical weather. It took a certain type of personality—stubborn, resilient, determined—to flourish in the terrible beauty of Santo Domingo.

As I sat marooned in a sea of chrome, a thud on my windshield shook me out of my thoughts. An old man with a mouthful of rotten teeth tipped a large cardboard crate toward me and gestured to the half-dozen newborn puppies within. I shook my head. He trudged away to try his luck with the drivers behind me.

Ahead, nothing was moving. On most days I would have started to panic. In my line of business, getting to work late was not an option. The first time you were warned; the second time you were fired. Today, however, I had plenty of time. I cranked up the air conditioner and the radio, trying to drown out the incessant honking.

Twenty minutes later I reached the quiet, tree-lined street where our villa was located. All the homes on Salvador Sturla had a neat, uniform look to them: surrounded on three sides by towering walls, with heavy wrought-iron gates protecting the entrance. Our villa also had a gardener tending the lawn, and an armed guard patrolling the premises. The only difference between our villa and the others in this residential neighborhood was that nobody actually lived here.

I parked my little blue Daihatsu next to Roger's red Cherokee, locked up, and slid the keys into my jeans. The guard opened the gate and I made my way toward the back of the house. From inside the open side door I heard the crackle of a transistor radio.

Peering into the kitchen, I saw Remo bent over the counter, peeling a mountain of potatoes. I snuck up and grabbed him around the waist. He dropped his knife and spun around, his gray eyes darting between me and the clock mounted on the wall. "I don't believe it!" he cried. "You're *early!*"

I stepped into what used to be the villa's formal dining room. Now it was known as the Big Office. Carmine was hunched over his desk, a garish Hawaiian shirt hanging off his bony frame. His eyes, magnified to owl-like proportions by his thick glasses, widened comically when he saw me. Before he could say anything, a fit of coughing erupted from the next room. I peered in. Roger was studying the racing form with a furrowed brow, alternately sucking on a Marlboro and gulping coffee.

The office ran on a strict schedule. Both men were busy preparing for the frantic day ahead. In twenty minutes the company van would arrive, dropping off the first group of clerks. A second group would arrive shortly afterward. By one o'clock, the phones would be ringing off the hook as we scrambled to record thousands of bets from all across the United States.

I sat at my desk. Roger had another coughing fit in the next room. "Time to quit, Roger!" I called.

Roger managed the Small Office, where bets on a single game were limited to a mere $2,000. I clerked for Carmine in the Big Office. We took wagers from the professional gamblers, customers we referred to as "wise guys" or "smart money." The kind of men whose daily bets could total $100,000.

I was addicted to the adrenaline rush that came with working there. At the moment, though, there was nothing to do. The phones were silent; the cubicles that lined the room were empty.

Suddenly, the stillness was shattered by loud shouts from outside. I looked out of the window and my heart tightened into a fist. Waves of heavily armed soldiers were swarming over the outer wall. A troop of machine-gun-toting men in combat fatigues rushed across the driveway. Our guard dropped his weapon and was brutally wrestled to the ground.

"What the hell's going on?" Carmine gasped as we peered out of the window. More and more soldiers were pouring over the wall. The sound of their heavy leather boots pounding against the concrete grew louder and louder. Roger came running over in alarm.

It's a coup, I thought. *It must be a revolution!* The country had been simmering with discontent for a long time. It wouldn't have been the first politically unstable country in this region to descend into martial law.

No other explanation made sense. I reached for the nearest phone and stabbed the numbers to Tony's cell. He would know what to do.

Pick up. Pick up.

With shouts and crashes the soldiers charged into the house from several different directions. I heard glass shattering, then crunching under heavy boots. They stormed into the room, weapons drawn, screaming at us in Spanish to put our hands up. Amidst the commotion I heard Tony answering his phone. Someone yelled, *"Drop the phone!"*

"Don't come in!" I blurted out. The blood rushing in my ears drowned out every other sound. I watched, frozen, as Carmine and Roger, both in their sixties, were roughly pushed up against the wall.

"Put the phone down! NOW!" A young soldier was advancing on me.

I stared at him but held tightly onto the receiver. Tony needed to hear what was going on. The soldier raised his hand to strike me. I flinched. When he came close, he stopped and took a step back. Even though I was wearing a baseball cap and a shapeless, baggy T-shirt, he recognized me instantly. To him I was the Constanza girl, the glamorous blonde model who lounged seductively on a boat strewn with pillows. The cigarette commercial ran constantly on the local channels.

The terrace doors crashed open and our lawyer, Gustavo Flores, was unceremoniously shoved inside. I'd never had much confidence in Gustavo's abilities as a lawyer. Right now, however, his flushed, jowly face was a welcome sight. He was always boasting about his powerful connections. Surely he would put a stop to this madness.

Gustavo flailed around comically before recovering his balance. He straightened up, and mustering whatever dignity he could, pulled his shirt back down over his potbelly. His eyes blazed with indignation and he addressed the soldiers in a booming voice: *"Soy Gustavo Medina Flores. Abogado!"*

All eyes swiveled toward the lawyer, and the room fell silent. Then a soldier viciously drove the butt of his rifle into Gustavo's belly, sending him crumpling to the floor.

Click.

I looked away from Gustavo and found myself staring down the barrel of a gun. The young soldier who had been gawping at me in surprise had regained his fierceness.

In a low, dangerous voice he said, *"Put . . . the . . . phone . . . down."*

I let the receiver slide out of my hand to the floor, hoping that Tony had heard enough.

Gustavo was dragged to a corner of the room. I was shoved to the opposite side, next to Carmine and Roger. One of the soldiers emptied a large burlap sack full of handcuffs onto Carmine's desk. We were ordered to face the wall, and our wrists were tightly cuffed behind our backs.

I closed my eyes and tried to fight the panic rising inside me. This was nothing more than a shakedown, I told myself, a misguided attempt by local police to get a cut of our lucrative gambling enterprise. Money would be exchanged, a bribe schedule made, and the affair would be smoothed over. Corruption was a fact of life on the island, after all. Still, one aspect of the operation didn't make sense. Why use an entire platoon of soldiers for a simple shakedown?

From somewhere behind me I heard Remo protesting his innocence. "I'm just a cook," he insisted, in fluent Spanish. Remo had a sweetness to his disposition that was unusual among the expat crowd. Santo Domingo was a frontier town in those days, and it attracted a fair number of people with shady pasts. Tony had worked hard to convince the good-natured young American to open the on-site cafeteria for us, and against his better instincts he'd agreed. Now he too was caught up in this insanity.

"He really *is* just the cook," I said.

Nobody reacted to my comment. Remo's breathing was erratic, and his face was ghostly white. His shirt was soaked through with sweat.

"Don't worry," I whispered, meeting his eye. Remo and I had been in the Dominican Republic long enough to know how the system worked. So long as Tony remained free and had access to money, we had nothing to worry about. I imagined him pushing his Jeep to the limit as he raced to intercept the company van.

The commanding officer barked into his radio that the house had been secured. We heard the distinctive tap of street shoes on the marble floor, and four men in dark suits appeared. The look on Remo's face told me all I needed to know. "Secret police," he whispered as the group headed straight for Tony's office, presumably looking for the safe.

Suddenly, a harsh white light illuminated us. We were being videotaped. Remo hunched over, trying to shield his face from the camera. I followed his lead. Soon the cameraman wandered off to film the rest of the house.

The phones started to ring. Within minutes, all thirty-seven phones installed throughout the house were ringing in unison as our customers tried to place their first bets of the day.

In our line of business an unanswered phone meant only one thing—a police raid. In another twenty minutes, rumors would spread like wildfire among the millions of Americans who gambled illegally on sports: Ron Sacco, the undisputed king of bookmakers and the man who had pioneered offshore gambling, had been busted.

"Silence the phones!"

The commander's men jumped into action, frenziedly ripping lines out of the walls. When they were done, the room settled into the same tense silence as before. The commander stalked from cubicle to cubicle, examining each desk in turn. His face was filled with barely concealed fury. He picked up a Don Best Sports booklet from one desk and glanced at it. "A *banca*," he snarled, flinging the pamphlet, pages fluttering, across the room. "This is nothing more than a *banca!*"

Bancas—or betting shops—were a big business in the Dominican Republic, as gambling was legal. Our company, Information Unlimited, was a legitimate corporation. The commander's fury actually made me calmer. This wasn't a shakedown, just a horrible mistake. The commander barked into his radio: *"Bring them in!"*

I heard more people entering the office. They were wearing sneakers. I heard them squeak across the floor toward us.

"Good afternoon, gentlemen," a distinctly American voice said from somewhere behind me.

"Agent Jack Peterson," I heard Roger whisper. "Fancy seeing *you* here."

"Jesus Christ!" Carmine groaned, shattering my fragile optimism. *Agent* Jack Peterson. This raid had clearly been orchestrated by the FBI. But how? They had no jurisdiction on the island.

"Guess you showed up a little early," Roger chuckled.

"Laugh it up, Bianchi," Peterson snarled. "I'm going to wipe that smile right off your fucking face."

It dawned on me that Agent Peterson had failed to take into account that Dominicans do not observe daylight savings time. Had the raid taken place an hour later, they would have caught the entire staff of Information Unlimited busily attending their phones.

"Who's Peterson?" I whispered to Roger.

"Had some dealings with him in the Bay Area, a few years ago."

A soldier barked at us to shut up. Roger dropped his voice further. "Don't recognize the others."

"For crissakes, shut up!" Remo whispered. "You're going to get us shot!"

No sooner had he said it than a young soldier drove the butt of his rifle into Remo's kidney, causing his knees to buckle. The three of us stood in shock, listening to Remo's agonized whimpers. The only sliver of hope I had then was that the clerks had not shown up. That meant Tony had intercepted them.

Once it became clear that no one else was coming into work, we were roughly marched outside under heavy guard. A crowd had gathered to watch the arrest unfold—a woman, two elderly men, and a cook being escorted away by a platoon of soldiers. They gathered across the street, behind bright-yellow tape bearing the legend POLICE LINE—DO NOT CROSS in English. The FBI had obviously been planning this raid for a while. They'd even brought their own crime-scene tape.

As Roger, Carmine, Remo, and I were shoved into an unmarked gray van, I cursed my bad luck. On the only day I had ever shown up to work early, the FBI raided our office. On any other day, I would still have been at home with my daughter. On any other day, my passport would be in the safe at home and not in my purse, which had been confiscated during the raid.

The four of us clambered into the scorching-hot van. "Where's Gustavo?" Carmine whispered.

Where was our lawyer? I wondered. I turned to look out of the back, but my view was blocked by the armed soldiers who climbed in after us. The doors slammed shut and our grim party roared away, sirens blaring. I closed my eyes tightly and thought about Tony. Surely by now he had alerted our lawyers stateside. All of my hopes were pinned on Tony. He would find a way to get us out of this mess.

1

East Los Angeles, October, 1986

"NO. NO FUCKING WAY!"

Tony was standing in the doorway of the warehouse, physically blocking us from getting through. It appeared that my career in the exciting world of illegal gambling was over before it had even begun. I'd left Vancouver for Los Angeles with the promise of accommodation and off-the-books pay; all I was supposed to do in return was answer phones for a few hours a day. My friend Jim had assured me it was a done deal. Apparently the boss of the operation hadn't gotten the memo.

"Forget it, Jim."

Tony was a tall, muscular man in his late twenties, olive-skinned—Italian, I guessed. Dressed in a faded T-shirt, leather jacket, and jeans, he didn't match the image I had in mind when Jim said I would be meeting "the boss."

"This is bullshit, Tony! You agreed to hire my friend!"

"I agreed to hire someone called 'RB.' What you neglected to mention, *Jim*, is that RB is a *girl!* I'm not taking responsibility for a girl. No girlfriends—no way, forget it."

Tony started to close the door, but I managed to wedge my foot inside. He looked at me as if he couldn't believe I'd have the audacity to contradict him. "I am not Jim's girlfriend!" I said.

I was offended by Tony's insinuation. While Jim was handsome in a grizzled, weather-beaten kind of way, he was in his late fifties, while I was just twenty-three. Jim was my racing partner in an upcoming endurance car rally. Our relationship was strictly professional.

Tony looked mildly amused by my outburst, but I pressed on. "I just drove all the way down from Vancouver to work here!"

Tony said nothing. He continued to stare at me in that self-satisfied, cocky way. It was infuriating.

"You know—Vancouver, Canada? As in, twenty-six hours away by car?"

His dark eyes seemed to be mocking me. I realized he wasn't going to budge. I gave him the dirtiest look I could muster and stomped away, heading back across the empty parking lot. I leaned against Jim's blue Mercedes and waited for him. As far as I was concerned, this Tony character could take his job and shove it.

Jim had invited me to co-drive in the upcoming Alcan 5000, a ten-day endurance and navigation competition. The 4,700-mile race was the longest held in North America, and I jumped at the opportunity. Jim was sponsoring the car; all I had to do was move to L.A. to train with him, and find a way to cover my expenses.

Jim financed his racing by rigging the phone lines for several L.A.-based bookmaking operations. He figured he could get me a job with Tony's outfit. Though I'd initially balked at the idea of working for an illegal gambling ring, Jim reassured me: "The police are paid to look the other way, so there's no danger of getting busted."

I watched the two men as they argued in the midday California sun. Tony had taken off his leather jacket, revealing strong arms and a lean torso. I squinted, trying to make out the image on his shirt. To my irritation it was of a nubile young woman in a bikini with the legend, "Dive a Virgin."

What a *jerk*.

The sound of the freeway drowned out their words, but their angry gestures told the story. I glanced around. The streets were deserted, apart from a hobo stumbling around. Gang graffiti covered the cracked concrete walls. The smell of fermenting garbage hung in the muggy air, and the ground was strewn with trash. At the far end of the block was a fortress of a liquor store, guarded by metal shutters and barbed wire.

I fidgeted with the strap of my purse. Did I really want to work for some male-chauvinist pig in a derelict building on the wrong side of town?

"RB!" Jim beckoned me over. I slid off the car and walked over to the two men. "Tony says you can work here for a couple of days. It'll give me time to find you something else. That cool with you?"

I nodded, giving Jim a faint smile. "Thanks."

"Don't thank me—thank Tony. I'll be back at five to pick you up."

Tony muttered something under his breath. Without another word he led me into the decrepit building. He slammed the door shut behind us and ratcheted several heavy bolts into place. I followed him down a dimly lit corridor into a room that smelled like a wet dog.

The mud-brown carpet was stained and worn through in places. The three small windows were all nailed shut with sheets of plywood. A row of neon tubes bathed the bare room in a harsh, unpleasant light. A workout bench occupied the middle of the room, some weights scattered around it. Straight ahead was an industrial-sized door, with glass panels offering a view of the depressing abandoned warehouse beyond. "Great," I mumbled.

Tony led me into a small, windowless room. It was thick with cigarette smoke and jammed full of office desks. A TV bolted to the wall was showing *The Young and the Restless*. The three men huddled inside, dressed in sweatshirts and jeans, were all in their late twenties or early thirties. They looked up as Tony led me in. I smiled awkwardly. The guy closest to me was an enormously overweight bear of a man, with shoulder-length blond hair and a shaggy beard. He smiled shyly at me.

Skipping the formalities, Tony pointed at an unoccupied desk in the far corner of the room and grunted, "Sit there." Tony took his seat at the desk nearest the door.

I silently sat down and found myself facing a blank wall. The silence was uncomfortable. I glanced over my shoulder and made eye contact with a man sitting at a desk nearby. He was tall and muscular, clean-shaven, with thick, wavy brown hair and pale blue eyes. He had a cigarette clamped between his lips. He got up and ambled over.

"You can call me Kyle," he said, offering his hand. He had a soft, deep voice with a thick Southern accent.

"How about she just calls you Dickhead like everyone else?" Tony's comment earned a few guffaws from the others.

I smiled and shook Kyle's hand. "I'm RB." Jim had advised me not to use my real name. RB—short for "Rally Babe"—was a name I'd acquired on the racing circuit.

Kyle headed back to his desk, and I turned my attention to the papers and booklets scattered in front of me. They were all sports-related, containing schedule listings for the upcoming college and pro football games. The desk itself was filthy: old coffee rings, crumbs, and cigarette ashes littered the surface.

Tony unfolded a copy of the *L.A. Times* and put his feet up on the desk. Jim had said Tony desperately needed someone to replace an employee who'd left the week before, but I couldn't understand why. As far as I could see, there was no *work* going on. The guys were engrossed in the soap opera, with the exception of the big shaggy guy, who appeared to be taking a nap. I glanced at my watch. In three hours I planned to walk out of this dump and never return.

"Jesus H. Christ!" someone yelled from behind me. A tall, lanky man emerged from the bathroom, a magazine tucked under his arm, zipping up his fly. "I think that Puerto Rican chick I banged last week gave me the clap," he announced. "Every time I take a piss, it feels like my nuts are on *fire*—"

He stopped short when he noticed me. Suddenly his whole demeanor changed. He ran his fingers through his hair and sauntered over. "Hey, sweet thing," he said, reaching out his hand. "The name's Danny." He shot me a dazzling smile. I could make out that the magazine under his arm was *Juggs*.

"RB," I said. I avoided taking his hand.

"Danny, leave her alone," Tony said from across the room. "She's not staying."

"We've never had a girl working here before," Kyle said. *No kidding*, I thought.

"She's not working here. She's just . . . helping out for a couple of days. Until Jim finds her a job," Tony said.

"Yeah," I said, looking around the sleepy office. "This line of work is obviously way too dangerous for a girl."

If only they knew, I thought. I had recently completed a twenty-one-day, twenty-three-thousand-kilometer endurance rally from Canada to Mexico and back up to Alaska. Along the way I had outraced a hurricane, changed countless tires, replaced shock absorbers and a right rear axle, and been robbed at gunpoint by Federales. I'd driven below sea level in Death Valley and up over twelve thousand feet in the heights of Colorado. I'd raced over everything from sand to snow, and I'd managed it all on an average of six hours' rest a day, much of which was spent maintaining the car.

I looked around this shabby room and at the oddball collection of men who populated it. I was tougher than any of these jokers knew, and more than capable of answering some silly phones.

"Sweetheart," Tony said, without taking his eyes off the newspaper, "in case you hadn't heard, what we do here is illegal. You could get arrested. Go to jail, even."

"Jim told me that the cops are on your payroll," I retorted.

Tony slammed the paper down. "Jim talks too much. Your boyfriend installs phones," he informed me. "He's got no idea what goes down here."

"He's not my boyfriend!"

"We *are* still paying off the cops, aren't we?" Kyle said. He sounded confused. "Because if we're not, I quit, T-bone."

This elicited a few laughs from the others. I resumed staring at the stained beige wall in front of me. Had I really quit my job and left my home, friends, and family to hang out in a filthy warehouse in East L.A. with this bunch of losers? I shuddered to think what my parents would say to see me sitting here.

It was bad enough that I'd disappointed them when I'd dropped out of college. Had my life gone as planned, I would have been studying at the Cooper Union School of Art in New York. But my portfolio disappeared shortly before my interview there. The body of work that I had poured my heart and soul into for the better part of a year had vanished—and with it my chances of being accepted at the prestigious art school. My parents were in the midst of a bitter divorce then, which brought out the worst in my mother and made life at home unbearable. I took refuge in the basement, where I could forget my mother's hysteria and threats of suicide and get lost in creating something beautiful instead. Studying at Cooper Union was all I had to look forward to, and my portfolio was my ticket there. Losing it devastated me.

My passion to draw evaporated. My art teacher, who had once lavished praise on me, gave me a failing grade instead. Desperate to escape the deteriorating environment at home, I applied to the University of British Columbia and moved to Vancouver when I was accepted. But the change of scenery did not inspire me to start drawing again. Adrift, I dropped out. I went to work full-time for a car-rental company that operated out of Vancouver Airport. It was a difficult, demoralizing time for me. For years I defined myself as an artist; now I had no idea who I was anymore.

That changed when I met a security officer at the airport. At first I found Doug pompous, and paid little attention to him until one day he complained that his co-driver had broken his leg, forcing him to pull out of an endurance rally. I had no idea that Doug had such an interesting hobby; clearly I had misjudged him.

I was seized by a sudden revelation that I would be great at it. Rally driving could be exhilarating. "I'll go!" I blurted out.

Now I sensed movement by my hand and spied a cockroach crawling lazily across the edge of the desk. I picked up one of the schedules and smashed it, sending crumbs, papers, old McDonald's wrappers, and roach guts flying in all directions. That did it. I had to clean up this mess, even if I was only working here a few hours. I marched to the bathroom. Gagging at the stench, I grabbed the only towel on the rack, rinsed it under the faucet and headed back to the desk.

Before I could start wiping the mess away, Tony stomped over and snatched the towel out of my hand. "That's there for a reason," he snapped.

I stared at him, radiating pure hatred. Tony tossed me a roll of paper towels and a bottle of Windex from underneath his desk. He sent Danny to replace the precious towel on the rack.

The phones began to ring with increasing frequency, and soon all the buttons on the phones were blinking. I watched in amazement as the room transformed. Tony began yelling out numbers and the others frantically jotted them down in their booklets. Bets were hastily written on slips of yellow paper, then tossed into an untidy pile on Tony's desk. Tony, phone cradled to his ear, would glance at them before tossing them back on the ever-growing mound. The atmosphere was frantic, electric even, and despite the grim surroundings, it reminded me of footage I'd seen of the trading floor at the New York Stock Exchange. There was that same testosterone-driven intensity as the guys barked into their phones in what sounded like a secret dialect.

"RB! Put people on hold!" Tony yelled. Then he gestured to the pile of yellow tickets. "And put these in order!"

Amid the cacophony all around me, I desperately shuffled through the tickets, trying to put them in numerical order. The more tickets I organized, the more got dumped on my desk. The same breakneck speed carried on for two and a half hours before—as quickly as it had begun—the chaos came to an end.

Tony yelled, "They're off!" and almost immediately the phones began to die down.

Cigarettes were lit as calmness descended. I watched—quietly horrified—as Kyle, a sugar donut clamped in his mouth, pulled up his T-shirt and slid an insulin syringe into his belly. Nobody batted an eyelid. The guys talked among themselves, and although I tried to follow their conversation, every sentence was peppered with words and phrases I didn't understand. All I really knew about gambling was that it was illegal. I quickly realized that the enterprise was vastly more complicated than I had imagined.

The overweight man with the long blond hair and shaggy beard came over. "I'm Mathew," he said, shaking my hand lightly. A slim, dark-haired man who sat directly behind me then smiled and introduced himself as Jay. Mathew wandered off to retrieve a pile of cassette tapes that he proceeded to label and store in a cardboard box. Kyle and Jay continued to answer stray phone calls, and Tony got on the phone to give a rundown of the day's events to someone.

Danny came over to help me sort the mountain of tickets. Once the stack was ordered, he showed me how to "rip" them, separating the original from the carbon copy. When we were finished, Danny secured both piles with rubber bands. He tossed one to Mathew and the other to Tony.

At five o'clock sharp, Kyle and Danny departed with a friendly goodbye. Mathew left a few minutes later, followed by Jay. I was left alone with Tony, who made no effort to speak to me. We sat there in an increasingly uncomfortable silence until Jim showed up.

"You found her someplace else to work?" Tony asked.

"Not yet."

"You've got till the end of the week. Then I want her out—no excuses."

I glared at Tony, appalled by his lack of manners. He pulled out a thick wad of hundred-dollar bills from the front pocket of his jeans, peeled one off, and slapped it down on the desk in front of me. "Be here at eleven forty-five tomorrow," he said. "Park around the block and bring lunch or a snack, because no one leaves again until five."

"Thanks," I said through gritted teeth.

Under any other circumstances I would have thrown the money back at him. But I needed it. I had car payments to make, and I owed money on my credit card. I had just earned the equivalent of 140 Canadian dollars, which was not bad for a few hours of work. Plus, I had to admit, it had been a fascinating afternoon.

"Lock up!" Tony called, leaving through the double doors and disappearing into the empty warehouse beyond.

"Is he always such an asshole?" I asked.

Jim shrugged. Then, brightening as if remembering something important, he took me by the arm and led me toward the bathroom. "I want to show you something."

Inside the filthy room, Jim went over to the towel rack and squatted down in front of it. The upper half of the wall was lined with cheap tiles, the lower half with ugly faux-marble linoleum. With a grunt, Jim pushed hard with both hands on the towel. Lo and behold, the entire length of the linoleum section of the wall flipped open like a long table. Nailed to the wooden backing was a row of tape recorders—fourteen in all.

I stared at this setup in disbelief. Secret panels? This was all getting very James Bond–like. Jim straightened up and grinned at me. "It's all done with hydraulics," he said. I came forward and examined the row of tape recorders. "Each one is hooked up to a separate phone line in the office," Jim continued. "All wagers are recorded. This way, if there's any discrepancy in a bet, they can check it against the tapes."

"So that's why Tony threw a fit when I picked up that stupid towel," I muttered.

"That stupid towel tells you exactly where to press. Plus, it makes sure that nobody leaves any suspicious handprints on that panel. You know, on the off-chance that someone comes snooping."

"Who'd come snooping? I thought the cops were paid off."

"They are." Jim shrugged. "But Tony doesn't like taking chances."

Despite my better judgment, the secret panel and hidden tape recorders made the enterprise seem even more attractive to me. I loved the intrigue of all these precautions.

Jim applied pressure to the underside of the panel, and the mechanism slipped neatly back into place with a soft whoosh. He eagerly explained how the wires were routed through the wall and into the office next door, proud of his cleverness.

"I'm impressed," I said.

"I don't just hide the tapes and install the phones. I also make them impossible to trace. Reroute the calls. If the cops try to trace the 1-800 number, they'll wind up at a potato farm in Idaho," he said with a laugh.

Outside, as Jim locked up, I peered around the deserted parking lot surrounded by a high chain-link fence. "Where's your car?"

"Down the street," he replied.

"Why didn't you just park here?"

Jangling the keys, Jim ambled over and pointed at a ragged plywood sign that said **FOR RENT**, with a phone number underneath. "That's my number. If anyone calls about renting the place, I tell 'em that it's already been taken. That's why we have to keep the parking lot empty and the windows boarded up. Maintains the illusion that we're not even here."

"Seems like a lot of precautions, don't you think? I mean, considering the LAPD are on your payroll already."

"Well," Jim said with a twinkle in his eye, "let's just say that the cops might not know exactly how *big* the operation is."

On the way back to the hotel, Jim told me that he had installed phone setups for a number of bookmakers in the area, so he was sure he'd be able to find me a similar position with another firm. The downside was that Tony's operation was the only one he knew of that provided accommodations.

"So what's his problem with having me work here?"

Jim shrugged. "It's not the kind of place where you see women hanging around. I guess Tony figures people might notice if a pretty girl starts coming and going. He's worried about you drawing heat, that's all."

When I turned up the next day, I was wearing the same uniform as the guys—a baggy sweatshirt, jeans, and sneakers. I'd skipped the lipstick and tucked my long blond hair under a baseball cap. Nothing about my appearance suggested I was a female—especially since, at five-foot-ten, I was taller than half the men in the office.

When Tony answered the door, he looked me up and down and mumbled, "That's better." As I pushed in past him, he added, "You're early."

The timing was deliberate. Before the rest of the crew showed up, I pulled on a pair of rubber gloves, sprayed the bathroom copiously with air freshener, and gave it a thorough scrubbing. In the office, I collected the garbage, cleaned the ashtrays, and wiped down all the surfaces. Tony pretended to be absorbed in paperwork while I worked, which was just fine by me. His desk was clean, so I kept out of his way.

When the others arrived, they were flabbergasted by the transformation and complimented me on my hard work. It was still a dump, but at least it wasn't a filthy dump now. I chatted with the guys, trying to get to know them a little better. Mathew pulled out his wallet to show me a picture of his wife. Just as I was starting to feel like one of the team, Tony called, "Opening line, listen up!"

The guys went to work, jotting down the numbers Tony called out as the phone lines started to buzz to life. I picked one up to put it on hold as I had done the day before, but I caught Tony's hostile gaze on me. "Don't touch that phone," he growled.

A large beige cordless telephone on Tony's desk started to ring. It looked like a brick with a thick rubber antenna on top. Although I had heard of them, this was the first cell phone I had ever seen. When Tony answered it, I had to smile. The thing looked ridiculous, and I was convinced that the invention would never catch on. The idea that someone would spend thousands of dollars on one of these outlandish contraptions was laughable. The phones continued to ring off the hook, but instead of answering them, the others looked at Tony expectantly.

"Changes!" Tony yelled out a series of numbers, and the guys scrambled to jot them down. All eyes turned to the clock. At exactly noon Tony yelled, "We're up!" and Danny, Mathew, Kyle, Jay, and Tony started answering the phones. The frantic pace continued until 1:45, then ground to an abrupt halt.

Danny went off to the bathroom, presumably to check the tapes. "Jesus, it looks like the Ritz in here!" he shouted. I smiled to myself, hoping my charm-offensive was doing some good. Without another word, Tony left the office. I caught a glimpse of him in the next room, furiously lifting weights. During a brief lull as the others smoked, ate, talked, and relaxed, I hovered on the periphery.

A short while later, Tony reentered the room, his T-shirt soaked with sweat. The phones began to ring again, and this time I was permitted to put people on hold and place the tickets in order. The afternoon proved to be even more frantic. I was soon struggling under a growing mountain of tickets. The ringing phones were unrelenting, and I realized how badly I needed to know the meaning of the terms I heard: *dog, favorite, teaser, dime, nickel, parlay, over and under.*

In a repeat of the previous day, at four-thirty Tony yelled out, "They're off!" and the phone calls started to recede. The afternoon had flown by. I was exhilarated to be a part of this strange covert world.

Hearing my nickname, I turned and saw Kyle speaking on the phone. "Oh yeah," he said in his soft, low voice, "she's real pretty." The room fell silent and I felt my cheeks redden. "Blond hair and blue eyes," he continued.

"Shut the fuck up, Kyle!" Tony barked. "She's *gone* already. It's her last day."

I turned to Tony. With a look of satisfaction he elaborated: "Jim found someplace else for you to work."

I tried to hide the crushing disappointment I felt. Just as I had started to enjoy being here, I was out. Tony had won.

The front door slammed. I looked up, expecting to see Jim. Instead a tall, red-haired man with piercing blue eyes sauntered in. He radiated the quiet confidence that comes with age and success. In one hand he was holding a cell phone; in the other was a huge cigar.

The men straightened up in their seats and greeted the man respectfully. He hovered in the doorway, taking in the scene. Pointing at me with his cigar, he asked, "Who's the girl?"

"Ah, don't worry about her," Tony said dismissively. "She'll be gone tomorrow."

The man appraised me silently. "The girl stays," he announced with an air of authority. "And Kyle—the next time someone asks what she looks like? Tell them she's *gorgeous.*"

2

I WOULD LATER DISCOVER that the person who had guaranteed my entry into the world of sports betting was none other than Ron "The Cigar" Sacco, the biggest independent bookmaker in America. He also happened to be Tony's boss. When Ron Sacco declared, "The girl stays," Tony had no choice but to accept it.

"Congratulations, kid," Ron said next. "You're officially on my payroll."

This sudden turnaround in my fortunes caught me off-guard, but I was smart enough to keep my mouth shut. I just said thanks. What made Ron see me as a potential asset could have been nothing more than the novelty of having a blond, blue-eyed girl working in his traditionally male-dominated office.

Whatever the reason, I was determined to repay his faith in me. Part of me wanted to rub Tony's nose in it by being a *great* clerk, someone who could do the job as well as any man. *I mean, really,* I thought—*how hard could it be?*

A few minutes later, I was driving my little red Renault Alliance, following the vague directions on a scrap of paper Tony had given me, toward my new home in Long Beach.

I was given a small, minimally furnished one-bedroom apartment in a modest complex. Still, the novelty of being able to walk out onto my balcony and look down onto a large swimming pool was intoxicating. The glittering blue water was incredibly seductive. I was temped to jump straight in. But instead, I darted back to my car to drive off in search of the ocean. Soon I was standing on the beach, dwarfed by the vast Pacific. Awestruck, I watched the water shimmering and undulating beneath a crystal-clear California sky.

I couldn't believe how quickly my life had transformed. I now had a job and an apartment a few blocks from the beach, and was training to compete in a prestigious car race.

Now that he was stuck with me, Tony was determined to get me up to speed. As soon as I walked into the bunker, he handed me a handful of booklets—the schedules for NBA, NFL, and college football games. "Sit next to Danny," he said. "You got work to do."

I pulled up a chair next to Danny, who assumed the role of instructor. "So, RB, what *do* you know about sports betting?"

"Um, well, I played basketball and softball in school."

"What else?"

I knotted my brow. "That's . . . it?"

"But you've watched sports on TV, right?"

I realized that the eyes of the entire room were on us. With a prickle of embarrassment I shook my head.

"But you know who . . . Joe Montana is?"

I shook my head again. Danny looked crestfallen.

"Magic Johnson?"

I gave another shake. Mathew burst out laughing.

Tony was livid. "That's great. Twenty million Americans follow sports religiously and Jim sends Shirley Temple to work for me." He stormed out of the room to lift weights.

His reaction seemed totally overblown. So what if I didn't know this stuff already? I was a quick learner. There were two teams per game, people backed one side or the other . . . how hard could it be?

Danny started fumbling around with a headset, his expression grim. He handed it to me and I slipped it over my head. "Just listen in for a while. It'll give you a feel for how the line works."

A few minutes later, Tony was back. He made a phone call. "Opening line, listen up!" he barked, hanging up. He began calling out a series of numbers.

Danny scribbled the numbers next to the corresponding teams in the booklets. "It's mid-October," he said as he wrote. "Pro football's in full swing. Pro basketball is just starting. College games are up and running. That means it's going to be a busy day."

It was almost noon and the phones in the office had started ringing. Nobody made any effort to answer them. When Tony's cell went off, however, he snatched it up immediately. His face furrowed with concentration. Then he hung up and called, "Changes—listen up!" He proceeded to reel off another series of numbers.

In the meantime, the phones continued to ring. Soon all fourteen lines were going at once. Danny leaned in and said, "They know we don't put the lines out until noon, but they always call early, hoping they'll be one of the top buttons. Everyone wants a crack at the opening line."

I nodded as if I understood all of this. What on earth was the "opening line"? It wasn't a good time to ask. A kind of pre-show tension had settled on the room. All eyes turned toward the clock as the second hand counted down toward noon.

"We're up!" At Tony's command, the office erupted into action. The guys started scrambling to answer the phones. I put my headset on and listened as Danny answered one call after another, frenziedly scribbling down wagers, shouting out bets, and penciling in new numbers when Tony called out a new set of changes. I found it impossible to keep up. Danny could deftly locate the correct team on the schedule in no time flat. By the time I had caught up, he had already moved on. His transactions were light-ning-quick and full of terms that I didn't understand.

The confidence and determination I felt yesterday were long gone. I was consumed with self-doubt. The clerks and customers might as well have been speaking Mandarin. *No wonder Tony doesn't want me around,* I thought miserably. Clerking was infinitely harder and more complex than I had imagined. It required an intimate knowledge of gambling and all its related terminology, plus math-ematical skills, steady nerves, quick reaction, and intense concen-tration. I could see it would take me months to pick up. I was relieved when the calls finally started to taper off.

"You look a little . . . perplexed," Tony chuckled. My cheeks reddened at his obvious delight. "RB . . . " He tapped his chin as if pondering some deep mystery. "RB, RB . . . I get it!" He snapped his fingers and grinned. "It stands for *Really Blond*, right?" He broke into a laugh and some of the others joined in. I was humili-ated, but vowed to prove him wrong if it was the last thing I did.

Eventually Tony composed himself and instructed Danny to give me a crash course in sports betting. Danny looked thoughtful, trying to figure out the best way to convey the basics to me.

"Okay, babe," he began. "Let's say Matt and I decide to play a game of basketball."

"Okay."

"Now, as you can see, I have the lithe, muscular physique of a trained athlete. But Matt . . . " Danny whistled. "Well, let's just say that his body isn't exactly a temple."

"It's more like a fucking drive-thru," Tony sneered, busting up the guys again.

"Given these circumstances, who do you think is going to win?"

"You."

"Exactly. Therefore, I'm *favored* to win. That makes me the favorite and poor Matt here the underdog. Or just the 'dog,' in Matt's case."

I nodded. So far, so good.

Danny addressed the room. "Who else thinks I can kick Matt's ass in basketball?" All hands, including Matt's, went up. Danny turned back to me. "Now, we got a problem. If everyone bets on me, then Sacco would be out a lot of money. Understand?"

"Su-ure," I said.

"There's no risk," he explained. "I would clearly win the game and everyone would collect. So what we got to do is level the playing field a little. That's the purpose of 'the line.' The line's also called 'the odds.' Same exact thing."

Danny swiveled around in his chair, clearly warming to the role of instructor. "So this is how it happens. Out in Vegas, the professional handicappers predict which team will win a game and by how many points. It's based on a bunch of different factors, like how the home court always has an advantage, or if a team's won the last three games in a row, then they've got a higher chance of winning the fourth. If Michael Jordan is sick and can't play, it'll affect the line on that game. If the guys in Vegas find out that a player's mother is terminally ill, that'll impact the line."

"But why does Vegas do the handicapping?"

Mathew chimed in. "Gambling's legal in Vegas. They put that information out there for their casinos. We just grab that same information for our players."

"Exactly," Danny said. "But today Tony is going to be our handicapper. T-bone, why dontcha give us the odds?"

Tony looked bored. "Danny minus 17."

"Great." Danny turned back to me. "Our handicapper predicts that I'll win the game by 17 points. So when the game is done, we're going to knock 17 points off my score. Matt will have 17 points *added*. We'll only determine the winner *after* we factor in those odds."

"So if I bet on Mathew and he loses, I could still win money?" I asked hesitantly.

"Bingo. Here's the deal. We want the same amount of money bet on Matt as on me. Ron's commission is ten percent. When the chart is even—when the same amount of money is bet on either side—then theoretically, Sacco isn't gambling. It doesn't matter to him whether I win or Matt wins. Sacco gets his commission either way—that's his profit, or the 'juice.' Out on the East Coast they call it the 'vig,' or the 'vigorish.'"

"The vigorish?"

"The juice, the vigorish . . . same thing. It means Ron Sacco—and the rest of us—get paid. Now Tony, his job is to adjust the line depending on how people are betting. If everybody's betting on me, then Tony's got to adjust the line to make it more desirable for people to bet on Matt. With me?"

Danny spun his chair around and addressed the room. "Bets, gentlemen!" The guys started yelling out bets on the fictional game.

"Danny minus seventeen for ten thousand!"

"Gimme Danny minus seventeen for fifty thousand!"

"Go to minus twenty on Danny," Tony called out.

"You caught that?" Danny swung around to face me again. "Tony just moved the line because he needs people to bet on Matt. So now at the end of our game Matt will have . . . what?"

"Twenty points added," I said.

"Right. And I'll have twenty points taken away."

"Give me Matt plus twenty," Mathew grinned, "for half a million!"

Danny looked at me expectantly.

"So Tony would move the line again?" I asked. "To Mathew plus ten?"

"Exactly," Danny smiled, relieved. "In reality the line rarely moves more than half a point at a time, but that's the general concept. We only take bets up until a game has started. Once it gets under way, it's off the boards. Simple, huh?"

He went on to explain the concept of "total" bets. These worked the same way—Vegas would predict the final score on a game and people could either bet over the total or under the total. "If everyone is betting over the total, Tony raises it to encourage people to bet *under*. So come on . . . tell me what you learned."

"Okay," I said. "Tony is the charter. He gets the line from the handicappers in Vegas and adjusts it based on how the players are betting. The chart is out when too many people bet on one side. So he moves the line and people will bet on the other side, making the chart even again."

"Good," he smiled. "Now, on to amounts. You've heard us use words like 'nickels' and 'dimes,' right?"

"Yeah." I nodded.

"Well, a 'dime' is a thousand dollars. A 'nickel' is five hundred. A 'buck' is a hundred, but don't worry about that 'cause we don't deal in bucks in this office. Minimum bet in this office is a nickel, maximum is ten thousand. When we write bets down, we leave off the last two zeroes. So a 'ten-dime' bet is . . . ?"

"Ten thousand dollars," I said, trying to keep the shock out of my voice. I was amazed that people would bet so much money on a game.

"Right. That's written as one-zero-zero."

I opened my mouth to ask why, but Tony cut me off. "It's quicker. And in the unlikely event that the cops raid this place and try to recover evidence, we don't want them to know the real amounts of money we're dealing with. So when you write down a five-dime bet, you make damn sure it reads five-zero."

"Got it," I said.

"And when you take a ten-dime bet, call it out so Tony can move the line right away," Danny added.

So far, so good—at least as far as the straight bets went. Danny was a natural teacher. However, when he started explaining variations—known as "gimmicks"—the business got trickier.

A "parlay," for instance, was a series of connected bets. All of the bets had to win for a payoff. The odds were stacked against you, but the payoff was bigger; a two-team parlay for five thousand dollars could net you a cool twelve grand. "Round robins," "teasers," and "wheels" were other kinds of bets with special terms and conditions that I would be required to learn. I would have to understand what all of them were, how they worked, and what they paid if they won.

At some point I raised my hand and stopped Danny, who was rattling off a dizzying series of names and phrases.

"Oh, shit," he said, noticing the look of utter confusion on my face. "Was I going too fast?"

■

ALL OF OUR PLAYERS accessed us via a 1-800 number, except for a special group of players known as the "Computer Group." This was a consortium of Ivy League graduates who'd pooled their knowledge to come up with their own points spread. The Computer Group's picks were so good that they were able to sell their information to other professional gamblers, who would bet on the games they picked for the maximum amount. These so-called "hot" games generated a lot of action, and necessitated frequent changes. The Computer Group was the only client who could use Tony's cell phone number to place bets before we officially opened.

Over the next few days I eased into life at the office. During the quieter moments I was allowed to read the lines to players, though I was still nowhere near ready to take bets from them. Gambling terminology was fluid and two or more phrases often meant the same thing. One player might ask for "ten dimes," another for "ten large" or "ten big." All of these equaled ten thousand dollars. Instead of asking for the favorite, some callers asked for "the chalk." "Gimmicks" were sometimes called "exotics," and instead of asking for us to give them the lines, some players would ask for "the price" or simply command, "run them." I listened to Danny taking bets for hour after hour, until I was itching to take the calls myself.

On Friday, Sacco showed up again, cigar clamped between his teeth. He tossed a paper bag to Tony, who pulled out five rubber-banded stacks of hundred-dollar bills. He tossed one packet to each of us, keeping the largest for himself. Ron removed the cigar from his mouth and surveyed the room. "Why doesn't the monkey play cards in the jungle?" he asked.

Nobody replied. I figured this was some more obscure gambling terminology.

"Too many cheetahs."

■

SEVERAL DAYS LATER I was with Jim, driving south to Hemet to pick up his new Mustang, which had just been fitted with roll bars. I asked Jim why gambling was illegal.

He shrugged. "I guess some folks can't handle it, you know? They get addicted. They'll gamble away the family home, their kid's college fund, you name it. Guess the government figures, if they legalize it, it'll be a problem."

"But it's legal in Vegas."

"Gambling also creates revenue. Jobs, all that good stuff. Hell, if it wasn't for gambling, Vegas'd just be another speck in the desert."

"So why doesn't Ron just move the office to Vegas?"

Jim laughed. "It doesn't work like that. Most of Ron's players are in California. If they called Vegas to place a bet, they'd be violating the Interstate Commerce Act. Anyway, there's a bigger problem with operating out of Vegas."

"What?" I asked.

"The mob! Wherever there's a casino, the mob is lurking close by. They're like flies on a turd."

I thought about Ron Sacco, with his red hair and preppy clothes. He definitely didn't fit the mob profile. Tony, on the other hand, with his classic Italian looks, seemed to fit the part. "So . . . Ron has nothing to do with the mob?"

To my relief, Jim shook his head. "There's no mob to speak of out here. Out on the East Coast, it's a different story. They have the whole gambling thing locked down tight. Hell, around there they'll let anyone place a bet with the neighborhood bookie, they don't care. Junkies, boozehounds, derelict gamblers, people on welfare . . . no questions asked." Jim went on. "Ron has all his major players screened. You only play with Ron what you can afford to lose. If for some reason you fall behind on your payments, Ron'll work out a plan with you. That's why he's a legend. Ron's got ethics; he runs a clean business. That's why the cops go so easy on him. If it wasn't for Ron, maybe the mob would have an operation out here, who knows?"

"So why does Ron have to pay off the LAPD?" I asked.

"Gambling's still illegal. Ron might not be causing trouble, but the heat's still entitled to something for looking the other way."

"I guess that makes sense," I mused.

"Sure it does. They still got to bust him every so often. But they only hit what we call the Baby Office, Ron's smallest office. And they call ahead to let him know when it's going to happen. That way it's a win-win. In the papers it looks like the cops are going after organized crime, but Ron stays in control of exactly what the cops recover. So long as you don't work in the Baby Office, you got nuthin' to worry about."

"So what's Tony's story?" I asked.

"Tony? He's been with Sacco twelve, thirteen years at least. Man, if it wasn't for Tony, Sacco would be lost, if you ask me. He started out as a clerk, just like you. But he had a real gift for it—a head for math, incredible memory. He'd adjust the line independently, by picking up on the patterns and tendencies among the players. When Tony started adding and shaving points, Sacco's profits soared. Sacco's a smart guy. He put Tony in charge of the office and gave him carte blanche to run it however he wanted."

Jim pointed toward a sign for Hemet. I followed his directions to Turner's garage and pulled into their parking lot. Jim jumped out and headed straight for his beloved Mustang, which was glittering in the morning sunlight. He got to work immediately, rolling up his sleeves and examining the newly added roll bars and shoulder harnesses. "Beautiful," he said, grinning.

Jim took me into the shop and introduced me to the professional driver who owned it. As Jim shared our plans for the Alcan 5000, I found myself getting excited about the upcoming race.

However, when the conversation turned to a lengthy debate over shock absorbers, I made my excuses and headed out on the long drive back to East L.A. It was 10:45 in the morning, and I knew I'd have to hustle to make it to the office in time for the opening line.

3

IN THE OFFICE I wore a uniform of baggy T-shirts, baseball caps, and sneakers, so I welcomed the excuse to dress like a woman again. The guys wanted to take me out to celebrate my first real day of bookmaking. Dinner was at eight at Vitello's, an Italian restaurant in Studio City, and I rushed home after work to get changed. I slipped into a figure-hugging dress and sandals and wore my hair down. I smiled approvingly at my reflection and dashed to my car.

When I arrived at Vitello's, the others were already seated. I apologized for being late and made my way over to the empty seat. Danny jumped to his feet and pulled out the chair for me, letting out a long, approving wolf whistle. "Damn, girl," he said, "I'd kinda forgot you were a woman."

From across the table, Tony was glowering. "Don't even think about it, Danny."

"Aw, come on, man."

"Come on, nothing. You don't shit where you eat."

Tony looked around the table. "Listen up," he said. "I just added another rule to office policy. No drugs. No hangovers. No lateness. And *no messing with RB*. If I catch any of you assholes looking at RB like she's a woman again, you're fired."

I was mortified by Tony's outburst. Even Danny looked embarrassed. Addressing me directly, Tony sneered, "Save the pretty dresses for Jim. And in the future, have the courtesy to show up on time."

I sat down, fuming. I was ten minutes late! As an awkward silence settled over the table, he picked up the oversized menu and opened it, shielding himself from my angry gaze. I grabbed my menu and tried to concentrate on my order. It was impossible. My mind kept drifting back to Tony and his ugly outburst. Everybody else treated me nicely; why couldn't he? He never gave me so much as a grunt of approval.

When the waiter arrived, however, Tony was all smiles. He addressed him by name and asked about his family, even recalling the ages of his children. Soon they were chatting away, chuckling at a shared joke. I was struck by the sudden change in Tony's demeanor. He could be quite charming when he wanted to. He just didn't want to be that way with *me*.

My bad mood didn't last long. The food was great and the conversation at the table soon flowed as easily as the wine. Away from the office, I learned a bit more about my coworkers. When Kyle wasn't taking bets, he dressed up as a cowboy, crashing through windows and busting through doors as a stunt man for Knotsberry Farm. This despite the fact that he had diabetes. Danny, as was typical in L.A., was an aspiring actor. Mathew was married to a kindergarten teacher, and he and his wife were trying for children. Jay was a part-time student, taking college classes in the evenings after work.

Even Tony relaxed after a glass of wine, and was soon regaling the table with stories from his childhood. "One of my biggest regrets is giving Mom the cell-phone number," he said. "She calls me sometimes, right in the middle of reading lines. I'm like, 'Ma! What?' and she says, 'Baby, are you taking your vitamins?'"

"So how old are you, Tony?"

The laughter at the table died right down. I sensed that I had crossed an unspoken line by asking a personal question. "Twenty-nine," he muttered.

Tony was six years older than me, I mused as I drove home that evening. I found my mind drifting back to our first encounter. He was rude, arrogant, and thuggish—an impression he seemed eager to reinforce at every given opportunity. But working so closely with him, I'd discovered that he was incredibly intelligent. He managed Ron's multimillion-dollar business with ease, a fact that became doubly impressive when I learned that he not only managed the office where I worked, but also oversaw two others: the "Small Office," dedicated to people with little gambling knowledge, and the "Baby Office," where the maximum bet was five hundred dollars. Tony was so good at moving the lines that other bookmakers paid to access them. He might not be engaged in a legitimate business, but he was a respected businessman all the same.

Plus, I couldn't deny the fact that Tony was quite . . . *likable.* He had a whiplash sense of humor and a mischievous smile that lit up his deep brown eyes. He had charisma. He was the kind of person who walked into a room and commanded it.

I wondered if Tony had a steady girlfriend. He was quite good-looking. Not my type, but handsome all the same. I could under-stand how women might find him attractive. Kyle had a girlfriend, as did Jay and Danny. Mathew was married. But Tony? I had no idea. All I really knew about his personal life were the snippets he had revealed over dinner. He kept his cards close to his chest.

Was I attracted to Tony? I pushed the thought out of my mind immediately. Of course I wasn't! The very idea was crazy—Tony wasn't my type. If I had a type, Tony would be the complete oppo-site of it. *Why am I even thinking about this?* I wondered. I supposed it might have been because he had declared me off-limits to everyone at the office. Was that the moment I had begun to think of him as attractive? It made sense in a weird way—it was typical of the way my mind worked. As soon as something was declared off-limits, I was intrigued.

I took a deep breath. I was being silly. Ridiculous. If Tony were to ask me out tomorrow, I'd say no. I wouldn't even have to think twice.

■

A WEEK LATER WHEN I arrived at the office, I found a ticket waiting for me on my desk. It read "SD-3 100," with a red circle around the 100, indicating that it had been graded the day before. "What's this?"

Tony was at his desk, reading the sports section. Without looking up he informed me, "We were never three on that game. We opened at three and a half, closed at four and a half."

I became defensive. "I never *had* three entered, Tony."

Tony sighed and put the paper down. That's when I saw the tape recorder. He pressed play.

"5056," said a player's voice, identifying himself. "What do you have on San Diego?"

Then I heard my voice. *Three and a half.* In the background I could hear the sounds of phones ringing furiously, bets being called out, and Tony yelling out the changes during the opening-line frenzy. "Gimme San Diego minus three for ten dimes," the voice said. I looked down at the ticket. Amidst all of the noise and confusion I'd obviously lost my concentration, because that's exactly what I wrote down. Minus three for ten dimes. Tony clicked the tape off.

"You just handed that joker half a point. Minus three and a half woulda been a loss for him. Minus three was a win. I had to credit him with ten dimes."

My blood ran cold. This wasn't just any mistake—this was a $10,000 mistake. I was convinced that Tony would fire me on the spot. But he didn't. He didn't say another word about it until the end of the day, when he called me over to his desk and handed me a stack of tickets a foot high. He informed me that I would be grading them tonight, his way of making sure that I would pay more attention in the future.

I knew I was going to have a long night. The other clerks always complained when it was their turn to correct the tickets, and I was about to find out why. At home, I called a toll-free number in Vegas at nine p.m. to get the final scores on the games. I entered these into the Don Best Sports booklet, then factored in the line to determine the winners and losers. I realized just how important those half-points were. Players who took the Lakers plus nine and a half won their wagers, but those who bet the game plus nine lost. With hundreds and hundreds of bets to grade, I came across countless examples of games that tied, or "pushed." One game even fell on a number—meaning both sides won.

The straight bets were simple enough, but the gimmicks were complicated and time-consuming to work out. My fingers cramped and my eyes ached as I worked my way methodically down the pile. Once I had completed the stack, I had to go back and calculate each player's total win or loss for the day and enter these figures next to their number on a long sheet of yellow legal paper. I worked my way through an entire pot of coffee, finishing my last cup at midnight, and eventually collapsed into bed at three in the morning.

As I drifted off to sleep, I thought of Tony again. I wasn't angry with him for making me grade. It was part of the clerk's job. But it baffled me how Tony managed to do this every night. Tony had to grade the original copies, and he boasted that it took him only a couple of hours. How did he do it?

The next step of grading was to meet with Tony in the morning to compare answers—a process known as "running numbers." I was walking toward the warehouse, clutching a plastic bag that contained roughly a million dollars in bets, when I heard the guttural roar of a motorcycle approaching. The engine revved furiously as the bike came closer. My workmates were constantly reminding me to be careful, as this was a dangerous neighborhood. Pulling my baseball cap lower on my face, I transferred the bag to my other hand. I picked up my pace as the motorcycle drew nearer. The warehouse was just ahead.

You're fine. Keep going. Almost there.

The bike pulled in sharply, blocking my way. A man wearing a helmet and a leather jacket sat astride a brutal-looking Harley. Through his featureless black helmet I couldn't make out the rider's face—just my own distorted reflection. I was considering running when the man flipped open the visor.

It was Tony. I tried to keep the panic out of my face. He fumbled for the keys and tossed them to me. "Let yourself in," he said. "I'll be there in a minute."

■

THE WEEKS FLEW BY, and before I knew it the Christmas holidays were approaching. This was the time of year when leading college teams faced off against each other, resulting in a frenzy of betting on bowl games.

"Well, there's the Super Bowl, of course," Danny explained. "That's the only pro football game. But then we've got the Orange Bowl, the Cotton Bowl, the Sugar Bowl . . . "

We were all expected to work through the holiday season, which was fine by me. I didn't relish the idea of flying to New York to join my family, where I would be bombarded with questions about my life in Los Angeles. Nobody would approve of the kind of work I was doing, no matter what kind of spin I put on it.

I was raised in a very different type of environment. Both of my parents are European, and my British-born father still traveled often for the U.N. I didn't even live in America until I was seven. During the sixties our family lived in Rome. At that time Italian mothers wore housedresses to the beach and settled under umbrellas to supervise their children. Our mother, by contrast, had long, thick blond hair, blue eyes, and a dazzling smile.

German-born, she looked like a movie star—not a housewife with three children born just fourteen months apart. Toned, tanned, and bikini-clad, she strode along the shoreline with the three of us toddling behind her. Even then I was aware of the attention she received.

My mother tongue was Italian, and the little English we had learned from my father seemed patently different from the slang and accents in America. It didn't help that my sister and I began attending school dressed in dirndls, traditional German frocks, with our long blond hair in braids. We just didn't fit in. We were Europeans living in the United States. Our furniture, the food we ate, the music we listened to, my parents' conservative values—all remained the same as they had been in Rome.

My brother Peter was promptly dispatched to boarding school in the U.K. to get a "proper education." He would grow up there, joining us only during summers and Christmases. There were few children in our upper-class neighborhood in Westchester, north of New York City, and in those early years my father was often traveling. We were a tiny family, living in a big house on a tree-lined esplanade. My sister Heather and I became fiercely close. Not only did we pass for twins, but we seemed to know each other's thoughts and did everything together.

When I was nine, my sister and I were taking ballet, piano, gymnastics, and ice-skating lessons, and attending private school. We went skiing in the winter and traveled to Vancouver or Europe in the summer. By contrast, my mother was nine when Hitler attacked Poland; eleven when she was dispatched to the countryside for safety; and thirteen when she made her way back to Hamburg, alone, only to find it reduced to rubble. All the unimaginable horrors of war that she endured in her childhood became a very real part of ours through her stories. It was clear that nothing I would ever go through in my life could ever compare to what she had suffered.

My mother was even more exotic in America than she had been in Rome. She was well traveled, spoke four languages, and was a talented ice skater, skier, pianist, climber, and gymnast. She got up at six a.m. every day to do calisthenics before going to work at Stauffer Chemicals, where she was a research chemist. She was required to wear a lab coat and metal-tipped shoes, and had hers custom-made into high heels. Every day she came home after work, prepared a nutritious dinner for us, then continued on to the local college, where she took courses to satisfy her insatiable thirst for knowledge. She always looked perfect: hair in a French twist, classic suits or dresses, stockings and high heels. She was elegant, sophisticated, driven. She knew how and when to be charming, and she clearly enjoyed being the center of attention; but there was an absence of warmth—a coldness—about her as well.

She kept my sister and me busy. We were responsible for keeping our big house and garden immaculate. There was always work to be done: a lawn that needed mowing, leaves to be raked, a huge driveway to be weeded, snow to be shoveled, tables to be set and cleared, dishes to be washed, rooms to be dusted and vacuumed. Everything had to look perfect, all the time. My father described our house as "sterile," which was a pretty accurate description.

Family meals became excruciating as the years passed. Conversation was forced, and restricted to current events and the weather. This polite adherence to the social niceties was merely a cover. Simmering under the surface was the unbearable strain of a marriage on the verge of fracturing. The open knowledge of my mother's serial infidelities—and the fact that my father seemed to prefer working in remote African villages, where food was scarce and malaria rampant, to being with his wife—poisoned the atmosphere at home. Whatever bond had first brought my parents together had long since come undone.

My father packed his things and left when I was seventeen. Peter was in college at UBC by that time, but my sister and I were still at home, and we had to deal with my mother's frequent and halfhearted suicide attempts, which were clearly meant to get my father back. She had spent years relentlessly berating him and carrying on with a string of lovers—one of whom bitterly complained to me when she broke off their relationship. She clearly didn't love my father, but divorce meant losing the status and perks she enjoyed as a "U.N. wife."

Even after I moved to Canada, I continued to field suicide calls from my mother. She would often call at four or five in the morning, Vancouver time, to tell me that she had a knife in her hand and was about to slash her wrists, or about to jump off someone's balcony, gas herself in the garage, or swallow some pills. This went on for months.

So I dropped out of school, became a rally driver, and ended up bookmaking in L.A., where no one had any way to contact me. I didn't have any intention of letting my parents know where I was or what I was doing; and for the time being, that meant staying put in L.A.

On Friday, December 26, Ron Sacco showed up at the office with a brown paper bag stuffed with our payroll and Christmas bonuses. When Tony distributed them and I discovered a thousand dollars in my envelope in addition to the week's salary, it felt like I'd won the lottery.

Ron perched himself on the edge of Mathew's desk, casually reached into his jacket pocket, and produced another envelope. He tossed it over to Tony. "Tickets for the Lakers–Houston game," he said. "Starts at seven." Ron looked around the room and winked. "Limo's on me."

An hour later, we were all piling into a stretch limo. The last time I had ridden in a limo, I was wearing a ridiculous fluffy dress and making awkward conversation on my way to the senior prom. Tonight was a different story. I was still dressed in my baggy sweatshirt, jeans, and baseball cap, with fifteen hundred-dollar bills stuffed into my pockets. I was on my way to my first live sporting event with my fellow bookmakers. It felt like the epitome of cool.

The atmosphere at the stadium was electric. As we made our way through the bustling crowd, I made sure to stick close to Tony. It was my express aim to wangle the seat next to his. When he found our row, however, he ushered me in first and let the others follow. He ended up sitting the farthest away from me. Disappointed, I wondered if he had done it intentionally.

The arena was buzzing, and soon I was caught up in the excitement along with everyone else. When the Lakers walked out onto the court, I rose to my feet and roared along with the rest of the crowd. With a surge of pride I realized that I knew not only the names of the players, but also the position that each of them played. I even recognized Pat Riley, the team's coach.

Before the game the Laker Girls did a cheerleading routine, showing off their flawless figures and acrobatic moves to the enthusiastic approval of the crowd. Their lithe, muscular bodies were barely covered by their tiny purple-and-gold uniforms. I snuck a glance at Tony as they performed, noting the intense scrutiny on his face as he watched them. I sat back and sighed.

What was wrong with me? Of course he found them attractive; what straight man wouldn't? I took off my hat and fluffed my hair in a vain attempt to make myself look more feminine. Why couldn't Tony look at me like that? What did I have to do to get his attention? I tried to put him out of my mind and focused instead on the game at hand. It turned into a decisive victory for the Lakers, who beat Houston 134–111. By the end of the game, I was hoarse from cheering.

When the limo dropped us off back at the warehouse, it was late. Tony disappeared into the office to grab the tickets. Game or not, he still had work to do.

"Who's grading?" I asked nonchalantly.

"Me," Kyle moaned.

"I'll do it, Kyle," I offered. "I mean, if you want."

Kyle couldn't believe his ears. "Really? I mean, you *sure?*"

If I graded, I would get to run the numbers with Tony in the morning. "Yeah. I'm sure."

Late that night, as I worked my way through a daunting pile of yellow slips, I found myself trying to explain my behavior. Over the past few weeks, Tony had been on my mind almost constantly.

I found myself seeking any excuse to look at him, scrutinizing him for faults or flaws. I wanted to find a reason to dislike him. But so far I hadn't found one. The more I got to know Tony, the more attracted to him I became. I liked his perfect teeth, his strong jawline, and his thick brown hair. I liked the curve of his neck, the shape of his nose, even the shape of his hands. I liked how he smelled.

Tony didn't smoke or gamble. He kept his desk spotless, he treated the players with courtesy, and he made the office a fun place to work with his easy wit and charisma. He didn't have a trace of arrogance, and he had an extraordinary mind. He was able to calculate the most complex bet instantly, even with a stinking hangover.

When Tony talked I was always listening, trying to glean any sliver of information that might give me more insight into his character. I learned that he had once been a talented football player. I discovered that his mother was Irish, and his father Sicilian. One day he made a casual reference to the fact that he skied, and I felt my heart leap suddenly as though I were a schoolgirl with a crush. *I can ski!* I thought, happy to have something in common with him.

A few weeks after the game, Tony bought us all tickets to see Bob Seger and the Silver Bullet Band. It was my day off and I had already committed to training with Jim; but without a second's hesitation I called him with a flimsy excuse and headed over to the Beverly Center instead. I splashed out on a new pair of jeans, a pale-blue gypsy blouse, and a pair of sandals. At home I showered again, shaved my legs, blow-dried my hair, and gave myself a manicure and pedicure. As I sat in front of the mirror carefully applying makeup, it occurred to me that I had never put this much effort into preparing for a date before. Tonight I would be going out with the entire office—I was hardly expecting it to be a romantic evening. The simple truth was, I wanted a reaction from Tony, some hint that he was looking at me with the same mixture of longing and curiosity that I felt for him.

Despite my careful preparations, however, he didn't so much as pay me a compliment. Nobody did. I started to think that I would always just be considered "one of the guys" in this office, and the realization stung.

As I drove home alone that night, I had the terrible feeling that I had been rejected somehow. I knew I was being ridiculous. I should be going out and meeting men, I thought. The sad truth was, I didn't want to meet other men. I wanted Tony.

I hated myself for being so attracted to him. I had hinted often enough that I was single, but he didn't seem to care. I'd even come into work once feigning exhaustion, as though I'd been out late the night before on a hot date—all in the hopes of making him feel a prickle of jealousy.

I tried to put him out of my head. I literally ached for him, and as illogical as it was, I couldn't control my feelings. Every time he talked about some girl he picked up at a club, it felt like a shard of ice stabbed through my heart. It took all of my self-control not to let my face betray the pain I felt, knowing that he had been with someone else. I began swimming lengths for hours in the evening, in a futile effort to clear my mind of him.

Jim was the first to notice that something was wrong. I no longer had my passion for racing. After a practice run one day, he turned to me.

"What the hell's wrong, RB? You're . . . sloppy. Is something up?"

I couldn't tell him. I'd have felt like a fool. I made a vague excuse and vowed to focus on the upcoming race. That was my whole reason for coming to L.A., after all.

But then the race fell through.

In late January, Jim's wife was hospitalized with a kidney infection, and went on to contract pneumonia. Jim was frantic, and I saw him age years overnight. She was discharged from the hospital in February—two days before the start of the Alcan—frail and in need of constant care.

Jim looked into having our entry fee transferred to the Alcan in October, but I barely cared. My mind was elsewhere. The original plan was for me to return to Vancouver in February, but I knew that I wasn't going anywhere. I couldn't leave Los Angeles.

As February turned into March, the pace at the office increased. It was "March Madness," when the NCAA tournament overlapped with the NBA schedule and offered seemingly unlimited games to bet on. The phones seemed never to stop ringing.

Just before closing time one day in late March, Ron showed up at the office unexpectedly. Looking unusually serious, he perched on Tony's desk and took the cigar out of his mouth. "The Small Office got busted earlier today," he said.

Mathew was the first to break the shocked silence. "You're kidding!"

"No warning call?" Tony asked.

Ron shook his head. "Nope."

This came as a shock. The mid-eighties were a troubled time in Los Angeles—gun crime, drugs, and gang violence were at an all-time high. Drive-by shootings were a common occurrence, as street gangs vied for control of the city's lucrative crack and heroin trade. Why would the police waste their time going after a group of people answering phones? Especially when they were being paid *not* to?

"What about the tapes and the diverters?" Tony asked.

"They didn't find them." Ron cleared his throat. "In light of this, I need to know if anybody wants out."

A long silence followed. I considered the possibility. I found the idea of not being around Tony infinitely more worrying than the possibility of being arrested.

"What would happen if we got busted?" I asked tentatively.

"Sweetheart, if you get arrested, your bail's going to arrive before you even get to jail. I guarantee that. I'll pay any fines or legal bills. So long as you work for me, I'll take care of you. I do the same for all of my clerks."

I nodded, my decision made. I trusted Ron. Some of the clerks had been with him for years, and nobody had a bad word to say about the man. The next Alcan was still seven long months away. I could pay off my car if I stayed until October. I'd work until then and quit after the race. I would go home afterward, finish college, do all of the things I was supposed to be doing. This was only temporary, after all. This wasn't my life.

The fact that I was a Canadian citizen also eased my worries. Even if I did get arrested in L.A., it wouldn't matter in Canada.

"I'm staying," I said. Tony started to say something, but I cut him off. "I'm staying," I repeated.

Ron smiled.

"Thatta girl."

The following day, everything was back to normal. It was as if the bust never happened. The Small Office was back in business, and no one mentioned the raid again. The weeks flew by in a flurry of work. Suddenly it was May, and I was preparing for the Kentucky Derby.

The 1987 Kentucky Derby at Churchill Downs proved to be one of the most dramatic races in its 113-year history. The bets came in fast and furious, and we struggled to keep up with the players' demands. As soon as the horses sprang from the starting gates, we gathered around the TV to watch what the pundits referred to as "the most exciting two minutes in sports."

As Alysheba, the eventual winner, roared ahead, a crash shook the foundation of our building. I thought for a brief moment that it was an earthquake. Yet the cause was all too human. As Alysheba thundered across the finishing line, the warehouse was swarmed by LAPD officers.

4

"HANDS AGAINST THE FUCKING walls!"

Police flooded in, weapons drawn, and within seconds the room was torn apart. Desks were flipped, chairs were kicked over, and papers were sent fluttering to the ground. In a daze I stood, raised my hands, and was shoved roughly against the wall.

It was nothing like the police shows on TV. The raid was violent and aggressive. The outraged demeanor of the police suggested they'd walked in on a child pornography ring, not a bunch of people taking sports bets.

Next to me, a terrified-looking Mathew was patted down. Out of the corner of my eye I saw his belly wobble as rough hands frisked him. Next to him, Danny was getting the same treatment. Behind us a cop yelled, "Look what we got here!"

I glanced over my shoulder and saw one of the officers triumphantly brandishing an insulin syringe.

"That's mine!" Kyle protested. "I'm a diabetic, for crissakes!"

I turned my head toward Tony, on my immediate left. We locked eyes. Gone was the impatient, dismissive stare that I was so familiar with. Instead, he radiated concern. Our hands were inches from each other, palms flat against the wall as we waited to be frisked. It felt strange to be standing there so quietly, with all the madness going on around us.

Slowly, I extended my pinkie finger toward his. I desperately wanted to touch him. I needed to touch him. My finger inched across the wall, closer, closer to his. When our fingers finally made contact it was as if all the noise of the raid suddenly receded. The shouting seemed far away, as if echoing from some distant place. All I could focus on was the sensation of Tony's finger against mine. He wasn't pulling away. We locked eyes again. This fleeting connection felt incredibly intense, after so many months of silent longing; for a brief, precious moment, everything seemed all right with the world.

Someone began patting Tony down. An officer grabbed a handful of his hair and wrenched his head back. With a sickening crunch, he smashed Tony's face into the wall. Tony's knees buckled, but he stayed on his feet. His eyes rolled back as his nose started to bleed. Out of the corner of my eye, I saw the policeman slip his hand into Tony's pocket and remove a thick wad of money. Throughout it all, Tony never moved his hand away from mine.

I was terrified of what might happen if I moved. There was something lawless, even dangerous about these men. We were just taking bets—nobody was armed. Nobody would have resisted.

Moments later I felt a pair of hands on my body, patting my legs, moving slowly up to my waist, then farther, farther up my body, until they reached my breasts. I felt my cheeks burn as the hands cupped them. The cop stopped, taking a step backward.

"Turn around."

Reluctantly, I removed my hand from Tony's. I turned to face the man who'd frisked me.

"I'll be damned," he said. "We got a female!"

I was marched into the room next door and directed to a chair next to Tony's workout bench. Seated across from me was an older man with a hard, weather-beaten face and small, beady eyes that radiated cold disdain. He was wearing a dandruff-flecked navy-blue slicker jacket with "LAPD" embossed in yellow above a shield logo. His badge read "Officer Gibson."

"Well, well," he said, his eyes traveling down my body. "What're you? The office bitch?"

I stared at him, dumbfounded.

"You fuck them all, correct?"

I was shocked. I had no idea how to respond.

"I'm just trying to figure out how it works around here," he continued. "Do they pay you to crawl under the desk and give 'em head?" I noticed the light reflecting off Gibson's gold wedding band and absently wondered if his wife knew what kind of a man she had married.

My mind drifted back to a decade earlier, when the police had responded to a burglary at our house in Westchester. The police officers had patiently followed my mother from room to room, listening with looks of concern as she tearfully recounted what had been stolen. They had taken notes and gently reassured her that they would do all they could to recover the missing goods. Back then I had felt so grateful for the protection of the police.

But now I was seeing another side to them. The harsh reality of being on the wrong side of the law was becoming very clear to me.

"Whattaya think, Mike?" Gibson asked one of his colleagues. "You think she fucks 'em one at a time, or all at once?"

As they debated this, some of Gibson's men tramped up and down the ramp that separated the office area from the warehouse, unaware that some of the evidence they were searching for was right under their feet. It was under this ramp that Jim had concealed the diverters, which were supposed to render the phones untraceable. How had the police found us?

So far they'd recovered only a stack of betting slips. Gibson was clearly frustrated at the haul.

"Check her for tracks," one of the officers suggested hopefully. Gibson forced my sleeve up. When he saw my healthy veins, he looked deflated and pushed my arms away. Another officer appeared behind Gibson, holding a small plastic baggie.

"We, uh, found this in the bathroom, sir."

I shook my head in disbelief. I kept that bathroom spotless, and whatever it was that he was holding definitely had not come from there. Gibson took my hand and placed the baggie on my palm. It was full of a fine white powder. I had never used it, but this was obviously cocaine. I stared at Gibson, perplexed. He grinned and forced my hand closed.

"That's not mine!"

"Yeah? Then why are your prints all over it?"

My mind flashed back to a speech Tony had given during my first week at the warehouse. "Whatever you do, don't bring drugs to the office," he'd ordered. "If we ever get busted, Sacco'll take care of you. But if you're caught with drugs, you're on your own."

Since I didn't drink or do drugs, I hadn't given much thought to his warning. But now, with Gibson forcing my hand closed over a baggie of planted cocaine, the memory made my blood run cold. From the next room I could hear Danny pleading with someone. Then I heard him yelp in pain.

The city of Los Angeles would later pay over $20 million to settle excessive-force cases. But back in 1987, the district attorney was still refusing to prosecute officers and sheriff's deputies accused of assault and brutality. The D.A. was essentially condoning their behavior. I knew the LAPD was corrupt—after all, it was taking regular payoffs from us. But nothing could justify the behavior I saw on display that day.

The atmosphere eased somewhat when a female officer stepped into the room. She was short and stocky, a tough-as-nails woman with a pair of torpedo-sized breasts that strained the buttons of her white uniform blouse. She greeted her colleagues jovially, then adopted a frosty expression when she turned to face me. "On your feet," she ordered.

She led me to the bathroom. Wordlessly she patted me down, running her fingers under my bra and through my hair. As she did this I noted with satisfaction that the towel was still on the rack, undisturbed.

When the search was over, Gibson handed the female officer a plastic sack. It contained my belongings—my wallet, keys, and Dr. Pepper–flavored lip-gloss. I noted with relief that the baggie of cocaine was not there. I was led out, pushed into the back of a waiting police car, and taken away, blue lights flashing.

True to Ron's word, my bail arrived at the Sybil Brand Institute for Women before I did. As my paperwork was being processed, I went over and over what had just happened. Had I witnessed the police as they really were?

An hour later I was standing outside of the prison, waiting for a taxi. The Armenian driver who collected me demanded to see the cash up-front before he'd agree to take me the short distance from Monterey Park to East L.A. By the time we got to the warehouse district it was completely deserted. My car was the only one remaining on the street. I was relieved to see it hadn't been broken into.

I pulled up at the nearest pay phone and dialed Jim's number. "Hello?"

"We got busted."

Jim was struck dumb but managed to gather himself together. "Jesus . . . RB, are you all right? Where are you? What number are you on?" I gave Jim the number of the pay phone. He told me to stay put, and hung up.

A minute later the phone rang.

"You okay?" It was Ron Sacco.

"Yes."

"You've got nothing to worry about," he assured me. "Listen, I want you to drive over to Mathew's place. We're going to meet there later. Do you have a pen?"

I jotted down the directions and hung up. I was grateful to have somewhere to go. The thought of spending the night alone in my apartment was unbearable. I needed to know that everybody was all right, especially Tony.

I pulled up in front of a pale-yellow 1950s-style house and double-checked the address Ron had given me. A pretty woman with a full face and curly auburn hair answered the door. I recognized her immediately as Mathew's wife, Patsy, from the photos I'd seen of her. She led me inside, chatting happily, and pointed me toward the bathroom. "There's some clean towels on the rack," she said breezily. "You'll probably want to clean up, after what you've been through."

She was right. I wanted to wash any traces of Gibson off me.

I left the bathroom and followed the smell of garlic to the kitchen. I found Patsy stirring an enormous bowl of spaghetti sauce. "Thought I'd make a start on dinner," she said. "The guys'll be starving when they get out." Patsy's reaction to the arrests seemed surreal. She acted as if it were normal for her husband to be carted off to jail.

The doorbell rang. I flinched, still jumpy from the events of the day. "That'll be Joanna!" Patsy cooed.

Joanna was Ron Sacco's girlfriend. I'd heard a lot about her, but this was the first time we'd met. She was a striking woman in her mid-thirties, dressed in burgundy leather slacks, a matching leather jacket, and high-heel suede boots. Her hair was bleached platinum blond and styled in full, soft waves around her luminous face. She should have looked cheap, but somehow she was undeniably glamorous.

"You must be RB." She smiled, revealing a row of perfect white teeth.

Joanna was obviously well acquainted with Patsy's kitchen. Soon she was taking olive oil, balsamic vinegar, and assorted herbs and spices out of the cupboards to prepare a salad dressing. "I'll be speaking with our lawyer tomorrow morning," she said. "In the meantime, I'll need to know exactly what happened. Every detail is important."

I recounted the bust to the best of my recollection. She frowned when I told her that the police had smashed down the door in lieu of presenting us with a search warrant. She seemed relieved that the sheriffs were not involved in the raid, as their jurisdiction was statewide.

"Did it seem that they were looking for something . . . specific?"

I shrugged. "They turned the place upside down, but they didn't find the diverters or the recorders. Not while I was there."

"Something doesn't add up," she mused. "We've always been on good terms with the LAPD."

After speaking with her for a while, I realized I'd been wrong in my assumption that Joanna was in her thirties. Based on her manner, intellect, and experience, I now decided that she was maybe a decade older. I liked that about Sacco. With his money he could have had any number of twenty-something bimbos on his arm. Instead he stuck with a woman who was not only close to his own age, but an asset to him professionally.

"What happens now?" I asked. I assumed that a bust of that magnitude would spell the end for the office.

"We'll open tomorrow from a backup location. Business as usual," Joanna said nonchalantly. "What about you?"

"Me?"

Joanne looked at me intently. "Ron likes you. The players like you. It would be . . . reassuring for them if you stayed on."

I considered the possibility of backing out, but quickly dismissed it. I had no moral issue with what we were doing. After seeing the way the police behaved today, I had no illusions about who the real bad guys were. Besides, I knew that the only way I could be sure of seeing Tony again would be to continue working for him.

"I'll be there."

Joanna leaned across and gave me a hug. When she broke away I glanced at my watch. It was getting late.

"This could take a while," she said. "It takes longer to process the guys."

"They probably won't be here until around one," Patsy called from the kitchen.

"You should go home and get some sleep," Joanna suggested.

But I didn't want to go home. I wanted to see Tony.

I thanked Patsy for her hospitality and followed Joanna outside, where she reassured me again that I didn't have anything to worry about. We said our goodbyes and I headed toward the car.

Stopping, I turned back to her. "By the way . . . do you have any idea where the guys have been taken to?"

Joanna smiled knowingly. "L.A. County Jail." She scrutinized me for a moment. "And in case you're wondering . . . it's Santino."

"Santino?" I repeated blankly.

"Tony's last name. Santino. You'll have to ask for him at the front desk."

I started laughing as I ran toward the car.

"Thanks, Joanna!"

As I barreled down the highway, it struck me that I was plotting to seduce a man I'd hated not so long ago. The more I'd learned about Tony, however, the more attracted I became to him. There was something old-fashioned about him, I decided—almost chivalrous. Even though he insisted that I be treated exactly like one of the guys, he always made sure that someone walked me to my car after work. He also had us put 5065 on hold every time he called for a month, because he'd screwed me out of that half-point. Tony was fiercely loyal to his friends, and I was touched by how involved in his siblings' lives he was. Despite his rough exterior, he was a smart, well-informed guy. He read the paper every day, and could wax lyrical about the ins and outs of the Iran-Contra affair currently in the headlines. When I started dreading my days off, I knew that my feelings for him were completely out of control. There was no stopping it now; my feelings were too strong. What I was about to do may have been madness, but I didn't care.

Gibson's assumption that I was having sex with the guys in the office couldn't have been further from the truth. I had been in Los

Angeles for seven long, celibate months. I was hoping that tonight was going to change all that. The moment I'd touched Tony's hand and he hadn't pulled away gave me all the incentive I needed.

I skidded to a halt in the parking lot outside the L.A. County Jail and brazenly marched toward the entrance. Before I got halfway to it, the doors swung open and Tony stepped out into the night. He didn't see me. He headed straight for a row of pay phones. I stopped in my tracks, suddenly frozen with indecision.

As he rummaged for change, I forced myself to continue walking. This was fate, I decided. A minute later and I would have missed him.

"Hi," I said.

He spun around. His expression softened when he saw me. We stood there staring at each other, saying nothing.

I reached out and ran my fingers softly over the blue lump where his forehead had connected with the wall.

"That's a nasty bruise."

"Yeah. Guess that's what I get for resisting arrest." He stared at me, as if he couldn't believe I had come. "What are you doing here?"

I shrugged, smiling nervously. "I thought you might need a ride."

5

TONY AND I SAT in my car in total silence. The moment we climbed into the little Renault, the atmosphere between us changed. We were together now, in tight quarters. I wondered if Tony also felt this unbearable tension.

"So . . . where to?"

I still didn't know which Tony I was sitting next to. Was it the other Tony, the good man I caught glimpses of at work? Or would I have to deal with the façade that Tony presented to the rest of the world?

"I've got to pick up my bike. It's still at the office."

"Now?"

Tony checked his watch. "I guess it can wait. Maybe we should just get some sleep."

Tony stared straight ahead, his expression unreadable. He pointed me toward the freeway, and we headed east.

"How's your head?" I asked.

"Fine." He brushed his fingers over the bruise.

"What about the others? When will they get out?"

"They got out about an hour ago." Tony sighed. "It always takes longer for me. Because of my name."

"Your name?"

Tony grunted. He seemed to consider saying more, but thought better of it. Instead he muttered, "It's complicated."

It was late and the roads were quiet. The only sound was the gentle hum of the engine. I couldn't stand the silence, so I tried another tack. "Was it rough in there?"

"It wasn't a picnic."

That effectively ended our conversation. Twenty painful minutes later, he instructed me to take the next exit. We entered a quiet residential area. My heart started to beat faster. We were heading toward his apartment.

"Here." He pointed at an empty spot in front of a charming 1920s two-story apartment complex. I pulled in and killed the engine.

Without a word Tony led me through the front entrance. He was always careful to keep details of his private life under wraps. Until now I didn't even know what neighborhood he lived in. Walking toward his apartment, I felt strange, almost like a voyeur. Tony stopped at a door, unlocked it, and switched on the lights. We stepped inside.

It was a small, minimal studio apartment. The few bits of furniture in the place were all a decade out of date—a sofa, a coffee table, a long, low 1970s-style sideboard. On top of the latter were several paperbacks and a small TV. Apart from these spare details, the place was bare. It looked hardly lived in. The walls were empty—no photographs or pictures. It was almost like I was being shown an apartment for rent.

"This is . . . nice," I said, glancing around the small, bare room.

It was certainly different from how I'd imagined Tony's place. With the money he was earning I was sure that he lived in some ostentatious bachelor pad.

"I don't spend a lot of time here," Tony said, as if reading my mind.

"It's . . . cozy." Tony closed the door after us. "Can I get you anything?"

I tried to play the situation to my advantage. "Well . . . a shower would be nice."

"Oh. Right, of course." As he went over to the linen closet, I wondered if I had successfully planted an image of my naked body in his mind. Tony pulled two towels from the top of a neat stack. "It's at the end of the hallway." He handed me the towels. "There's extra toothbrushes in the cabinet."

The bathroom revealed a little more about Tony than the rest of the apartment had. The medicine cabinet was stocked with top-of-the-line shaving creams and razors, toothpaste, toothbrushes, and mouthwash. He certainly didn't skimp on toiletries. With the door closed behind me I picked up a bottle, removed the cap and inhaled the familiar scent of Tony. As I brushed my teeth, I found myself staring blankly at the label.

Obsession.

I undressed, making sure to leave the bathroom door unlocked. I wondered if he would try to join me in the shower. As I stood under the powerful jets, the pounding hot water eased the muscles in my neck and shoulders. I soaped myself sensuously, all the while glancing over to the door. It did not open. After a while I realized that he wasn't coming. With disappointment, I turned off the faucet.

I stepped out of the steamy bathroom with one towel wrapped around my head and the other covering my body. I walked bare-foot into the living room. Tony was sitting on the couch, staring blankly at the TV. He seemed a million miles away. On-screen, Janet Jackson was skipping through an alley singing "When I Think of You," wearing an oversized blazer with huge shoulder pads and even bigger hair.

Tony sensed me behind him and stood up. He looked stiff, uncomfortable in my presence. "I guess I'll take a shower," he muttered, walking past me.

While Tony showered I glanced around the rest of the apartment, noticing that he didn't even have a bed. I went to the sofa, where I presumed he slept, and positioned myself as seductively as I could. When Tony returned he was freshly shaved, with a towel wrapped around his waist. I tried my best to not to stare at his broad shoulders, his muscular arms, or the thin line of hair that started at his chest and ran down his flat stomach. Instead I tried to focus on those clear brown eyes.

He looked more alert now. The exhaustion had left his face and it was as if the water had awoken him to the reality of the situation. We were feet away from each other, naked except for our towels. He looked unsure of what he was doing. This was not the Tony I was used to seeing. His unflappable self-confidence had seemingly deserted him.

"Listen, RB . . . " He ran his fingers through his damp hair. "I really don't think this is a good idea."

"Marisa," I said. "My name is Marisa." I stood up and dropped my towel to the floor. His mouth fell open a little. I stepped toward him. My heart was pounding and I felt light-headed. There was no way back now. I noticed that his eyes did not stray from my face. The perfect gentleman. But that look of uncertainty remained.

I was utterly exposed, in more ways than one. I was standing naked in front of my boss. I had made my feelings clear. I knew that if he were to send me home now, I would never be able to face him again.

"Look . . . Marisa . . . "

I leaned forward and pressed my lips gently against his. He did not resist.

I kissed him again, just as softly. This time he put his arms around me and pulled me closer. Our kisses became more passionate. He reached for the nape of my neck and entwined his fingers in my hair. The months of longing, the evenings I had spent alone aching for him, had all led up to this. I was dizzy with desire. I reached blindly for his towel and tugged at it. It fell away to the floor. My eyes traveled down his taut, muscular body, then returned to his face. He met my gaze with a look of such intensity that it took my breath away.

He stepped away from me and pulled open what I had assumed were a pair of closet doors. Instead, a cast-iron Murphy bed popped out of the wall. Laughter bubbled up inside me; it was absurd, comical, like something you'd see on a sitcom. But when Tony kissed me again and gently pushed me onto the mattress, I forgot about everything . . . everything except him.

■

THE INCESSANT RINGING OF a telephone woke me up early the next morning. I felt Tony shifting around, groaning, sitting up to get the phone.

"Yeah?"

I opened my eyes. The sunlight was already creeping around the heavy curtains, bathing the room in dim light. Tony was sitting on the edge of the bed, phone to his ear. I could make out the defined muscles of his back and shoulders in the early morning gloom. I sat up and crawled catlike toward him, pressing my bare breasts against his back.

I could hear Ron on the other end, talking about how the agents had been in touch with the players. Everybody had the new 1-800 number. Today would be business as usual.

I kissed the nape of Tony's neck and ran my hands across his chest. Tony did his best to end the conversation. Ron wasn't finished, though. "Carmine's going to join you guys," I heard him say. "And RB's staying."

"Okay."

"She doesn't have the backup address. You'll need to get in touch with her."

Tony turned his head slightly and nuzzled my cheek. "I'll get right on it . . . "

After hanging up the phone Tony turned his attention back to me, pushing me playfully back on the bed. As he began to kiss the nape of my neck, his lips slowly traveling down my naked body, I silently thanked every woman Tony had ever made love to. As upset as I'd been to hear about the other women in his life, last night I'd learned that all of those conquests added up to a man who really knew his way around the female body.

An hour later, we were completely spent. Tony was next to me, our limbs entwined, the only sound in the room the steady rhythm of our breathing. He looked at me reluctantly.

"We'd better get ready," he said. I got up and walked shakily toward the bathroom.

Half an hour later, we were outside the warehouse. Tony needed to pick up his motorcycle. Before he got out of the car, he leaned across and kissed me deeply. "By the way," he said, "about last night." I raised an eyebrow. "I don't think we should mention it to anyone, okay?"

The smile froze on my face. I felt a sudden sick lurch in my guts. With a slam of the door he was gone, heading back to his bike. I watched him jump on, start the engine, and roar away. I followed close behind, my mind whirring. What did he mean, *I don't think we should mention it to anyone?* Did he think this was some kind of one-night stand, some little secret he could keep under wraps?

I didn't do one-night stands. I took a deep breath and tried to get my thoughts under control, to look at the evidence logically and dispassionately. He had taken me to his apartment. Not a hotel, his apartment. That had to count for something. And the sex . . . I knew it wasn't just my imagination. I had really felt something, a special connection that only comes when two people care about each other.

Soon we were pulling into the employee parking lot at Olympic Produce and Cold Storage, an enormous warehouse in the middle of the bustling produce district of L.A. Tony went in first, and I followed behind him as nonchalantly as I could.

The warehouse, the size of an aircraft hangar, was bustling with activity. The wailing of a Spanish love ballad on the radio echoed around the cavernous space, punctuated by bangs, yells, and the discordant noises of a loading bay in full swing. Nobody glanced at us as we walked past hundreds of piled wooden crates. A black dwarf with a cigar gripped between his teeth zoomed past us on a forklift, yelling something at a gaggle of workers loading crates of iceberg lettuce into a refrigerated truck.

Tony headed briskly toward the back wall of the warehouse. It was much darker back here, and the concrete floor was sticky with decaying produce. He stopped in front of what appeared to be a dead end: a wall lined with stainless-steel industrial-sized refrigerators. He beckoned me over. I watched in astonishment as he squeezed into the crevice between the wall and the first fridge, until he was completely out of sight.

I peered into the tight, dark space. "Tony?"

"Come on in," I heard him call back. "The water's fine."

I turned and squeezed myself into the gap. I had to shuffle sideways down a long, narrow, pitch-black passageway. My chest was pressed against the wall in front of me, with my back against the cold steel of the fridge. The noise of the warehouse receded. Tony's hand reached out and took mine, pulling me gently out into a small room. He slid a panel into place, concealing the tiny gap from which we had just emerged. Beyond the door was a brightly lit office, no wider than a corridor.

Danny and Kyle had already claimed their places at the long, crude "desk"—a plank of unvarnished wood balanced on crates spanning the length of the cinder-block wall. *"Amigos!"* Kyle called. *"Como estas?"*

They scooted their chairs forward to allow us to pass. I slid into a metal folding chair at the far end of the room. If the last office had reminded me of an underground bunker, this one was like sitting in an oversized coffin. Yet despite the claustrophobic space, I was relieved to see Danny and Kyle seemingly unscathed after last night's ordeal.

"It's basic, but functional," Danny said, waving his hands around the tight space. "If I were an L.A. realtor, I'd say . . . *cozy.* "

"It's a dump," Kyle grumbled. I surveyed the minimal setup.

There were no TVs, no diverters, and no clever system to hide the tape recorders. They were simply connected to the phones, which were spaced at intervals along the wooden plank.

"Just remember to press the 'record' button every time you take a bet," Kyle said. "Other than that, we're golden."

Jay arrived. He slapped palms with the guys and took his place at the table. I looked around the room.

"Where's Mathew?"

Tony chuckled. "Mathew can't make it."

The others smiled knowingly, but I was still missing the obvious. "Oh . . . is he okay?"

"He's okay." Danny gestured over to the tight space we had all just squeezed through. "But he's about a hundred pounds away from being able to fit his ass through the entrance."

The door opened again, and someone I didn't recognize entered the room. He was wearing a dreadful flower-print Hawaiian shirt and thick glasses that comically magnified his brown eyes.

"Carmine!" everyone chorused. As he edged into the room, people jumped up to shake his hand.

"Make way for an old-timer," he said in a voice like whiskey and razor blades. He slid into the seat next to mine. Turning to me he smiled, revealing a set of gleaming dentures. "Carmine," he said, offering his hand.

Despite the less-than-ideal office situation, my spirits were high as the day got under way. I was happy to be back at work, and felt safe tucked away in this tiny secret office. Plus, I was just a few feet away from Tony. I stole a sideward glance at him, and my heart soared when he returned my smile.

When the calls tapered off after the opening rush, the conversation turned to the bust. "Tell us about your cellmates, RB," Danny said. "Any lesbian action?"

"I was only there for about an hour!"

"I dunno, RB. I feel like *something* happened while you were in that prison. You look different today. You might say . . . glowing." Kyle chuckled.

"Really?" The guys were amused by something, but I couldn't understand what. "Thanks, I guess."

Kyle popped his feet up on the desk, warming to the theme. "You know"—he winked—"maybe you should go to prison more often."

Tony cleared his throat. "All right, guys, that's enough."

"Hey, Tony," Danny said, "you remember last year, the all-star break? When we all went down to Magic Mountain?"

Tony smiled. He was happy to steer the conversation away from me. "Sure."

"You remember how they reversed the trains on one side of the Colossus? And you wanted to ride it backward?" Danny was chuckling at the memory now. "And then we went on the Log Jammer, and you got, like, soaking wet, 'cause you sat up front?"

Now Kyle and Jay were cracking up as well. Tony smiled faintly and said, "Yeah."

"And you remember how Kyle said he didn't want to spend the rest of the afternoon looking at your hairy nipples poking through your wet shirt? So he went and bought you a T-shirt?" Danny and Kyle were both convulsing now.

Tony's expression froze on his face. Realization dawned on me.

I looked down at the T-shirt Tony had lent me that morning. He'd pulled it out from the bottom of a stack, where I imagined it had been sitting for years. Over a silkscreened image of a giant roller coaster was the legend "Six Flags, Magic Mountain." My cheeks burned red as the guys howled with laughter and high-fived each other.

After the initial embarrassment, I was actually glad that everything was out in the open. The guys teased Tony relentlessly over his biased office policy, but it was all good-natured. I wanted a real relationship with Tony, and I interpreted their friendly ribbing as a sign of approval. Even Tony seemed less uptight about the situation.

Later, when all the games were off the boards and we were busy ripping the tickets, Tony's cell rang. It was Ron. Normally this would have been a routine call. He'd inquire about the chart and ask for an estimate of how much we'd taken in bets. Ten minutes later, though, Tony was still on the phone. From the look on his face I knew it wasn't good news. By the time he'd hung up, his expression was bleak.

"Listen up. Ron wants everyone at Dan Tana's tonight. No excuses."

My heart sank as the guys started protesting. I'd been hoping to lure Tony to my apartment that evening.

"That's not all," he added. "Effective immediately, no one is to call, meet with, or speak to Jim Arnold."

Although he was addressing the room, Tony's gaze was fixed on me. Everybody knew that I was the only one who had any contact with Jim outside of the office. My mouth turned bone-dry.

"Why?" I managed to croak.

"Because Jim's the reason we got arrested."

6

"I DON'T BELIEVE IT."

I looked imploringly from Ron to Tony. The three of us were huddled together in a red leather booth at Dan Tana's, an Italian restaurant in West Hollywood.

Ron smiled sadly and shook his head. "It's true, RB."

"Ron. I know Jim. He'd never do anything to put me, or anyone else, in danger. It's got to be a mistake."

Tony leaned forward, his face illuminated by the soft glow of the flickering candle. "We're not saying he did it intentionally."

I opened my mouth to say something, but Ron cut me off. His voice was soft, full of compassion.

"I'm not the only person Jim works for, RB. Jim installs diverters and recorders for other bookmakers in California. Guys in Vegas, too—legitimate operations. Jim makes it seem as though all the calls are coming from within Nevada, as required by the gaming commission."

I glanced around the dining room. The other clerks were sitting in booths all around us, but Tony and Ron needed to resolve the Jim situation with me before mingling.

"But . . . so what?"

"Last March, one of the biggest independent gaming centers in Vegas went out of business. The owner vanished, owed his customers millions. Guess whose name came up in the ensuing investigation?"

"Well, I assume you're going to say Jim. But—"

"Not long after that, another legit bookmaker, the Santa Anita, was closed down by the marshals. The gaming commission was all over it, went through the phone records with a fine-tooth comb . . . and guess whose name came up. Again."

"But that doesn't prove anything," I insisted.

"It proves that the authorities know exactly who James Samuel Arnold is," Ron said, with an air of finality. "Tampering with phone lines is a federal offence, RB. Of course, the LAPD were alerted to his activities. And it's not as if Jim is exactly a . . . low-profile kind of guy."

"He's a publicity whore," Tony said flatly. "The bottom line is, his name's out there. He races. You can see pictures of him in the paper, posing next to his car. It wasn't tough for the cops to get a line on him. They tailed him to the Small Office and from there to the Big Office. The cops thought they'd stumbled on a major bookmaking operation. So they went in guns blazing. That's why we didn't get a warning—they didn't realize they were busting *us*."

Ron took a puff on his cigar. "Look, Jim's just too hot right now. The cops are tailing him. He understands the way it's got to be; there's no hard feelings. Jim's job for the next few months is to stay away from us. No one—and I mean *no one*—is to contact him."

I knew what he was implying. I had a choice to make: race in the next Alcan with Jim and quit bookmaking, or drop Jim and stay on. A few months ago I would have just quit my job. But not anymore.

"You shouldn't even be considering this," Tony said with a hint of annoyance.

Ron shushed him. "She's a big girl. Let her make her own decision."

Tony was right—racing was thrilling and exciting. I looked at him in the flickering candlelight. Gazing into his eyes, I felt my heart lurch. My desire to be with him was overwhelming. The idea of walking away from him just as things were starting to go so well was inconceivable to me. No other man had ever made me feel the way Tony did—not even close.

"Jim won't have a problem finding another driver," I said finally. "He's got ages before the start of the race. I'm staying."

Ron beamed at my choice. I avoided Tony's gaze. I knew he was trying to protect me. But the truth was, bookmaking was probably the safer choice.

"Hey, RB." Carmine was standing next to a tall, well-dressed man with salt-and-pepper hair. "I wanted to introduce ya to Roger from the Small Office."

As I introduced myself, I noticed more clerks filing into the place. Within minutes we numbered twenty-one, filling the entire section of the restaurant. It really hammered home the scale of Ron's operation to me. His staff was a cross-section of people who looked like they had nothing in common with each other—but they all revolved around Ron Sacco.

He made the rounds from table to table, chatting amiably with his employees. It didn't matter who they were, Ron could relate to them on their level. It occurred to me that he could probably have a successful career in politics—though maybe he was a little too honest for that.

By the time Ron made it back to our booth, the food had arrived. He tucked into his steak. "Gibson remains an issue," he said, punctuating his words with a jab of the steak knife. "It's just our luck we've got the only straight cop in L.A. sniffing around. I want everyone on high alert. Make sure you're not being fol-lowed. Park farther away from the office."

"What about Jim?" I asked, thinking about his expert crafts-manship. "I mean, how will you replace him?"

"Already have. 5043 put me in touch with a couple of guys who do top-of-the-line work."

"5043 . . . Dale Calhoun," Tony pondered aloud. "The Beverly Hills Bookmaker." I recognized the number. He was one of our players.

"The very same. When he heard what happened, he called me and recommended the services of two security experts."

Ron dabbed the sides of his mouth with a napkin. "Dale hired them because he suspected that one of his clerks had hooked up with a player and was ripping him off. Within days they had audio and video proof for him. Dale was singing their praises. I did a bit of digging, and liked what I found."

Tony took a sip of wine. "And?"

"One of them, Dan Hanks, did a tour of duty in Vietnam."

"Doing what?"

"Placing wiretaps for Naval Intelligence. Got his honorable discharge, then spent the better part of a decade in and out of prison—petty stuff, mostly. The other guy goes by the name 'Mad Dog' Valis, and comes with glowing references from the Gambinos."

"The Gambinos? Aren't they *Mafia?*" I interrupted. But neither Ron nor Tony reacted.

"The two of them hooked up in detective school, of all places. Pooled their resources and went into bounty hunting." Ron took a long, thoughtful puff on his cigar. "I met 'em last night. Exactly the kind of people I like on my payroll: bright, talented, creative."

He blew on the glowing tip of his cigar. "When these guys get done, the new offices are going to be bust-proof. Mark my words."

■

WHILE HANKS AND VALIS were busy securing the new premises, we went on working in the claustrophobic, smoky backup office

at Olympic Produce and Cold Storage. I didn't mind the conditions. Tony was nearby, and at the end of the day I had him all to
myself. With the help of his Harley, he was introducing me to the
chaotic, messy splendor of Los Angeles. I held onto him tightly
as he roared around the hairpin curves and over the blind crests
of Sunset Boulevard. We raced up through the winding streets of
the Hollywood Hills, past multimillion-dollar mansions perched
over the smog-choked city below. We zoomed across Mulholland
Drive, taking in some of the most incredible views the city had to
offer.

My feelings for Tony continued to intensify. The Tony that I
knew outside of the office was a completely different man from
the snarling, angry person I had met all those months ago. I was
experiencing the first flush of real love. Though he didn't ver-
balize it, I felt that he cared deeply about me too.

My parents wouldn't approve of my boyfriend or my job, so I
simply didn't keep them informed. Not dealing with my father
was easy. He had moved into an apartment in Manhattan after the
divorce, and was still traveling extensively. Avoiding my mother
was more complicated. I usually called her when I knew she would
be in her yoga class, but that tactic couldn't work on Mother's Day.
I rang her at noon, New York time, hoping she might be having
brunch with a girlfriend. She picked up on the first ring, as if
she'd been sitting by the phone waiting for my call. I froze, nearly
hanging up on her.

"Marisa? Is that you?"

Recovering my composure I said, "Hi, Mom," as brightly as I
could. "I'm calling to wish you a happy Mother's Day!"

"Where are you? What are you doing?" Hearing the concern
in her voice threw me off. "I haven't spoken to you in months!
Neither has your father!" The fact that my parents were worried
enough to actually speak to each other after their bitter divorce
set off alarm bells.

Flustered, I said the first thing that popped into my head.
"Mom, I'm fine," I said. "I'm working for a . . . produce company."

"You're doing *what?*" She sounded like I had announced that I'd decided to pursue a career in exotic dancing. I took a deep breath and began to describe my fictional life at the warehouse, basing my description on the observations I'd made there. I babbled about crates of vegetables, refrigerated trucks, and my Mexican coworkers.

The silence on the other end was excruciating. This only spurred me on to say even more nonsense. I realized I didn't even know what I was talking about anymore. I stopped and tried to rescue the situation.

"I'm really happy," I said definitively. This, at least, wasn't a lie. "I've met a wonderful guy. And I'm living in an apartment right next to the beach."

She put me through another long, ominous silence. "So you have a green card?" she asked in a tense, clipped tone.

"I don't need one—I'm working off the books. The Mexicans all do it. It's not a big deal."

"This boyfriend of yours is . . . Mexican?"

I fought the urge to laugh. "No, Mom. Italian. He manages the company." I'd hoped this last detail might help, but she had no interest at all.

"And school? Surely you have some ambition beyond . . . packing fruit."

"Yes. Of course I'm going to go back . . . one day. Just not right now."

When we finally hung up, I was miserable. Not only had I ruined Mother's Day, I had the impression I'd just shattered her whole world. Yet her reaction was exactly what I'd expected. I cringed at the thought of introducing my parents to Tony, but I knew that it was inevitable. My boyfriend came from a world that was completely alien to them. They would simply have to learn to deal with each other. I'd never felt this way about anyone before. I rationalized that they would like him once they got to know him.

Tony and I were together almost 24-7. I concentrated on being the perfect girlfriend. I put my domestic skills to work, taking over the shopping, laundry, and cleaning. I'd even begun to think about the possibility of marriage. This was remarkable, given the fact that my parents' marriage had long ago poisoned my idea of wedded bliss.

Moving in together seemed like the next natural step. Tony and I divided our time between my apartment in Long Beach and his at Bimini Place. It seemed silly to keep two separate homes, given that we were always together. I dropped hints, but they were ignored. I knew Tony well enough not to push the issue.

Ron eventually solved the problem. "I want you to move in together," he announced one day, as he casually tossed the payroll on Tony's desk. He let the comment hang for a moment before adding, "I mean, all of you."

"You want us to move in together?" Kyle asked, his brow furrowing.

"Just until the heat dies down. Gibson's determined to close me down. You saw how easy it was for him to follow Jim. He could do the same to any of you."

"So why do we have to move in together?"

"The cops can't follow you if they can't see you," Ron said. "There's a high-rise on Franklyn Avenue with underground parking. Imagine—you travel to and from the office together in a blacked-out van. Nobody sees you coming or going." He noted the astonished expression on our faces. "It wouldn't be forever. Just until Gibson thinks I've closed up shop."

The suggestion had caught everyone off-guard. The first person to object was Carmine. "Jesus, Ron, I'm too old for fucking roommates. I need my space. No offense to these guys, but I already see too much of them."

Ron seemed to have anticipated Carmine's objection. Instead of persuading him, he focused his energies on convincing the rest of us.

"This building's beautiful. There's a swimming pool on the third-floor terrace, a sauna, and wraparound balconies overlooking the ocean."

"I'm in," I volunteered. Kyle and Danny immediately followed suit. Tony and Jay remained silent.

"It'll cut down on travel time to the office," Ron said, continuing to whittle away at them.

Jay shook his head. "Can't do it. I've got college, Ron. I'm already too far away from campus. Any farther out, and I couldn't make it. Anyway, I need peace and quiet to study. Sorry."

Ron was well aware that Tony and I were an item. I expected that this was simply a case of "too much, too soon" for Tony. My heart soared when he sighed. "Okay, I guess." He added sourly, "But I'm not giving up Bimini!"

That didn't matter to me. All I cared about was the fact that Tony and I would be living together.

And his reluctance faded when he got a look at our new residence. It was a luxury high-rise, with its own doorman, concierge, and valet service. Our apartment was beautiful—the master bedroom alone was bigger than Tony's old place, with its own walk-in closet, bathroom, and ocean-view balcony. The other bedrooms were at the opposite end of the apartment, so it was private—almost like having our own separate living space. The swimming pool was huge, surrounded by plush deck chairs. I squeezed Tony's hand, giddy with excitement.

At the Franklyn Avenue apartment, our lives followed a dependable routine. Each morning we'd meet Carmine and Jay in the underground parking garage. We'd all hop into the new van, which resembled a fortress on wheels. The windows were tinted, and it was equipped with a police radio. The wing mirrors faced upward, so we could make sure helicopters weren't following us. Tony was the designated driver, and Jay's job was to listen to the radio for any sign of suspicious police activity. I found the whole thing undeniably exciting, as if we were playing a giant game of cat-and-mouse with the LAPD.

One morning in June, we got the news we'd all been anxiously awaiting. The new office was ready. Ron gave us the address and the time to meet. Mathew rejoined the team and we met him in the garage before we all piled into the van. We headed north on Highway 10 and drove to Bay Street, in downtown L.A. We pulled up to an unimpressive-looking building splattered with graffiti, its windows boarded up and painted a murky shade of white. Above a wooden door was a sign that read "Gumms Lighting, By Appointment Only." A number was listed underneath. We peered out of the van and I noticed Ron's Mustang parked across the street. He got out and we followed him to the front door.

It opened from the inside, revealing a tall, stocky man with tight strawberry-blond curls. A pair of reflective aviator shades covered his eyes, making it hard to guess his age. Then I noticed his guns. He had two tucked into the leather holster pulled tight around his waist. As we filed in past him, another man approached us from down the hallway. He was slightly shorter and very lean, with sleepy eyes and dark, shoulder-length feathered hair. He was dressed from head to toe in black, with a pair of snakeskin cowboy boots and a gun casually tucked into his belt.

These were Hanks and Valis, the security experts Ron had hired. They introduced themselves, however, as "Red" and "Duke." I glanced over at Tony; he looked less than impressed by the sight of this strange duo.

Red and Duke proceeded to give us a guided tour of the new space. Red, with his strawberry-blond mullet, did most of the talking. "Take a look at this," he said. "Looks like an ordinary wood door from the outside, right? But if you look here, you can see it's reinforced with steel. We put a safety bar here, just to be sure." Duke picked up the heavy steel bar and lowered it into the brackets. It extended a foot on either side of the entrance. Mathew whistled appreciatively. The door was virtually impenetrable. "Ain't nobody going to be sneaking up on you in here."

We followed the odd couple down a brightly lit corridor until we reached the main office. It was a huge improvement on the old place: large and clean, with desks and chairs lining the perimeter of the room. It smelled of fresh paint. A couple of TVs were mounted on the wall, and two monitors sat on a desk. Red walked over to the monitors and tapped one lightly.

"These babies are your eyes and ears. We have two surveillance cameras mounted on the roof that give you a clear view of both streets. No one can approach the building without you seeing them first." He gave Ron a crooked smile. "No surprises."

On the screens we could see cars parked as far as a couple of blocks away.

"Shredder," announced Red next, pointing to a box-like device by the wall. "In the unlikely event that you see the cops heading your way, you just feed the tickets in here to destroy 'em." He picked up a couple of blank tickets and fed them into the machine. The blades reduced them to spaghetti-like strands.

The next stop was the enormous warehouse. Tony's workout bench and weights had been set up underneath a barred window. We still had plenty of space to park the van inside. We followed Red and Duke over to a set of pallet shelves set against the wall.

"Here you have an ordinary set of shelves," Duke said, gesturing to the wall like a magician about to perform a trick. "But with one subtle application of pressure—" He crouched down, reached under the bottom shelf, and pulled out a hidden drawer. The recorders were installed seamlessly inside.

Danny crouched down to take a close look. "That's kick-ass," he said.

The diverters were also cleverly hidden, disguised within the body of a fully functional workbench. Even Tony seemed grudgingly impressed by the craftsmanship.

Red pointed to the exit at the end of the warehouse. "The doors back there are reinforced with steel as well," he said. "Impenetrable."

As far as I was concerned, having shared a restroom with the guys at the office for months, the most exciting new feature was the two bathrooms.

When we all crowded back into the office, Red asked Ron to dial the office's 1-800 number from his cell phone. A moment later the digital phones on the desk began to ring, lights blinking in unison. Duke handed Tony a silver ballpoint pen. "Click it," Duke instructed. When Tony clicked the pen, the ringing stopped abruptly and the blinking lights went off. Tony clicked again and the phones sprang back to life. Danny laughed, delighted by this clever device. Ron looked thoroughly impressed.

"And there you have it," said Red. "Your new office. Word of advice—vary your route to work. Routine is your enemy. And don't forget the basics—check your rearview mirrors, and don't open the door until you confirm the street is clear. You stick to that, you're going to be real happy here. Any questions?"

Nobody said a word. Red grabbed his shiny black Members Only jacket from the back of a chair and zipped it on, concealing his guns. Duke readjusted his shirt to cover the gun jutting out of his jeans, and slipped a pair of sunglasses over his face. "Good luck," Red said, and they left, Ron seeing them out. We watched on the monitors as the three of them ambled outside, Duke and Red swaggering off to a Buick at the end of the block.

"Jesus, Ron," Mathew said as Ron walked back into the office. "They're a bit over the top, aren't they? Like a couple of cartoon characters."

Tony snorted, "Dale recommended those clowns?"

"Highly recommended," Ron said, in a placating tone.

Tony shook his head, watching the Buick pull away. "I'd take Jim any day over those two jokers. Even with the cops following him."

■

THAT EVENING WE DROVE over to Bimini Place to pick up the last of Tony's things. I was excited: this was the final step before we were officially cohabiting. As we opened the door, I immediately sensed that something was wrong. The curtains were closed. We hadn't slept there in a few days, but I was sure I'd left them open. Then I noticed a strange, stale odor.

I felt Tony stiffen. "Wait," he muttered.

As he flipped on the light, I gasped. A man was sitting on the edge of the bed. He was shirtless, hunched over, his back to us. Without turning around, he growled, "Turn off the fucking light." Before Tony plunged the room into darkness again I caught an image of the man on the bed. His skin was pallid and shiny with sweat. The upper body was muscular and fully developed, yet he seemed the size of a child. A long scar ran from the base of his neck all the way down his spine. Seeing him hunched over like that, shielding his eyes from the light, my first impression was of some subterranean creature that had been unexpectedly exposed to the sun. Tony switched on a dim table lamp.

I stood frozen as the stranger turned to face Tony. In the half-light he looked even more sinister. He had sandy-blond hair and light eyes that looked heavily medicated, glassy and dead. His face unnerved me. There was something demonic about it—yet strangely familiar. The man pointed to one of the barstools and deadpanned, "Happy thirtieth." I followed his finger to a neat pile of white powder on the stool by the kitchen counter.

"That was two weeks ago," Tony said.

With dismay I realized why the man looked so familiar. It wasn't just the face—they had that same powerful upper-body shape too.

So Tony's father *wasn't* dead, as I'd assumed. I looked at the pile of powder. "Tony doesn't do drugs," I said. I was appalled at the idea of a parent encouraging their child to use narcotics.

Tony's father turned toward me slowly. He laughed—a horrible, wheezy sound, like a tire deflating. It was a laugh designed to tell me just how wrong I was. I waited for Tony to back me up. Instead he averted his eyes.

"Where the fuck did you find Dorothy?" his father sniggered.

Tears welled in my eyes. I turned to leave, but Tony strode across the room and took my arm.

"Don't go." He looked back at his father. "Get dressed!" he told him.

The little man stood up and pulled on a wrinkled shirt he'd left lying on the sofa. As he dressed, I couldn't help staring at his tiny body with a kind of horrified fascination. He buttoned up his shirt and walked past me without a word. Tony followed him.

I closed the door behind them and turned on the light again. This encounter had jarred my perception, and I saw the place as it was for the first time. I had once thought of it as cozy, but it wasn't. It was a dump. The paint was chipped. The wallpaper was peeling. The parquet floors were scratched. It was a crummy apartment, in a rundown building, in a bad neighborhood. And I was standing in it—next to what looked like thousands of dollars' worth of cocaine.

Everything was wrong. I'd been arrested. I was working illegally. I was deeply in love with a criminal. A despairing sob rose in my throat, and I struggled to hold it back. What was I doing? I looked around the tiny apartment again, and realized with a chill that I didn't know Tony at all.

7

"I can't believe that man is your father."

We were sitting together on the sand, looking out on the vast, unfathomable ocean. It was a relief to be away from Bimini Place. Tony's father had cast a sinister shadow over the whole building.

Tony tried to put his arm around me, but I stiffened.

"Don't judge me by my father, Marisa," he said. "I barely know the man." The rays of the setting sun cast a golden glow over Tony's face as he stared out to sea.

"How come?"

Tony took a deep breath. "He wasn't exactly what you'd call a role model. He was barely even a father. He would disappear for months, sometimes years at a time. We never relied on him for anything. Once in a while he'd just . . . show up. Act like he'd never been away."

"And your mom would just let him in?"

Tony smiled sadly. "Oh, she hated him. Used to call him a no-good short son of a bitch. But she always took him back. Always."

I thought about my parents' bitter relationship, which suddenly seemed rosy in comparison.

"When I was thirteen he pulled up, out of the blue, in a brand-new silver Caddy. We were dirt-poor at the time. And there's my pop in the coolest car I'd ever laid eyes on. He took me out for a spin, and . . . I can't tell you how good it felt when my friends saw me driving around in this kick-ass Cadillac." Tony was smiling now. I could see from the faraway look in his eyes that he was wistfully reliving that day. Then a shadow fell across his face.

"Go on," I whispered.

"Dad said he had something to take care of. I didn't ask what. I didn't want to say anything to rock the boat, now he was back. We drove to the Tenderloin, and it was a war zone down there. The stores were all shuttered. Bums sitting on the corners drinking outta paper bags. Hookers parading up and down. And Dad, he slows down to a crawl, peering up and down the street, muttering to himself. Finally he sees the guy he's looking for. Some black guy on the corner. Dad pulls over and tells me to roll down the window and call the guy over, you know? So I roll it down, and yell Hey, mister! The guy struts over to the car, real cool, and leans in.

"The next thing I know . . . *Crack!* Pop takes off, full tilt. It takes me a moment to realize that he just shot the guy in the face. And I'm sitting there covered in blood and brains."

I was stunned into silence. "He killed him?" I said at last. "Just like that—right in front of you?"

"Blew the guy's face off. You shoulda heard Mom yelling when he dropped me off at home. I looked like I'd just got done slaughtering cattle. Dad tells her I got a nosebleed. After that he disappeared again. We didn't see or hear anything from him for almost four years. I figured he was in jail or dead. Then one day he calls the house. I was seventeen."

"What did he want?"

"He's got a job for me in Los Angeles. He hooked me in by promising that I'd be going back home in a few weeks with a lot of money for Mom and the girls. I took two weeks off work and drove down to L.A. He opens the door and the place is a mess—needles, burnt spoons, the works. He's strung out on heroin, barely coherent. He was supposed to be answering phones for Sacco."

"Ron?" I could not fathom that Ron would ever associate with someone like Tony's father. "Your father worked for Sacco?"

"They were old friends. Dad and Sacco started taking bets together twenty years ago. They were partners until Dad fucked it up as usual. He got into drug trafficking, started hanging around shady people. Ron was smart enough to realize that Dad was bad for business, so he bought him out. Five years later, he calls Ron, flat broke, begging for a job. I guess Sacco felt he owed him, so he gave him a job clerking. Back then Sacco had satellite offices—one clerk, one phone per apartment, taking bets from a group of players. He had seven of them at Bimini Place. The building was falling apart, so the owner didn't care what went on as long as the rent was paid. Sacco set Dad up in one of the apartments, and the landlord turned a blind eye.

"Only Dad was all fucked up and he wasn't answering the phones. Ron starts getting complaints from the players, so he goes to check on Dad and finds him out cold. He gives Pop one last chance to get it together, and that's when Pop called me. When I got down there, he was in no state to work. That was my crash course in the art of bookmaking."

Although I was saddened by Tony's story, I was also grimly intrigued. This was the most he had ever told me about his past.

"Jim told me that Sacco didn't really start making money until you came along," I said.

Tony smiled. "I always had a head for numbers. Bookmaking just made sense to me straightaway. There are patterns, you know. . . I paid attention to how the players were betting. I began to adjust the lines myself. If we were three on San Diego and a player had already bet it twice, I'd give it to him at minus four. Back then the whole system was still in its infancy. Ron would call every few hours with the changes. But I didn't need his changes, because I was making my own. My office was the only one consistently making money. Funny thing was, Ron had no idea I was even working there. Not until we got busted. That was twelve years ago—my first arrest, the day after my eighteenth birthday. It was the only time the cops didn't confuse me with my dad. You remember I told you that my name causes me problems? That's because when they put it in the computer, Pop's record shows up as well. And believe me, he's been busted for a whole lot more than bookmaking."

I thought of the pallid little man I had encountered earlier. Even when he wasn't around, he was wreaking havoc with Tony's life.

"Sacco came down to the station to bail us out. He recognized me straightaway, even thought he hadn't seen me since I was a kid. He paid the fines, asked me to stay on. I figured, what the hell? I already had a record. So Ron rents a warehouse, puts all the satellite offices under one roof and gives me the job of running it. Business started booming. I've made Ron a lot of money, but he's always been good to me in return. If not for Ron, I wouldn't be able to take care of my mom and sisters. I bought them a house in northern California, put my little sisters in Catholic school and helped my brother-in-law start his own business."

"All the things your father should have been doing," I said.

"Ron's been more of a father to me than mine ever was."

I took a deep breath. I was glad to know more about where Tony came from, but it didn't solve the problem of his father being back in the picture. "So how often do you see your father?"

Tony shrugged. "Not often. Whenever he needs something. The only reason I see him at all is because he knows where to find me."

"Maybe you should move."

"It's not that easy, Marisa. Larry—the manager of Bimini Place—he's an old friend. When Ron pulled the satellite offices out of the building, it was a huge blow to him. Larry's always been good to me. That's why I stayed there and why I'll keep renting the apartment, even if I don't live in it. Larry's like family."

I nodded. I knew that loyalty was very important to Tony, a quality that made him completely different from his father.

"What happened to your father's back?" I asked tentatively. "Was he stabbed?"

"No . . . when he was a little kid, he had a lump on his back that just kept growing and growing. Back then the family couldn't afford to take him to a doctor. By the time he was eleven, it had grown into a huge hump. The doctors had to cut him open. Inside they found a bunch of hair, flesh, and teeth. The doctors said that my pop had absorbed his twin brother in the womb, and the twin was using his body, like a parasite, to keep growing. They removed it, but the operation stunted his growth."

I shuddered, but it seemed oddly appropriate—Tony's father, the evil twin that ate its brother.

"Did your father really come here for your birthday?"

Tony put his arms around me and pulled me close. I did not resist this time. Amusement flecked his voice as he said, "That's what's so sweet about you, Marisa. You always look for the good in people. No, he didn't come for my birthday. Not even close."

"What, then?"

"Dad's importing heroin from Thailand. He came because he needs a favor."

"Heroin? You mean, that powder in your apartment was heroin?"

"Yeah. China white. Worth a small fortune."

To me the word heroin was synonymous with death. "Do you do heroin?" I whispered.

"I tried it once. Just once. Look, Marisa, I've been in L.A. a long time. You're the only person I've ever met who doesn't drink or get high."

"So you do drugs." I felt my chest tightening. "What drugs?"

"Coke." I broke free of his embrace, and he quickly added, "I've been doing a lot less of it recently."

"Why, though? Why do you do it?"

I never understood the appeal of getting drunk or high. I was a risk taker, but I always wanted to be in control. The idea of being dependent on a substance was insane to me. I couldn't respect someone who took drugs. And without respect, no relationship can survive.

"Why do I do coke?" Tony pondered the question. "There's the practical reason—I do it to stay awake. I work six days a week and grade nights. I need something to keep me functioning."

"You should try coffee," I sniffed.

"But"—Tony placed his hand on my arm—"ever since we've been together, I've barely touched it. I've been spending a lot more of my time in bed these days."

I knew he was trying to lighten the mood, but it didn't matter. My eyes started tearing.

"Hey," he said softly. "Come here. Look, I think it's great that you don't do drugs. I love that about you. I'd never want you to start."

The tears started coming. I wasn't angry, though. I was simply crying for the little boy that Tony had once been. I felt desperately sorry for him. His childhood, his entire life, could not have been any more different from mine. He pulled me close and I buried my face in his neck. *If he loves me,* I thought, *he won't need drugs.* I breathed in the clean, warm scent of his skin.

"I love you," I whispered.

■

BACK AT THE OFFICE, the workload eased off. Baseball season was in full swing, and that sport was decidedly less popular with our players. Many of them opted to take the entire season off. With the lighter workload came more free time. Tony and I made the most of it, exploring southern California together on his Harley.

One evening Tony took me to Tale O The Pup, an iconic Los Angeles hot dog stand shaped like a giant hot dog. It was one of the last survivors of the 1950s trend of buildings created to mimic the products sold in them. I had my first chili dog there, sitting outside on a balmy summer night. I told Tony again, "I love you," hoping that he would say it back to me.

He didn't understand how much I needed to hear him say those words. I knew, deep down, that he must love me. How could he not? What we had was so incredibly intense, passionate, and tender. I knew he felt it as well. Why couldn't he say it?

■

"GOD" WAS THE MONIKER that the guys came up with for the pen-shaped device Tony used to silence the phones. God turned out to be an extremely useful gadget. Being able to shut the phones off until we opened gave us some much-needed peace and quiet.

One Saturday in June, however, Tony was pissed. "Where the fuck is God?" he demanded, storming around the office. His pointed question drew the usual round of wisecracks from the guys.

"God is everywhere!"

Tony continued rummaging around the desks.

"Actually, Danny, Nietzsche postulated that God is dead," Mathew pointed out, with the assumed air of a philosophy professor.

Tony, who had little time for philosophy—especially moments before the opening line—replied with a decisive "Shut up and help me look!"

As Tony stormed past me, I noticed something slim and silver poking out of his back pocket. I reached over and plucked it out.

"God was with you the whole time," I said. With a click, the phones screamed to life.

As usual, I checked the monitor periodically. Sergeant Gibson seemed to have forgotten about us, but we remained on high alert. The screens showed an unchanging picture of the deserted streets in front of the building—just another day at the office.

However, at the back of the warehouse, sheriffs, officers, detectives, and electronics specialists were quietly assembling. Red and

Duke had indeed reinforced the garage door and rear exit with steel, as promised. They'd also loosened the hinges on the back door, allowing Gibson's men to wedge it open with a crowbar. One by one, this grim assemblage filed into the warehouse like shadows. They crept past the parked van, weapons drawn. The incessant ringing of the phones and our harried voices, frantically taking bets, drowned out their approach.

I was reading a player the line when I saw a subtle movement out of the corner of my eye. I glanced up and spotted Sergeant Gibson. For a moment, I thought he was a hallucination. The apparition didn't make a sound—he just stood there, face twisted in a humorless grin. As I opened my mouth to warn the others, the officers swarmed in.

This raid was a much bigger deal than the one before. From the number of cops I knew there was no way we'd be answering phones from a backup office in the morning. A deep, heavy sadness flooded me as the cops swarmed around us with practiced efficiency. I sensed that this would be the end of everything.

"Up against the walls."

Plainclothes officers slipped into our vacated seats, answering phones and smoothly recording wagers. The transition was flawless. Our players didn't notice that they were placing bets with undercover detectives.

Gibson was rummaging around on the desks, clearly looking for something in particular. He was a lot calmer this time around. He had really done his homework. Suddenly his eyes lit up and he made for Tony, plucking God from where it was clipped onto Tony's T-shirt. Without hesitating, Gibson depressed the button and the phones were instantly silenced. He winked at Tony, letting us all know that he was in on the joke. This intimate knowledge could only mean one thing—Red and Duke had set us up.

We would later learn that they had been working undercover for the FBI and the DEA for over a decade. Their bust of Ron Sacco subsequently blew their cover for good.

Handcuffed and lined up against the wall, we gravely listened to the angry thump of hammers and the whining roar of power saws as the secret drawer and workbench were expertly dismantled. This time around, the authorities were not going to miss out on any vital evidence. Their smooth, coordinated precision was almost more frightening than the violent and chaotic raid that had preceded it. No screaming, no threats, no physical violence. They had specialists on hand to take the office apart in minutes.

As the raid went on, the sobering reality of the consequences I now faced became apparent. What was I doing here, sitting on the floor in handcuffs, alongside this ragtag bunch of lawbreakers and misfits? Me—cosmopolitan, educated, with a father who worked for the United Nations? What was I thinking? How could I have been so stupid? Did I really believe that breaking the law could be so easy, that I wouldn't have to pay the price?

A camera crew arrived, and then another, and another. We were making national news. In fact, we were headlining. As the office turned into a media circus, Sergeant Gibson came over, squatted in front of me and looked me in the eye. "Look who's fucked now," he breathed, casually knocking my baseball cap off my head and exposing my face to the cameras. I desperately twisted away, hoping my parents wouldn't recognize their daughter's face when they turned on the evening news.

Eventually, the reporters and the camera crews were ushered out along with the sheriffs and detectives, leaving the LAPD to finish up. I looked miserably at Tony. He was staring off into the distance, lost in thought. I felt a pang of despair as I realized I would probably not see him again for a very long time.

Two female officers came over and helped me to my feet. I looked back at Tony one last, desperate time. He looked up and our eyes locked.

"I love you," he mouthed.

8

I WAS IN PRISON. Again. I could barely believe I'd allowed myself to sink this far.

Ron had again ensured that my bail was posted before I'd set foot in the maximum-security women's prison. But thanks to a special request from Sergeant Gibson—immediately granted by the warden—I was to be held for twenty-four hours regardless. I was going to be locked up with hardened criminals. I concentrated on preparing myself mentally for the horrors that I imagined awaited me.

The guard—a tall, pinch-faced blonde squeezed into a too-tight uniform—led me and another woman toward the holding cell. My companion was a squat, hard-looking Mexican with a crudely inked dagger etched on her cheek. She'd caught me staring at it during the booking process and shot me a look filled with bone-chilling malice.

The guard removed the keys from her belt and took off our handcuffs. We were put into the holding cell. Four other women were cooped up in there, all sharing a hard wooden bench that ran the length of the wall. I took my place on the empty bench opposite them, staring down at my feet.

The Mexican girl flopped down next to me. "Fucking *puta!*" she announced to no one in particular. I'd ascertained from her familiarity with the booking process that this wasn't her first time in Sybil Brand, either. I snuck a sideways glance at her. Her eyes were boring right into me. The India-ink knife creased as her mouth twitched in distaste.

"Go on, bitch. Surprise me. What the fuck you in for?"

I felt the eyes of the women on the opposite bench upon me. "Bookmaking," I answered, trying to keep my voice steady. "How about you?"

"Possession with intent."

I rested my head back against the concrete wall and closed my eyes. I'd been replaying the last moments of the bust on a constant loop for the past few hours. Just as I'd been dragged away, Tony had said the three words I'd been longing to hear. *I love you.*

At least I knew it now. Even though we had been cruelly torn apart, for who knew how long.

A loud clanging shook me out of my thoughts. The door to the holding cell was being unlocked. An enormous trustee with tightly cropped gray hair waddled into the cell. She began to distribute sandwiches under the watchful gaze of a guard. She handed one to each of us. "Dinner, ladies," she announced. When she reached our end of the bench, she greeted the Mexican girl with the familiarity of an old friend. "Lupe! Whatchoo doin' here, girl?"

"Shit. Same as you. Got fucking popped."

They chatted excitedly in Spanish until the guard told them to shut up. A sandwich landed on my lap, and the trustee waddled out of the cell. The bread holding it together was stiff and dry. Peeling it back, I discovered a discolored slice of baloney underneath, curling up at the rim. Beneath that was a smear of mayonnaise that had a distinctly unhealthy sheen to it. My stomach gurgled. I hadn't eaten since breakfast, but I wasn't going to risk salmonella by putting this in my mouth. I knew I was due to be released sometime tomorrow. I'd have to tough it out until then. I placed the sandwich on the bench next to me and started to massage the red marks where the handcuffs had dug into my wrists.

An uneasy silence had fallen over the cell. I looked up. The women on the other bench were staring at me. An air of antagonism was quickly poisoning the cell. Maybe they figured me for some snobby white princess who thought she was too good to eat the same food as everyone else. I picked up the sandwich and held it out to them. "I'm not hungry," I said.

The prisoner directly across from me—a large black woman with a shaved head—snatched it from my hand and wolfed it down in two bites. For now, at least, the tension passed.

Soon the guard returned to our cell and called out my name along with two others. We were marched down a corridor and ushered into a bare room bathed in harsh fluorescent light. Here we were photographed and checked for lice. Afterward, we were stripped and subjected to a humiliating body search. Finally, I was given a pair of shapeless gray pants with a matching top. My new uniform.

They couldn't find a pair of prison-issue shoes to fit me, so I was allowed to wear my own sneakers. I'd bought them because of their chunky soles—the extra height helped me to maintain the illusion of masculinity when I'd worked in the seedy warehouse district. I absently hoped that the inches they added might give me a slim advantage in prison.

Once dressed, we were taken to a second holding cell. It began to fill up as more and more women were processed. We waited in abject, miserable silence. The last to arrive was the Mexican girl, Lupe. She swaggered in with the confident air of someone who knew this routine by heart. She had nothing to fear. She had friends on the inside, which put her at the top of the cell's hierarchy. I soon noticed another trustee languidly dragging a broom down the hallway outside the cell, covertly assessing the newcomers. Lupe sprang to her feet and ambled over to the bars.

She and the trustee exchanged hurried whispers. In the blink of an eye the trustee reached into the waistband of her pants, produced a cigarette, and dropped it to the floor. She swept it under the bars and into the waiting hands of Lupe, who expertly tucked the contraband into the cuff of her rolled-up pants. Triumphant, she sauntered away and sat down next to me. She pointed a stubby finger at my chest.

"Bitch, I heard you wuz on the news."

"Really?"

"Yeah, bitch, really. Your white ass is all over the TV! You want to know something else? Word is, they going to fuck you *up* in here."

■

THE INMATES' JEERS AND screams bounced off the oppressive pink walls as we followed the guard down a long hallway. Inmates pressed themselves against the bars, catcalling at the new arrivals. The guard seemed impervious to the noise, dropping each prisoner off at the allocated cellblock. One by one, our numbers diminished. Soon just Lupe and I were following the guard. We approached the gate at the end of the hallway, and were ushered through. A crowd of rough, menacing women eyed me as the barred door clanked shut behind us.

Straight ahead was a bustling area where women milled around aimlessly, seemingly free to come and go as they pleased. Instinct told me to keep moving. A couple of women jostled me, but I kept right on walking, eyes glued to the floor. Suddenly I sensed something large blocking my path.

Looking up, I realized that I was standing in front of a muscular black man. His Afro was covered by a black hairnet, knotted at the front. His pants hung low on his waist, cut off at the knees, exposing a pair of strong, hairy legs. He had a pack of cigarettes tucked into the rolled-up sleeve of his tight T-shirt, and glistening, muscular arms. I was momentarily too shocked to react. What was a man doing in a women's prison?

The man's nostrils flared as he sized me up. Then I heard a familiar, mocking voice behind him. *Lupe.*

"That's her. That's that white bitch from the news. Fuck her up, Pretty Boy!"

At her command the man took a step toward me. His eyes glinted dangerously. I realized that I was wrong. Pretty Boy was a 200-pound woman.

How I reacted here would determine how I was treated for the rest of my stay. If I cowered, I would be easy prey for anyone who wanted to use me as a punching bag. I curled my fingers into fists. My breathing became shallow. I had done nothing to provoke this creature. It was the end of a long, difficult day. All I wanted was to be left alone. I felt a rush of adrenaline kick in, fueling the rage that had been simmering inside.

"Leave me alone!" I threatened.

The eyes of the entire cellblock swiveled in our direction. She glared at me, but didn't make a move.

"I mean it! Leave me alone!"

On any other day, Pretty Boy would have ripped me apart in a fight. But not today. This wasn't justice. I did not deserve to be here, or at the mercy of this beast.

"Come on! Fuck—her—*up!*" Lupe, again. Hungry for violence.

Pretty Boy leaned forward, her face inches from mine. She recognized from the hostility in my eyes that this wasn't going to be an easy beat-down.

"You better stay the fuck outta my way," she growled.

She walked off, with her disappointed instigator tagging along behind. The small crowd that had gathered around looked disappointed that the white girl wouldn't be hammered.

Heading farther into the cellblock, I ended up at a wall of metal shelves, where bundles of linens were stored. An elderly inmate instructed me to take a bundle, then directed me toward the sleeping area. After seeing many movies set in prison, I'd imagined that I would be sleeping in a cell with a bunk bed and a toilet. Instead I entered a dormitory containing row after row of metal bunks. At least a hundred women were detained in this large, open, and virtually unsupervised section of the prison. The lack of guards terrified me. I was sure that violent outbursts were a part of everyday life here.

My bundle contained a towel, sheets, a pillow, a pillowcase, and a blanket. I found an unoccupied bunk and threw it down. Although I wanted to avoid the prison bathroom, nature was calling.

Like the dormitory, the bathrooms were huge. Rows of shower stalls lined one wall. Against the other were toilet stalls with tiny, lockless doors that afforded little privacy. The place was packed with women, who seemed to gather here to talk and hang out. I snuck into an unoccupied stall.

Over by the sinks, a group of women were engrossed in some strange activity. I looked on in quiet fascination as a woman dismantled a ballpoint pen and squeezed the ink from it onto several blobs of white toothpaste. Then she blended the mixture with her fingers on the ceramic tiles. I realized that she was creating the latest range of Sybil Brand cosmetics. Red ink mixed with toothpaste produced a palette of lipstick and blush shades, from pale pink to bright red. Blue ink was used for eye shadow, and was copiously applied with fingertips. The women began to dip their fingers in the stuff and paint their faces. If you could ignore the surroundings, they looked like a bunch of high-school girls getting ready to watch a football game. I noticed that even their baggy, sexless prison uniforms had been carefully adjusted to show off their legs, breasts, and waists to maximum effect.

Rage simmered in the air, and every few moments I heard outbursts of shouts and curses. I decided to hide out on my bunk until lights-out. When I got there, I discovered someone had taken my blanket. I knew that I'd never be able to get it back. There were too many beds, too many prisoners; and anyway, what would I do? Ask politely? I wasn't prepared to risk a beating—or worse—over an itchy prison-issue blanket, so I resigned myself to sleeping without one.

All of my former bravado had ebbed out of me now. Instead I felt exhausted, drained. I climbed up on the top bunk and tried to get comfortable. The mattress gave off a series of disconcerting creaks and pops as I clambered onto it. I closed my eyes and my mind drifted back to Tony. I wondered what he was going through at that very moment. Was he thinking of me?

Unlike the majority of these women, I would be free tomorrow. But what then? Would Tony and the others go back to work for Sacco? I couldn't. I would never risk coming back here again. The thought of being locked up for more than twenty-four hours alongside these violent, hardened women was inconceivable.

Hours later, the rest of the inmates started filing into the huge dormitory. The atmosphere became tense as women argued over cigarettes or missing clothes. My stomach rumbled and my mouth tasted stale and sour. I hadn't eaten in a long time, and breakfast was still hours away. I needed to sleep; I needed to keep my strength up.

Guards roamed up and down the rows of beds, monitoring the women as they settled in for the night. I watched one pass by me. She was wearing a paper dunce cap, with the word "PUSSY" scrawled across it in crude block letters. She stopped by my bed and glared at me.

"Shoes off."

I removed my sneakers and tucked them under the scratchy threadbare sheet. I wrapped the laces around my hand in case someone tried to steal them in the night.

At nine o'clock a guard called, "Lights out," and the dormitory fell into darkness. I lay there, rooted to the spot. I heard whispers, giggles, padding footsteps as women maneuvered around the room, crawling into different bunks. I turned on my side, hoping that tomorrow would come quickly. The last thing I remembered before I fell into a fitful sleep was seeing a flare of light somewhere in the darkness, and then smelling the unmistakable aroma of marijuana.

9

40-MILLION-A-YEAR BOOKIE RING BROKEN!

The gang from the Big Office was crowded around the Formica table gaping at the *L.A. Times* headline. We had also made the front pages of the *San Francisco Chronicle* and *USA Today.* We made headlines all across America.

"Read it out!"

We were at the Pantry, a downtown Los Angeles institution famous for its blue-collar cooking, enormous portions, and all-day breakfasts. We were all in serious need of comfort food after twenty-four hours in prison. I glanced around nervously. After seeing how massive this news story had become, I was sure that all eyes were upon us.

"What . . . here?"

"Nobody's looking," Mathew said gently. "Go on."

I started to read.

"A sophisticated bookmaking operation that used toll-free numbers to rake in at least 40 million dollars on sports bets was raided Saturday by the Los Angeles County sheriff's vice detectives. Six people face charges of bookmaking, a felony that carries a maximum three- to five-year jail sentence upon conviction."

I felt the color drain out of my face. Three to five years?

"Babe . . . are you okay?"

Tony's eyes radiated concern. I nodded quickly, tried to refocus my eyes on the newspaper. The waitress appeared and I jumped in surprise as she started refilling our coffee cups.

"Go on," Danny urged.

Tony reached under the table and gave my thigh a reassuring squeeze. "Trust me, babe. You are not going to jail."

"But it says here—"

"Trust me." His eyes bored into mine. "You'll get a fine. A slap on the wrist."

"Just read it, RB!" Danny said again.

I forced my attention back to the paper. *"The organization, which operated out of six fictitious businesses, was headquartered in an East Los Angeles building, where officers recovered electronic gear used to record wagers. The organization took bets from out of state and used a hookup to forward incoming calls to locations known only to organization employees, so the calls could not be traced."*

The article went on to describe our activities loosely, even dedicating a sentence to "God": *"Detectives found a wireless transmitter concealed in a fountain pen that, when activated, shut off phone service to the office."*

The piece ended with a list of the names and ages of those arrested. I cringed when I saw my name in print. Even if my father had somehow missed the evening news on TV the night before, he would surely read it in today's paper.

"Oh, God," I moaned, "this is going to kill my parents . . . "

Tony shook his head. "It's your first offense. You'll get a fine."

"Actually, it's her *second* offense."

Tony shot Mathew a poisonous look. "Thanks, Mathew. Now shut the fuck up."

I tried to focus on the positives. I knew Tony had been arrested half a dozen times, and he'd never received any more than a fine and probation—even on his felony convictions. Surely that was a good sign.

Danny leafed through *USA Today*, whistling to himself. "Damn, we're hot!"

With all of the murders, rapes, drug trafficking and gang wars that were happening in America, how on earth was a bookmaking operation the biggest story of the day?

"We can thank Duke and Red for that," Mathew scowled.

Tony shook his head in frustrated agreement. "They charge Sacco an arm and a leg to keep us safe from the cops, and then lead 'em right to us."

Six steaming plates piled high with hotcakes, home fries, and thick slices of sweet cured ham arrived at the table. Famished, I doused my hotcakes in maple syrup. "So what happens now?"

Tony had been through this routine many times before. He reeled off the next steps with an air of professional detachment. "They charge us. Bookmaking and conspiracy. After that, we'll get a fine and a caution. That's it."

"What about Ron?" I lowered my voice. "It's over, right? He can't get past something like this."

"Are you *kidding?*" Tony tapped the newspapers for emphasis. "You read what his business is worth. He's not going to walk away from that kinda money."

"But surely the cops will just close him down again?"

"He'll find a way. He always does."

"Well, good for him," I said with a trace of bitterness. "But I am out. There's no way I'm going back to that place. I couldn't."

As I'd lain in my bunk at Sybil Brand in the quiet moments before the dawn, I'd made a decision. I did not belong in a women's prison. I belonged in school. I'd thought about a time in my life when all I wanted to do was to draw and sketch and paint. I had lost that part of myself. But no longer. I would be an artist again.

"I'm going back to college." As soon as the words were out, I felt a huge sense of relief.

Tony nodded. "I already told Ron you quit."

"What?"

Tony's brown eyes twinkled. "I wouldn't have let you come back, even if you'd begged me. This life isn't for you. You've got more going on than this."

I leaned over and kissed him deeply. Normally, I would have been furious with someone for making a decision for me. Considering the circumstances, however, I felt nothing but relief.

"What about the rest of you?"

"Nothing changes for me," Mathew said, shoving a forkful of hotcakes into his mouth. "Cops didn't find the backup office or the Baby Office. They don't even know about the Franklyn Avenue apartment. I ain't worried."

"Anyway, those assholes set us up," Danny sneered. "If it wasn't for Duke and Red, Gibson woulda never found us."

I knew that Tony would be staying on with Ron. He couldn't earn the kind of money he made running the office in any legal way.

Meanwhile, the noose continued to tighten. A few days later, Ron and Joanna were arrested at their home in Chino for conspiracy to commit bookmaking. According to the newspapers, Sacco was "the suspected ringleader of a multimillion-dollar nationwide bookmaking ring." Ron paid their bail in cash and they danced out of jail.

We all reconvened at Dan Tana's that evening. Despite the grim developments, there was a palpable excitement in the air. Everybody was eager to see what Ron's next move would be.

"Staten Island," he announced. A murmur of surprise went around the table. "We're heading east. Jim's out there already hooking up the lines."

The reason Staten Island was chosen as the new base was twofold. The unwanted attention from Sergeant Gibson necessitated a move out of state. And Staten Island was the only place in America where bookmaking was a misdemeanor, as opposed to a felony.

"The worst-case scenario on Staten Island is that we get a fine," Ron said. "And I can afford a fine."

Ron had already rented four houses on the island borough of New York. Everything was set up and ready to go. Most of the guys had no reservations about trekking cross-country for him. Mathew joked that his wife loved the East Coast because there was less pressure to look thin there. That night Ron only lost one clerk, Jay, who refused to relocate because of school.

As the meeting went on, I began to feel more and more excited. I was thrilled at the prospect of heading east. I would be closer to my parents, but not too close. Suddenly, getting my life back on track seemed easy. Perhaps I would end up going to the Cooper Union School of Art after all. I would work on putting together a portfolio, and reapply.

Unfortunately, Ron had other plans for Tony. He asked us to stay behind after the meeting. After seeing everyone else out, he sat down at our table, puffing on his second cigar of the evening. He leaned back in his chair and grinned at Tony.

"I'm getting you a gambling stamp," he announced.

Tony didn't seem too enthralled with the prospect.

"What's a gambling stamp?" I asked.

"It will allow Tony to operate a legitimate office in Las Vegas, licensed by the Nevada gambling commission. Just think about it," he said, directing his smoldering cigar toward Tony, "you'll be handling our biggest players."

From Tony's reaction I realized the conversation had a subtext. "And?" Tony asked coolly.

"And you'll have direct lines to Staten Island. So you can . . . keep an eye on things there. Make sure everything's running smoothly."

I wondered why Ron didn't want Tony moving to the East Coast with the rest of the office. Something didn't add up.

Tony leaned across the table and dropped his voice. "Ron," he asked, "you got permission to do this?"

Ron checked his watch. "It's after midnight," he said mildly. Then, turning to me: "Sweetheart, you must be exhausted. Why don't you head on home? Get some sleep."

I got the message. I told him, "Sure," and kissed Tony goodbye so they could talk in private.

■

BACK AT THE APARTMENT I was debating whether or not to call my parents. I knew they must have heard about the bust by now. I couldn't avoid them forever. But I chickened out, calling my sister Heather instead. I knew I could rely on her to do some damage control for me. I dialed her number in Vancouver and waited breathlessly for her to pick up.

As soon as she answered the phone, I knew I was in the clear. She sounded so cheerful, I knew she hadn't heard about my arrest. If Heather didn't know, then my parents must also be in the dark. I couldn't believe my luck.

"You sound really happy," my sister observed.

"I've never been happier."

Instead of having a long difficult conversation about my lifestyle choices, we chatted for an hour about our respective boyfriends. This is the way it had always been.

We had always confided in each other.

That dated all the way back to childhood, to whenever we literally got hurt. My mother treated all our wounds with the same indifference. We were simply hauled to our feet or told to "get up," "keep going," "stop crying," or "move on." Gashes that should have been tended to in the emergency room were merely bandaged at home instead. My mother didn't have the luxury of medical attention during the war, so why should we?

When I was sixteen, I became aware of a lump growing on the back of my neck and another close to my right ear. It was a fight to get my mother to take me to a doctor. She finally relented but took me to her "doctor," a psychiatrist. I felt betrayed and humiliated. I wasn't imagining the lumps; something was growing in my head, but I felt powerless to do anything about it.

The first mass was eventually removed, leaving an unsightly scar on my neck. My father, who was still traveling extensively, arranged for a plastic surgeon to remove the second, a large histolytic hyperplasia that had grown through the facial muscles and was pushing out the skin on my cheek. Once again, my mother showed not the slightest sign of empathy.

This indifference on my mother's part drove me further and further from her. Did she want me to be tough, or was she simply incapable of nurturing? Or was it just that she didn't care? That's the way I interpreted it. As the years went on, I stopped divulging any pain I had to her, physical or mental, because I knew that it didn't matter.

As always, I enjoyed catching up with my sister, but when I heard the sound of the key turning in the door, I said a hurried goodbye. I had to find out what had happened to Tony.

"What was all that about? Why did Ron send me away?" I asked.

"Babe, it's late."

Yet Tony wasn't going to sleep without answering my questions.

"Why does Ron need permission to move the office to Staten Island? Permission from whom?"

Tony took off his shirt and flopped back on the bed, bare-chested. "Politics. You can't move a high-profile, multimillion-dollar bookmaking operation across the country without permission."

"Permission from whom, Tony?"

"From the mob."

"You told me we don't work for the mob," I said in a voice that was barely a croak.

"We don't. Ron doesn't. It's more complicated than that. He still has to operate with their consent."

"I don't get it. Why?"

"Years ago, way before I came on board, Ron lost money on a game that fell on the number. It crippled him financially. He had to borrow money to pay his players. When you need that kinda cash in a hurry, there's only one place to go."

"The Mafia."

"Yup. Ron went to see a couple of retired mob guys who own a vineyard out in Napa Valley. He had a solid reputation even then, so they loaned him the money. And Ron paid it back, every cent, plus interest."

"And?"

"A few years ago, a couple of Italians showed up at my door in Bimini. I didn't have a clue who they were, but they sure seemed to know me." Tony put on a thick East Coast accent. "'Tomorrow you work for us!'"

The change in dialect startled me. I was not liking where this story was going.

"So I called Ron as soon as they left. Half an hour later, we're driving out to Napa Valley. The two old mob guys welcome us like we're old friends. They gave us a tour of the vineyard, had us stay for grappa and Cohibas. They told us that the Italians who showed up at my place were from the Cleveland crime family. They'd been trying to muscle their way into California for a while. The old guys promised to take care of it. And they did. We didn't hear from the Cleveland family again. After that, Sacco figured it would be smart to borrow money on a regular basis. I mean, we didn't need to. But Ron figured the interest they earned would give them an incentive to protect us from any future takeover attempts."

"So Ron pays protection money to the mob."

"Not protection, exactly. More like insurance."

"So these two guys, the ones out in Napa Valley—they're the ones who gave him permission to move the office to the East Coast?"

"Yes. Under one condition." Tony turned his attention to my underwear and started tugging it down.

"What's the condition?"

"I can't go."

A recent power struggle within the Gambino family had turned bloody. Tony had a reputation and the two mobsters felt that his presence might add fuel to the already volatile climate out East.

There was so much more I wanted to ask, but by now I was half naked and all thoughts of the mob had left my mind.

I laid next to Tony for hours, listening to him breathe. I thought about Las Vegas. It was not the kind of place I'd ever imagined living. I'd miss the ocean. I'd miss the life we had started to build here. I tried to comfort myself with the thought that I would be too busy with school to spend my days wandering along the beach.

■

A WEEK LATER I made my first appearance in court. At 8:50 on Friday, July 3, 1987, Kyle, Jay, Mathew, Danny, Tony, and I walked up the imposing steps to the Los Angeles County Courthouse. We checked in with the clerk's desk to face charges.

Ron's lawyer, Harold Fisher, was a squat man with a pencil mustache. He explained what was about to happen. We would enter the courtroom when summoned. We would be formally charged with one count of felony bookmaking and one count of conspiracy each. We would be advised of our constitutional rights and asked to enter a plea of guilty or not guilty.

Harold caught my eye. "Plead not guilty," he instructed.

Tony had the bored, detached air of someone in line at the DMV. I alternated between nervously wringing my hands and obsessively checking my watch. Tony had reminded the others to dress appropriately, and they looked ridiculous in their ill-fitting suits and silly ties. Tony, on the other hand, looked more like a lawyer than a career criminal in his classic black double-breasted suit. How could he be so calm?

"I'm going to the bathroom," I blurted.

Once in the ladies' room, I headed straight for the mirror. I checked under my arms and was relieved to discover that my nerves were at least not visible through my jacket. I smoothed my clothes and touched up my lipstick. With one final glance at my reflection I headed out, my high heels echoing in the empty hallway.

I found everybody gone except for Tony. "What happened?"

"The D.A.'s office hasn't pressed charges yet. We have to come back on Monday."

"But what about Vegas?" We were due to leave town later the same day.

"Doesn't change anything. We'll just drive back here Sunday night."

■

EVEN THOUGH I HAD never been there, Las Vegas looked strangely familiar: the glittering pink and green lights outside the casinos, the screaming come-ons from the barkers roping in the tourists, the enormous neon cowboy outside the Pioneer Club. Thanks to the movies, I felt as though I had seen it all before. Far from being dazzled by the glitz, I found it all rather tacky and tasteless. As far as I could see, Vegas offered nothing but gambling, boozing, shopping, and weddings, twenty-four hours a day. The thought of living here permanently filled me with dread.

I followed the U-Haul truck as it turned into a large, dusty parking lot in front of the Majestic View apartments. I turned off the ignition and stepped out into the scorching desert heat.

"I guess this is it," Tony said, checking the address.

The generic pale-gray two-story building had none of the charm of our old Hollywood apartment. I followed him up the stairs and down the gray-carpeted hallway to number 212. Tony unlocked the door and switched on a light, revealing an empty one-bedroom apartment. I looked around, not saying a word. With a sigh Tony said, "Let's unload the truck."

Two days later, we returned to the courthouse in L.A. with Kyle, Danny, Mathew, and Jay. Once again we were informed that charges had not yet been filed. We were told to appear again on August 27.

Mathew was furious. "It's ridiculous!" he said. He, Kyle, and Danny would have to fly back from New York for a third time to make their appearance.

"I can't believe they can just waste our time like this," I complained. "We drove five hours for nothing. Why haven't they pressed charges? The bust was in May. How much more time do they need?"

Tony laughed at my naïveté. "Babe, they can do whatever they want, whenever they want. We're at their mercy now."

We stopped for gas on the way back to Vegas. We were leaving the station when I noticed the headline in the display rack.

BAY AREA BOOKIE BUSTED!

I nudged Tony and picked up a copy. Tony glanced at the paper and then at the long line of people in front of the cashier. With a shrug he placed it back on the rack. "Forget it. That was San Francisco. It's got nothing to do with us."

Had we bought the paper, we would have read about a man called Anthony "Sonny" LoBue, a bookmaker operating out of San Francisco who had been charged with extortion, game-fixing and bribery, along with illegal gambling and conspiracy. Little did I know that LoBue's name would haunt me in the coming years.

■

I WAS EXHAUSTED BY the time we got back to Vegas. Every muscle in my body ached from the move. All I wanted to do was to have a long soak in the bathtub and crawl into bed. The stress of the last few days had drained me completely.

"What the hell?" Tony breathed as soon as he unlocked the door. Unfamiliar papers were strewn across the dining room table. Tony grabbed a handful and leafed through them. The pages were covered in handwritten lists of names, numbers, and monetary amounts. Somebody had left them in the apartment.

Suddenly we stiffened upright at a loud, insistent knock at the door.

"Open up!"

Tony and I glanced at each other, then instantly jumped to the same conclusion. We were being set up. I grabbed the papers and hurried into the bathroom, locking the door behind me. I ripped up the papers frenziedly, dumping them into the toilet bowl, and flushing periodically. My hands were shaking and my breath came in gasps. Outside, I could hear the police threatening to break the door down. I gave the toilet one last flush and ran to Tony's side just as the door burst open.

Sergeant Gibson tossed a search warrant at Tony. "Cuff him!" he spat at his men. An officer stepped toward me with handcuffs, but Gibson gestured for him to stop. "Not her. She hasn't been convicted. Yet."

I watched in numb shock as the officers began searching the apartment, presumably looking for the incriminating papers. They left minutes later, taking Tony along with them, still dressed in the suit he wore to court in L.A. only hours earlier.

I slumped onto the sofa, bewildered. My mind began to spin. What had just happened? Why were they taking Tony? And who planted the list of numbers? I needed to call Ron, but we didn't have a phone yet. I considered leaving the apartment to find a pay phone, but what if Gibson had his men waiting outside, ready to follow me? I burst into tears, feeling overwhelmed and helpless.

Tony returned less than two hours later. I flung my arms around him. "Are you okay? What happened?"

"We're leaving, babe. Right now. We're done here."

Gibson had tried to have Tony thrown in jail, but reconsidered when Tony demanded to speak with his lawyer. Instead he settled on giving Tony a warning. "You tell Sacco that if he tries to set up in Vegas, it'll be an automatic twenty years."

It turned out that, as a convicted felon, Tony was required by Nevada law to register with the local police if he was planning even to visit the state. They gave Tony forty-eight hours to comply or go to jail.

"I chose the third option," Tony said with a sad smile.

"Which is?"

"I retired."

I stared at Tony blankly. "I don't understand."

"As of today, I'm retired. No more bookmaking."

This was incomprehensible to me. After thirteen years with Ron, after everything Tony had told me about their relationship, he was just going to leave?

"What are we going to do?"

"Same as everyone else. We're going to be regular people."

Tony left to find another rental truck, leaving me with the arduous task of packing up again. As I was putting everything back into the boxes I'd just unpacked twenty-four hours ago, Tony's words swirled around in my head. What did he mean, regular people?

When Tony returned, he began methodically filling boxes and packing suitcases. He showed a renewed vigor, determined to leave the city as soon as possible. "I'm too Italian for this town," he fumed. "They want to keep the mob outta Vegas, and I look like mob."

In all of the chaos following Tony's announcement, I realized I had failed to ask one rather important question.

"Where are we *going?*"

Tony stopped what he was doing and mopped his brow with his T-shirt. "Red Bluff," he said, as if it were the most obvious answer in the world. Noting the look of bewilderment on my face, he elaborated, "Where my mom and sisters live."

"Where's that?"

"Northern California."

Tony continued shoving our belongings into boxes. I was too exhausted to argue. I did, though, want some idea of what to expect next.

"Tony . . . does Red Bluff have a university?"

He just gave a slight shake of the head and continued packing.

Hours later, I slumped behind the wheel of my Renault and followed Tony in the rented truck as he sped out of Las Vegas, bombing down another anonymous stretch of highway. We passed through miles and miles of dry, dusty land. The air became thick with the terrible stench of packed herds of cattle, waiting for slaughter.

I'm moving to the middle of nowhere, I thought, as a feeling of dread traveled to the pit of my stomach.

10

Red Bluff, California, July, 1987

"My baby!"

Sophia Santino bounced through the screen door and flung her substantial arms around her son. Tony staggered backward as she grabbed him in a powerful bear hug.

"My baby's home!"

As she buried Tony in a flurry of kisses, she glanced over his shoulder, shooting me a cold, appraising glance. Sophia struck me as someone who would have no trouble at all surviving a three-to-five stretch in Sybil Brand.

She finally let go, smoothing back her thinning brown hair, which was pulled into a scraggly ponytail. She cupped his face in her hands. All of the hardness seemed to melt away. Her eyes brimmed over with tears. "My baby's home," she whispered. Then she hollered into the house, "Girls! Get over here! Your brother's home!"

She led us inside and we entered a small, shabbily decorated living room. A television set was blaring in one corner. Bounding over from the blue-corduroy sectional sofa came two teenage girls. In the lead was Dina Santino, Tony's fourteen-year-old sister. Dina was wearing a tiny halter top and hot pants that barely covered her lean, young body. Her shoulder-length brown hair had been elaborately curled and she was wearing a thick layer of makeup. She planted a kiss on her brother's cheek. Tony held her at arm's length and took a good, long look at her.

"Go wash that goop off your face," he scowled. "And put some clothes on, for crissakes."

"Mo-om!" Dina looked at her mother with pleading eyes.

"Do what your brother says. No arguments!"

While Dina stomped out of the room, Tony introduced me to seventeen-year-old Leanne. She was chewing a great wad of bright-pink bubble gum. "Nice to meet you, Leanne," I said. By way of response she flashed me a smile, popped a large bubble, and flopped back on the couch. She turned her attention back to *All My Children*.

Tony and I followed his mother into the kitchen. Sophia pulled three cans of Budweiser out of the fridge and clanked them down on the counter. She ripped the tab back on one and passed it to Tony. Then she offered one to me. "You want a beer, hon? It's five o'clock somewhere."

I declined as cheerfully as possible. I was about to explain that I didn't drink, but Sophia had already shifted her attention back to her son.

"Here's to my baby!" Sophia raised her beer to him before taking a long pull from the can. She stubbed out her cigarette, produced another, and lit it. Dina re-appeared, wearing a black T-shirt with the words "Bon Jovi—LET IT ROCK" written in bold yellow letters. Her face was freshly scrubbed.

"There's my little sis!" Tony grinned, giving her a playful hug. Dina rolled her eyes, and went off to join her sister in the living room.

Sophia took a drag of her cigarette and exhaled a cloud of smoke. "So, did you come all the way up here just to introduce me to your pretty . . . girlfriend?" she asked, with a barely concealed edge of condescension.

"No, Ma. I've got news." Tony grinned. "*Big* news."

Tony's mom looked at me sourly. "You going to have a baby or something?"

"No, Ma! I've retired from bookmaking. I'm going straight. We're back home . . . for good."

Sophia's face dropped slightly. She struggled to regain her composure. As she held her cigarette to her lips I noticed her hand quivering.

"Oh," she said weakly. "Well, how about that . . . "

I was puzzled by her reaction. I had assumed that she would be ecstatic at the news. Her son was giving up his life of crime and moving close to his family.

The subject turned to money, and the reason for Sophia's reaction became clearer. She began nervously rattling off a laundry list of unexpected expenses that she had recently incurred.

I felt awkward. My parents had never discussed their finances around me. Yet here I was, sitting with Tony's mother for the first time, listening to a detailed catalogue of financial hardship. I excused myself and stepped outside to give them some privacy.

I sat down on the stoop, gazing at the unkempt lawn. Large brown patches had been scorched by the sun. Parked in the driveway was a silver Cadillac. I assumed it was the one that Tony had surprised his mother with two years earlier on Mother's Day. It sat there now, baking in the mid-afternoon sun. The windows were dusty, a hubcap was missing and an ugly dent marred one side. I looked around this barren vista and wondered—not for the first time that day—what I was doing here.

When Tony joined me, his mood was black.

"Let's get outta here," he growled, storming across the lawn. He wrenched open the door of the Renault. "She lost my fucking money!" he spat. "I moved her here specifically to keep her away from Bay Meadows, and she . . . " Tony shook his head in futile anger.

Bay Meadows was a famous San Francisco racetrack. Sophia was a gambler. Having Tony's cash at her disposal had proved to be too much of a temptation for her. I resisted asking how much of his money she had lost. From the incandescent look on Tony's face I knew it had to be substantial. Tony sped through the small town of Red Bluff, whizzing past the church, the school, and a couple of sunbaked stores. In a blink Red Bluff was shrinking in our rear view. We crossed over the interstate and drove through a couple of miles of open land.

Tony turned onto a gravel road and pulled up to a large fenced-off lot. At the rear were piles of rocks, ranging in size from tiny pebbles to large boulders. Tiles, paving stones and bags of various kinds of soil were stored neatly on the property. He parked in front of a one-story wooden building with a sign that read, "Accardo Landscaping." I recognized it as his brother-in-law's company, in which Tony told me he had invested.

Slamming the car door behind him, Tony stormed toward the front entrance. I followed him inside. The office was small, minimally decorated, and blissfully cool. The surprised-looking man behind the desk jumped to his feet as Tony burst through the door and barked, "Where's Angela?"

"Tony! I wasn't expecting . . . uh, Angela's out back."

He led us out the back door. We walked across a dusty lot toward a brand-new mobile home. Trying to break the awkward silence, I introduced myself to the man whom I assumed was Tony's brother-in-law. "Dominic Accardo," he confirmed, shaking my hand.

Dominic led the way onto a deck that had been added to make the residence look more like a house and less like a trailer. A pretty brunette with the same coloring and eyes as Tony answered the door. His oldest sister, Angela.

"Tony," she said with a wry smile. "Long time no see."

Tony cut straight to the chase. "Ma's gambling again!"

Angela's eyes widened in surprise, but she said nothing.

"How could you not have known, Angie? You're, like, five minutes away!"

Angela looked past her brother and gave me a faint smile. "You'd better come in."

As we filed into the trailer, I saw two children running around. Tony, completely oblivious, was still accusing Angela of keeping him in the dark about Sophia's gambling.

Finally Angela snapped, "What am I? Her goddamned babysitter? I've got two kids and a business to run, Tony. Give me a break!"

Tony and Angela continued their heated discussion while they followed Dominic back to the office. I stayed behind in the trailer with Angela's kids: Cynthia, four, and Jason, three. I had a terrible feeling that Tony's plans had gone up in smoke. I tried to distract myself from this disconcerting thought by introducing myself to the children.

"So," I asked cheerfully, "What do you two do for fun?"

Jason smiled, exposing gaps where several baby teeth were missing. "Fishing."

"Really? That's great. Have you caught anything recently?"

"Uh-huh." Jason spread his arms wide, and nearly toppled over with the effort. "I caught a striped bass with Daddy. Down on the river. It was *this big!*"

I laughed. They were a cute pair. "That's wonderful! And what else do you like to do?"

Jason plopped down on the carpet and sighed dramatically. "There ain't nuthin' else *to* do."

Next door, Angela was giving Tony a detailed breakdown of how they had spent his seed money for the landscaping company. I had no doubt that Sophia was still sitting in her kitchen, nursing a beer and brooding on life's cruel twists. I'm sure it never occurred to her that Tony might quit his lucrative career in bookmaking. There would be no more trips to Bay Meadows now that Tony was in Red Bluff. Now she would never get the chance to win back the money she had frittered away.

Tony walked out of Accardo Landscaping with a company T-shirt, a matching hat, and a full-time job. I left with the name and address of a company in Redding—a town half an hour north—where I had an interview lined up for the following morning. As luck would have it, the company that made signs for Accardo was looking for a new office manager. Tony drove back to his mother's house in silence. I realized now that we were completely broke.

"I guess we really *are* just regular people now," I said, in a vain attempt to lighten the mood.

■

THE MOMENT I STEPPED into the showroom of Autographics in Redding, I knew I wanted the job. Gary Stamper, the owner, had long hair and was wearing a paint-splattered Grateful Dead T-shirt and jeans.

"Heeey," he said with an easy grin. "You must be Marisa. Right on—come in, take a look around . . . "

Gary was a talented artist who had found his niche customizing trucks and cars, and designing and manufacturing signs. The showroom was partly an artist's studio, and exhibited a wide range of Gary's work in various media. I inhaled the smell of turpentine and fresh paint. Tony's world had been a culture shock to me. But the familiar sights and smells of oil paint, pre-stretched canvases, spray cans, and the general disarray of an artist at work were incredibly comforting.

"Come on, let's go through to the office," Gary said. "The wife's dying to meet you."

Gary's wife, Sheila, was eight months pregnant and looked every bit as much the hippie poster child as her husband. She conducted the interview with a squirming one-year-old on her lap. She explained that they were looking for someone who could answer the phone, give estimates, make appointments, organize Gary's schedule, order supplies, keep the building clean, and take money to the bank every day. I nodded enthusiastically.

"You're not afraid of dogs, are you?"

"Dogs?" I wondered what that had to do with anything. "No, not at all."

Sheila gave a loud whistle and two enormous Doberman pinschers, Shadow and Shady, came bounding into the room via a large dog-door in the office wall.

"Good!" Sheila said. "I guess you're hired."

Tony and I rented a small house in Red Bluff, and settled into our new lives working full-time on minimum-wage salaries. I got my California driver's license and we got health insurance, car insurance, and a phone jointly registered in our names. We became just like any other young couple struggling to make a life for themselves—except that we were still waiting for the police to formally press criminal charges against us.

We returned to L.A. in August for our next court appearance, only to be informed that, yet again, no charges had been filed. We returned again in September and were told the same thing.

Being in Los Angeles, surrounded by my former friends and colleagues, was a bittersweet experience. The city held so many cherished memories for me. I'd hoped that it would also remind Tony of everything we had left behind, but sadly, it didn't. He completely slammed the door on his old life. As we waited around in the courthouse, he never once enquired about Ron, or the Staten Island offices. Instead he enthusiastically told the guys about the hunting trip that he and Dominic were planning in the fall.

My God, I thought, *he's really happy living in Red Bluff.* In a way I envied his happiness. I resented it too. I found small-town life claustrophobic. Those brief, frustrating trips back to L.A. were a powerful reminder of everything we had left behind. I missed the freedom of living in the city, and began to dread that long, depressing drive back to Red Bluff.

Life took an abrupt turn for the worse when we learned that Tony's father had passed away in Mexico. Anthony Vittorio Santino died of liver failure, a result of decades of abusing his body with heroin and other drugs. Tony and Angela had to make the long drive down to Chihuahua to identify a shriveled, yellow corpse as the man who had once been their father.

The memorial service was held in St. Bruno's Catholic Church in San Francisco. Sophia's loud cries echoed around the church— she wept throughout the long, solemn service. As the ceremony dragged on, I began to feel queasy. Then a powerful wave of nausea hit me. I clamped my hand over my mouth and bolted down the aisle in my high heels. Throwing open the heavy wooden doors, I made it to a nearby row of neat shrubbery and vomited.

■

A HORRIFIED LAUGH BURST out of me when Sophia suggested that I might be pregnant. I had been taking the pill faithfully, and having a baby was not part of our game plan. His father's untimely death had cost Tony dearly: he'd had to pay for his father's substantial medical bills before the hospital would agree to release the body. Then there were the cremation and funeral expenses. There was no way we could afford a child.

Tony insisted on buying a pregnancy test on the way back to Red Bluff. As I sat on the edge of the bathtub at home, I stared in mute disbelief at the red plus sign that slowly appeared. I burst into tears. Tony knocked on the bathroom door.

"Well?"

I handed him the little plastic stick and proceeded to sob bitterly. He stared intently at the test. Then a huge grin appeared on his face.

"We're having a baby!" he laughed. "Marisa—we're having a *baby!*" He flung his arms around me. As shocked as I was about the pregnancy, I couldn't helped but be pleased by Tony's reaction. He looked me in the eye and wiped away my tears with his thumbs.

"I guess we'd better get married," he said.

My heart soared. Even though I knew the timing was all wrong, this still felt right. Tony was the only man I had ever really loved.

Thinking of the potential horrors of a wedding in Red Bluff with both our families present, I said hopefully, "Let's elope—drive down to Vegas, make a holiday of it."

"Vegas?" Tony said. "You forgotten what happened the last time we set foot in that place?"

Like it or not, I was soon swept up in plans for an elaborate white wedding. Tony's family wouldn't hear of anything else; for the eldest child and only son in a proud Italian family, nothing else would do. For me, however, that meant I had to do something I had been dreading from the moment I accepted Tony's proposal.

"Hi, Mom." I got straight to the point. As chirpily as possible I blurted, "I'm getting married! Isn't that great? . . . Mom?"

A deathly silence lingered as my mom absorbed the shocking news. "So you're pregnant," she said flatly.

I struggled to regain my composure, having rehearsed this call a dozen times before making it.

"Why yes, Mom, I am." Silence. "You're going to be a grandmother!" Well, I thought, as the silence stretched out painfully, at least she doesn't know I'm up on felony charges.

When we mailed out the invitations for our November 28th wedding, I didn't invite a single friend. They were college graduates with fabulous jobs, boyfriends, and lives. I, on the other hand, was pregnant, facing criminal charges, and getting married to a man who mowed lawns for a living. I invited only my immediate family, and even then I dreaded to think how my mother would react when she met her future in-laws.

My own relationship with Tony's family had soured since I announced that I would be keeping my maiden name. I was overwhelmed with all the sudden changes in my life, and the thought of losing my last name only added to my anxiety. Sophia's outraged objection only served to strengthen my resolve. I clung to "Lankester" as if my very survival depended on it.

I knew I could count on my father to lighten up the tense atmosphere. He was practiced and smooth in any social occasion. He had taught me to be resourceful, to enjoy life, and to make the best of any situation. He too had suffered during World War II, but his reaction to that awful time was completely different from my mother's. My mother couldn't seem to let go of her past; my father had simply buried his.

I learned about the fate of my father's family from his father when I spent part of the summer in England with him. I was 16 then, and had no idea that my father had suffered such unimaginable losses during the war. In 1940 his mother, brother, aunts, and cousins were killed when a German bomb struck the Lankester house in Leicester. My father was the only survivor.

My parents' marriage was hanging by a thread when he bought land in the Catskill Mountains. This effectively excused the two of them from spending weekends together. My mother opted to drive into Manhattan to visit museums and galleries. I joined my father camping on his property in the woods. Staying there was a welcome escape from the strict rules and oppressive atmosphere at home. Away from my mother, my dad was relaxed and happy. One day he announced plans to build a road up the hill to a clearing where there was a view. Piles of shale rock arrived, which we later smashed into stones with sledgehammers.

Then an old factory was torn down in Phoenicia, close to the land we owned, prompting my father to reclaim the old wood. Suddenly he was building a house, with the help of his children. Heavy machinery was used to dig the foundation and pits for the septic tanks, but we did almost everything else. We mixed cement and concrete, laid cinder blocks, and used saws, hammers, and every other tool imaginable. We installed dry wall, insulation, tarpaper, and tongue-and-groove flooring. It took years, but finishing that house taught me that anything is possible, no matter how outrageous the goal. My father very much believed that women could do anything men could do, including using a chain saw, chopping wood, and digging ditches. At home I was constantly criticized and critiqued by my mother. In the Catskills I felt useful, empowered, and capable.

Heather and Peter arrived in town a few days before the wedding, in time to help me plan the critical seating arrangements.

I welcomed their support. Since the divorce, my mother's moods had fluctuated between bitterness and depression, and she was about to come face-to-face with the man she blamed for her misery. My father, on the other hand, was happily remarried to an attractive, successful woman, who also happened to be a decade younger than my mother. Just the thought of having my parents and stepmother in the same room caused me overwhelming anxiety. On top of that, I had to consider the effect of adding the Santino clan to that already toxic atmosphere.

"He looks Mexican," my mother remarked when she met Tony at the rehearsal dinner. Working long hours under the scorching California sun had turned Tony's skin deep brown. I bit my tongue. It was pointless to say anything. I knew that Tony could never measure up to her expectations.

I guessed that meeting her future son-in-law was one of the lowest points in my mother's life. As far as she was concerned, I was a monumental failure. All those hours of piano lessons, ballet, and gymnastics; all the trips to galleries and museums; my expensive education—all of it wasted on Tony and his "white trash" family. She had expected so much more from me when it came to men.

My mother's eyes trailed Tony as he made a beeline across the room to introduce himself to my father and his wife Kristen, who had just arrived. They greeted Tony with warm smiles. My mother turned stiffly and mumbled "strumpet" under her breath.

Heather and Peter broke away to watch my mother so I could join Tony and greet my father and Kristen. To my relief the three of them were talking about golf. Tony had played from time to time, and soon my father was eagerly giving him tips on form and technique. Across the room I noticed a look of horror cross my mother's face. I followed her shocked gaze to a slightly-worse-for-wear-looking Sophia. She had stumbled, and was trying to steady herself against a wall with a beer in one hand and a cigarette in the other.

A slight chill tinged the air the next morning, as the bridal party climbed the steps to the little church. Tony's sisters fussed over each other for a last-minute hair and makeup check, while Dad and I peered through the heavy wooden doors at the guests gathered inside. Tony's cousins, aunts, uncles, and fellow Accardo Landscaping employees occupied one side of the half-filled church. My mother sat on the other, wearing her pale-blue Chanel suit and Hermès scarf, resolutely facing forward. Next to her was my brother, and behind them my stepmother Kristen, who suddenly looked over her shoulder and gave a supportive smile when she made eye contact with Dad. His face melted into a smile. I couldn't recall seeing him as happy as he looked then.

The music started, cueing the bridesmaids. One by one they slowly walked down the aisle. Heather, who was acting as my maid of honor, dramatically fluffed the full skirt of her ridiculous gown and winked at me before sashaying behind her future sisters-in-law toward the altar.

"Are you really certain you want to go through with this?" my father asked. His eyes were filled with paternal concern. I had always confided in him, and part of me wanted to share everything that was wrong in my life. In the past he had always made things better. But I was no longer his little girl. Telling him the truth would devastate him. I put on my best smile.

"Yes," I said. "Of course I'm sure."

I smiled at Peter, who snapped a picture as the organ struck up "The Wedding March." My father, his arm intertwined with mine, pulled me slightly closer. As I walked down the aisle with my father, ready to say my vows to love and honor Tony, I was convinced that I was doing the right thing. The love we had for each other was undoubtedly strong enough to handle whatever life was going to throw at us.

■

I LOVED BEING MARRIED, but I was feeling worse with every passing day. Morning sickness followed me into the second trimester. It felt as if the child inside me was growing stronger while

I became weaker and weaker. I detested being pregnant. Being in control had always been vitally important to me, and now I was at the mercy of a process that I had zero control over.

Tony was fast becoming frustrated with his inability to ease my fears about winding up in jail. I couldn't stop worrying. Why hadn't we heard anything? What was going on? As the weeks passed, I became more and more convinced that something terrible was about to happen.

I was eight and a half months pregnant, and at my most vulnerable, when two men wearing suits walked into Autographics. The sight of them instantly set off alarm bells. I took a sharp intake of breath and dropped my hands to my belly, as if I could somehow protect my unborn child from what I knew was coming next.

The men approached the glass divider and flashed their badges. "We're looking for Marisa Lankester."

"That's me," I managed to squeak.

The men came charging into the office, grabbed my arms, and pulled them behind my back. While one of them cuffed me, the other pushed my head onto my desk. This quick, vicious movement squeezed the last of the air out of my already squashed lungs.

Shadow and Shady heard the commotion and came charging into the office. Their deep growls caught the officers off-guard, and they released me.

"Call off your dogs," one of them growled. "Call off those fucking dogs, now!"

I tried to speak but I couldn't catch my breath. The officers drew their weapons, ready to shoot the dogs. I managed to scream, "No!"

Gary came flying out of his studio. With his palette knife in one hand and his wild hair flying all over the place, he looked more like a dangerous lunatic than the gentle artist he really was. I felt a sharp pain in my abdomen as the room started to recede.

It felt as though someone were pushing down very hard on the top of my head. And then blackness.

"YOU GUYS ARE OUT of your minds!"

I could hear Gary's voice, bleary and indistinct, as I started to come around. "She's no fugitive! No way, man . . . she's been working here for a year."

I blinked. The room came back into focus. Gary was gesturing wildly at the officers as they dumped the contents of my purse on the desk. Nobody seemed to have noticed that I'd blacked out. One of them checked my ID against the name on the warrant. "It's a match," he said.

The officer asked, "Where do you live?" and I gave them the address. The same as on my ID. The cops looked at each other quizzically. "When was the last time you visited Staten Island, Ms. Lankester?"

"I've never been there."

He fixed me in a humorless glare. "We got a warrant that says different."

Gary could barely believe what was going on. "You're making a mistake! Here, look at this." He reached for the accounting book. "I've got all the salary entries right here. I'm telling you, she's been working here, full-time, for almost a year."

"The name on the warrant matches her driver's license. We've got no choice; she's coming with us."

I was taken to Shasta County's high-security detention center— a bleak, ugly building surrounded by an imposing barbed-wire fence and miles of desert sand. After I was photographed and fingerprinted, the admissions officer ran my name through the computer. She looked puzzled by what she saw on the screen. A quick phone call to the L.A. county clerk confirmed that I had not missed a scheduled court appearance. It was becoming abundantly clear that I was no fugitive.

"How can there be an out-of-state warrant for my arrest if I haven't been out of state, and I can prove it? It doesn't make sense."

The officer shrugged and carried on typing. "Ms. Lankester, it doesn't matter if it makes sense or not. The fact is, I'm obliged to transport you to Los Angeles County, where you'll be incarcerated until your court appearance on"—she squinted at the screen— "May 30th."

It felt as though the world had stopped. Incarcerated? "But I'm due to give birth on the 27th!"

With the cold, unwavering voice of authority, she replied, "In that case, we'll need the name of a relative who will be willing to take custody of the child when it's born."

I stared blankly at her, looking for any trace of humanity in those cold, gray eyes. I found none. My head swam. My child? Born in Sybil Brand, then snatched away from me?

"Ma'am, I'll need a name?" Heavy tears began to roll down my cheeks.

"No," I said, shaking my head.

"You've got plenty of time to come up with a name."

■

As soon as the guard closed the cell door behind me, I slumped to the floor. Sobs wracked my body. I couldn't decide what was worse: the thought of giving birth in that hellhole, or the fact that I would then have my daughter taken from me as soon as she was born. I'd never felt such despair before.

Around five o'clock, the cell door swung open again. "Your husband's here," a male guard said. I assumed this meant Tony was now also in custody at Shasta County Jail. "Come on. On your feet." He helped me up and led me out to the admission area.

To my astonishment, Tony wasn't in handcuffs. He came over and embraced me tightly.

Moments later I was sitting in an Accardo Landscaping truck with Tony, driving home. I could barely believe this sudden reversal of fortune.

"What happened? Why didn't they go after you?" I asked him.

"Gary called to warn me, thank God." Tony turned onto the freeway, heading toward Red Bluff. "So I took off. Called Ron to find out what the hell was going on. Turns out the Staten Island offices were busted in March. Gibson."

I shuddered hearing his name.

"Gibson formed a task force. Headed out east to shut down the whole operation. He was working with the local cops out there."

"But what does that have to do with us?" I asked.

"Nothing. But Gibson was convinced that we were working there, too. Apparently, Danny managed to escape during the raid. Jumped out a side window, left a bunch of his crap behind. Gibson found some of his clothes and thought they were mine. They found some of his girlfriend's things, too, and I guess Gibson assumed they were yours."

I shook my head. "Are you telling me that's all he needed to put a warrant out for us? Some stupid clothes that didn't belong to us?" It was scary that one man could wield so much unchecked power.

"It's not just that, babe. The cops know I've been with Sacco thirteen years. I guess Gibson's having a hard time believing that

I've really retired. He put two and two together, got five, and we became fugitives."

We drove in silence for a while.

"How come we never heard about Staten Island getting busted?" I asked quietly.

"Why would we?" There was a trace of bitterness in Tony's voice. "I told Ron to keep all of that stuff to himself. But since I had to call him, he put me in the loop . . . you heard of the RICO Act, right?"

"Sure."

The Racketeer Influenced and Corrupt Organizations, or RICO, Act had been making headlines since it was passed in 1970 with Mafia crimes in mind. It ruled that any persons working for a criminal organization who had committed two crimes within a ten-year period—from a specified list of thirty-five, including gambling—could be charged with racketeering. This usually led to large fines, heavy jail sentences, and confiscations of assets.

"Ron thinks the only reason Gibson was given permission to go to Staten Island was because he cited RICO. That prick is trying to go after Ron's assets."

"Poor Ron," I said. I really did feel for him. Still, I was mostly concerned about what would happen to us. "So what now?"

"You go back to work tomorrow, just like any other day."

"Do you really think Gary and Sheila would want me back? I almost got their dogs shot!"

"I told them the whole story, babe. They want you back. They insist on it."

I started tearing up, touched by their friendship and loyalty. "But what about us? I was one step away from having our baby in prison. We've still got two cases pending, and now this mess. I feel like we're being punished for going straight."

"Ron told me that getting out was the best decision I ever made. He says we should just go on with our lives as if today never happened. Look, babe, we've been straight for almost a year. In the eyes of the law, we're the model of reformed criminals. Fisher can prove that we've never been to Staten Island. He's going to make Gibson look like an idiot in court. He says the judge is going to go easy on us at sentencing."

"Go easy on us?"

Tony had always insisted that we'd never go to jail, but I sensed a distinct shift in what he was telling me now.

Tony responded without answering my question. "Harold got your court date postponed. So you can give birth right here, just like we planned."

I was so relieved at this news that I ignored the fact that Tony had dodged my question. "And you'll be there with me, right?"

"Of course. There is one thing, though. I gotta go to Vegas in the morning. I got an outstanding warrant I gotta take care of."

"What? Why? We were only in Vegas for three days."

"It's a formality. I just show up, turn myself in, post bail, and come back." He leaned across and kissed me on the forehead. I was emotionally strung out.

We pulled into our driveway and saw the search warrant taped on the front door. In our absence the police had torn our house apart.

I stalked from room to room, my anger rising. Carelessly strewn across the floor in the baby's room were the tiny baby clothes I had worked so hard for. I silently collected the little pink-and-yellow outfits. When I had gathered them all up, despite Tony's protests I stormed to the kitchen and dumped them in the trash. There was no way I would dress my baby in these clothes.

Tony placed a protective arm around me and brought me over to the couch. He sat next to me. His eyes never left mine. "You know there was no way I could have let you stay in jail, right?"

"Of course."

"You also know that there's only one person in the world I know with access to the kind of money I needed to pay your bail and mine today. By the time this mess is cleared up, it's going to end up costing us thousands and thousands in legal bills and fines."

I nodded slowly. He was telling me that this last arrest had ruined us financially.

"Ron offered to cover everything. All of our legal expenses, everything. On two conditions."

"Go on."

"The first one is, he wants me to plead guilty to the three felony charges they've got against him. He needs me to tell the cops that I was the boss back in L.A."

"No!" I shook my head decisively. "There has to be another way. We could borrow the money. From my family."

"I would never borrow money from your family," Tony said firmly. "Look, I'm not pleading guilty to anything relating to Staten Island. I'm just taking responsibility for the last two arrests. Prior to Vegas. Harold says the judge will be sympathetic to us, given the circumstances. Think about it—we were leading a life of crime but we fell in love, retired from bookmaking, got married, went to work regular jobs, and started a family. We have overwhelming evidence to back up our story. Harold says we're a defense attorney's dream. There'd be nothing to gain from sending me away. Harold's convinced we're looking at a fine, community service, and probation—nothing more. He says my worst-case scenario is a year inside."

When Tony said this, I felt the bottom dropping out of my stomach. I imagined raising our child alone while Tony served a year in prison.

"And what about me?" I breathed.

"A fine and probation."

I sat there, dumbfounded by what my husband was telling me. "And what's Ron's second condition?"

Tony paused. I prepared myself for the worst.

"Ron wants us to move to the Dominican Republic. Set up our offices there."

At first I was convinced I'd misheard. "Where?"

"Santo Domingo. He's been working for months with lawyers here and out there. He wants to relocate to the Dominican

Republic because gambling is legal there. And the American government has no jurisdiction. We'd be safe from all of . . . this."

Santo Domingo. The name conjured up images of white sandy beaches and palm trees swaying softly in the breeze. I had taken holidays in nearby Bermuda and Puerto Rico, and fallen in love with both places. After months of feeling as if the walls were closing in around me, the idea of relocating to the Dominican Republic filled me with a sense of upcoming adventure. Freedom.

"So we'd move to Santo Domingo to live?"

Tony nodded heavily. He was happy with small-town life. I suppose he relished being free from the extraordinary pressure of working for Ron. He enjoyed being a regular Joe who worked nine-to-five with weekends off. He liked being close to his family and going hunting and fishing with his friends. To Tony, Red Bluff was paradise. I could barely disguise my joy at the prospect of leaving.

"How soon would we go?"

Tony shrugged. "Well, we gotta get the court case over with. Harold thinks we could have it all wrapped up by September."

I had the curious sense that all of the dark clouds that had been hanging over us the past year were lifting. September was only four months away. For the first time since Los Angeles, I was actually looking forward to the future.

■

THE NEXT MORNING, TONY flew to Vegas and I left for work. Gary and Sheila welcomed me back. Their trust in me was unshaken, despite my arrest, and I continued running the office as if nothing had happened.

By the time I got home, Tony was back from Vegas. He'd posted bail, but was still facing a legal nightmare in Nevada. He would have several more court appearances, in both Las Vegas and Los Angeles. Beyond that, he refused to go into detail. His mantra over the coming weeks was that everything was being taken care of, and I should relax. "Focus on the pregnancy," he said, protectively caressing my sizeable belly.

My due date came and went. Three days later, Tony reluctantly left me in Red Bluff for his next court date in L.A., worried he would miss the most important day of our lives. There he was charged with nine counts in all. Afterward, he handed Harold Fisher a slew of documents, including our tax returns, that proved without a shadow of a doubt that neither he nor I had so much as set foot in Staten Island.

I was still pregnant two weeks later when Tony returned from his second court appearance on June 10. Early the following morning, I finally went into labor. Later that night, Tony and I were huddled together, marveling at our beautiful newborn daughter.

"Justine," I whispered, kissing the top of her head.

"Justine," Tony repeated.

We had chosen the name for its meaning: justice.

One week after Justine was born, I appeared in the courthouse in Los Angeles. Before going in, Harold Fisher advised me of what would happen.

"Plead guilty," he said as I clutched Justine tightly. "They'll drop the last charge. That will reduce your maximum jail time from five years to three."

Although we had already discussed this, I was still terrified to walk into a courtroom and plead guilty to a serious crime.

As per his agreement with Sacco, Tony had already pled guilty to three felonies and taken responsibility for the operation. Danny, Kyle, Mathew, and Jay had all pled guilty too. I knew I had no choice but to do the same. Reluctantly, I handed Justine over to her father. I gave her a last, lingering kiss and composed myself. Then I followed Harold into the court.

The courtroom was crowded and hot. Gibson was standing beside his colleagues, arms crossed, with a smug look on his face. I tried to keep my expression neutral. Harold cued me when to sit and stand.

The judge launched into a long monologue, filled with legal jargon, explaining what my rights were. Then he addressed me directly. "Have you been threatened?"

"No," I replied.

"Have any promises been made to you?"

"No." He read out the charges. I was asked to enter a plea. I took a deep breath.

"Guilty," I said.

Sentencing was scheduled for July 25. I was free on bail until then. Court was adjourned.

■

THE NEXT MORNING, TONY flew out to the Dominican Republic to meet with a lawyer and a representative of the local phone company. Back in Red Bluff I began the arduous task of packing everything we owned into storage. Within a week I'd sold my car, settled our bills, handed over the house, and said a bittersweet goodbye to Gary, Sheila, and Tony's family.

Late that afternoon, Justine and I arrived at the 7th Avenue bus depot, where Tony was waiting to collect us. He tossed our luggage in the back of Joanna's car and drove to the passport office. We picked up the application for Justine. Traveling to the Dominican Republic only required a birth certificate and photo ID, so Tony had no trouble entering the country. He looked over Justine's form and on the spur of the moment, asked for another. Even though felons were prohibited from holding a passport, he decided to apply anyway. "The worst they can say is no."

When we returned to court for sentencing, Tony was up first. He received 350 hours of community service, a $15,000 fine and three years' formal probation. I watched with satisfaction as Gibson stormed out of the court, furious that Tony hadn't been sent to prison. We breathed a collective sigh of relief, knowing that if Tony wasn't going to jail, nobody else was either.

That afternoon, it was my turn: a $3,000 fine and two years of informal probation. The legal nightmare that had been hanging over our heads for a year was over.

Tony, Justine, and I moved into a spacious bedroom suite on the second floor of Joanna and Ron's beautiful home. We soon settled into a routine. Every morning at seven o'clock Tony would roar off on his Harley to L.A. County Jail. There he would change into an orange jumpsuit and spend the next ten hours collecting trash from the side of the freeway. Ron would leave mid-morning to take care of his business, and Joanna left for Decorators Choice, the luxury-goods company where she was a partner.

I stayed behind with Justine. My only responsibility was signing for the many boxes and packages that arrived via FedEx for Ron. They contained hundreds of thousands of dollars in cash. Ron would frequently call the house and ask me to open up a particular package and count the money inside. I gave him the total the same way I used to write tickets—leaving off the last two zeros.

One morning, two envelopes arrived addressed to Tony and me. I signed for both, tearing the first open to find Justine's passport inside. In the second envelope was another passport. This one was in Tony's name. It had been issued without question. For once the clumsy machinations of government bureaucracy had worked in our favor.

As the weeks went on, I felt happier than I had in a long time. The house had a crystal-clear pool in the backyard, where I swam laps whenever Justine napped. My days of feeling big, clumsy, and depressed were truly behind me. I felt lean and strong again— both physically and mentally. I actually preferred the way my body looked after giving birth; I felt more womanly and feminine than I had before. It was a side effect of motherhood that Tony enjoyed as well.

For all his reluctance to leave Red Bluff, I was grateful to see that Tony had slipped back into his old life effortlessly. He threw himself into the task of setting up the Dominican office. On the basis of his brief visit, however, his impressions of the country were less than favorable. I felt that his complaints could all be boiled down to a single issue: it wasn't America. Given this, I felt almost guilty about how much I was looking forward to the move.

Tony's probation officer was a tough, no-nonsense lady named Ruth Gordon. In mid-August Tony, Justine, and I met her for the first time at her Crenshaw office. Tony gave our address as 117 Bimini Place, and described, with a straight face, his full-time occupation installing lavish and elaborate window dressings for Decorator's Choice. The terms of Tony's probation required that he fill out weekly reports and mail them to Ms. Gordon. He was also required to meet with her face-to-face once a month for the next two years. This meant Tony would have to fly from Santo Domingo to L.A. every month, and convince her that he had spent the last four weeks hanging window treatments for a living.

I shivered as she sternly reminded him that his movements were restricted to Los Angeles and San Bernardino County. "And of course," she added, "you are prohibited from associating with other bookmakers."

12

Santo Domingo, September, 1988

SHIELDING MY EYES FROM the blinding sunshine, I hoisted Justine on my hip and followed Tony off the plane and onto the scorching tarmac. A group of grinning men in flowery bell-bottoms and ruffled shirts played a frantic merengue song. As they swirled their hips in unison, another group handed cups of rum-and-Coke to the disembarking tourists. The air was hot and salty. Justine's slick body squirmed against mine with the shock of the humidity.

We walked briskly to the relative cool of Santo Domingo's tiny airport terminal. A short, fat man in an ill-fitting gray linen suit strode toward us, hand outstretched. Two imposing soldiers in full army fatigues flanked him.

"Señor Santino," the man purred, taking Tony's hand. "Welcome back to Santo Domingo."

"Marisa, this is Gustavo Flores, our lawyer," Tony explained. "Gustavo—my wife, Marisa."

The little man flashed me a smile as slick and insincere as any politician's, and gave a little bow. "*Encantado.*"

We were led farther inside the shabby building to buy tourist visas. On Gustavo's advice we claimed we were visiting for pleasure, not business. Gustavo handed our paperwork to one of the soldiers. The man shoved his way to the front of the long, slow-moving immigration line. With barely a glance from the official behind the desk, our papers were stamped and we were waved through. Our fellow travelers watched us curiously, muttering to themselves, as we headed for the baggage area. Tony was clearly enjoying the VIP treatment. I wondered how much, or how little, it had cost to arrange.

We collected our belongings and moved on to customs, where we received the same preferential treatment. We cut straight past the long lines of tables where other new arrivals watched aghast as their cases were emptied and unceremoniously picked through by opportunistic customs agents. Beyond customs a swarm of Dominican porters rushed to our side, all competing for the chance to load our luggage onto their rusty carts.

"Taxi! Taxi!"

"Change money! Good rates, change money!"

"Hotel, hotel, nice hotel for you!"

I gripped Justine closer to me, threatened by the chaotic swarm around us. The metal barrier tipped and rocked as crowds of mostly dark-skinned locals pressed against it, hands outstretched, vying for our attention. Others held scraps of paper with the names of arriving passengers scrawled on them. Dozens of barefoot children trailed after us, begging for change. Gustavo swatted them away as if they were mosquitoes. I wanted to reach into my purse, but I was afraid to get detached from our group. When the airport soldiers chased the children off, I felt a guilty sense of relief.

By the time we'd reached the parking lot, our party seemed to have tripled. For every piece of luggage there were at least three or four men helping to carry it. I felt someone tugging at my purse, offering to carry it for me. "No, *gracias!*" I snapped. I kept my eyes glued on Tony's wallet, which was sticking casually out of his back pocket. Justine whimpered again, uncomfortable in the extreme heat. As we finally got the cases loaded into Gustavo's battered black Pinto and the military Jeep next to it, a dozen sets of hands were thrust into our vehicles, demanding payment. Tony distributed ten-dollar bills to the original porters, causing a near riot.

Gustavo's Pinto roared out of the airport and began to bounce along a pothole-riddled road. I searched around in vain for seatbelts, gave up, and clutched Justine to me. While Gustavo and Tony chatted, I gazed in awe at the rocky coastline and glistening turquoise waters. It was a thrilling feeling—a new beginning. We would have beaches to explore, a new culture to adopt, and another language to learn.

My mother had been baffled as to why we'd want to relocate to what she considered a third-world country. Hearing that Tony had a job offer in Santo Domingo didn't placate her in the slightest. Tony had instructed me what to tell people if they asked, and that's exactly what I told her: "He's going to manage a company selling sensitive information on short-term, high-risk ventures." My mother—who had no idea of the problems we were leaving behind—was less than convinced.

"Really. And that's something he couldn't do in the United States?"

"The phone company offers favorable rates there." I knew it was a weak excuse, but it was the best I had.

The abject poverty that my father had warned me about was everywhere on display as we drove. Tumble-down tin shacks dotted the countryside. Children played barefoot in the dirt, occasionally darting across the road in front of us like they were playing some high-stakes game of chicken. A steady stream of locals walked along the side of the road, carrying plastic bottles filled with drinking water. The highway turned inland, and the traffic increased dramatically as we drew closer to the city. The air turned hazy with the smoke from dozens of burning piles of garbage. We passed dilapidated buses and ancient, smoke-belching cars, all crammed with people. A motorcycle whizzed past with what looked like an entire family perched precariously on it.

We drove over the Juan Pablo Duarte Bridge onto a newly paved street. At first glance the street appeared to be lined with new apartments. Looking closer, I realized that the front-facing buildings were merely a façade—an illusion created by the government to disguise the maze of decrepit tin shacks just behind them. At the top of a hill I spotted a once-beautiful colonial mansion, now in a state of utter disrepair. It had seemingly been taken over by squatters pitching makeshift tents on the crumbling balconies. The city had undoubtedly seen better days.

Whenever we stopped at an intersection, beggars and hawkers beset Gustavo's Pinto. One man limped over on a pair of wooden crutches and attempted to clean the windshield by rubbing a filthy rag across it. An old woman pressed herself against the window, tapping pathetically with a gnarled finger, and pleaded for a few pesos. I made eye contact with her and she smiled, revealing a mouth devoid of teeth.

"Tony . . . give her some coins. Please."

Gustavo snorted contemptuously. "Mr. Santino, don't pay any attention. If you give one beggar money, twenty more will appear." Gustavo yelled something in Spanish at the woman. She trudged dejectedly away to the next car in line.

The traffic was painfully slow and the air was alive with the futile honks of frustrated drivers. We continued crawling toward the sparkling Caribbean, then turned right on Avenida George Washington, which hugged the coastline. "No power," Gustavo said, pointing at an unlit traffic signal. That sight would become extremely familiar to me in the coming years.

Our surroundings gradually changed. Soon we were driving down a street lined with magnificent villas, all protected by high stone walls and armed guards. We turned into a driveway bordered with lush tropical plants and pulled up to the Jaragua, the newest five-star hotel on the island. A doorman wearing a peaked cap and white gloves greeted us.

Two uniformed porters led us through the enormous lobby to the reception area. The air conditioning cooled the damp clothes against my skin. In the background was the subtle tinkling of a jazzy piano song. I could have been in any luxury hotel in the United States. The place was at once beautiful and utterly anonymous.

"The Jaragua has its own generators, so the electricity never goes off," Gustavo said as I glanced around the mirror-lined lobby. "There are three restaurants, a spa, a beauty salon, several bars, shops, boutiques, tennis courts, swimming pool . . . " He shot me another curiously insincere smile. "Mrs. Santino, you will never want to leave."

Something about Gustavo's manner really bothered me. As beautiful as the hotel looked, I was tired of living out of suitcases and eager for Tony and me to have a place of our own. When I mentioned this, Gustavo insisted that he was looking for a "beautiful villa" for us, somewhere away from the noise and grime of Santo Domingo. This was the last thing I wanted to hear. I'd had enough peace and quiet in Red Bluff.

"I'd like to live somewhere more urban," I said. "I want to be able to buy fresh produce daily from the markets."

Gustavo laughed heartily. "You will have a driver and staff to take care of the shopping for you. Just relax. Visit the spa. Don't worry about shopping. Worry about taking care of this beautiful little girl." He grinned at Justine and patted her on the head like a dog. "Let me worry about everything else."

■

"GUSTAVO CAN TAKE HIS villa and shove it," I said as soon as the elevator doors closed. "I don't want to live out in the country with a staff."

"He's just trying to be helpful, babe."

"I don't like him. Did you see the way he patted Justine on the head? Ugh. Where did Ron find him anyway?"

"Ron? Ron's never met him. He came via Edwin Walker."

"Who?"

"Edwin Walker. He's an American who works for Codetel, the phone company here. Walker helped turn Codetel into the most sophisticated telecommunications system in Latin America. And he gambles with the Small Office. Has been for years."

"So what's the deal between Walker and Gustavo? And where does Ron fit in?"

"Walker told Sacco he could offer him the same service here that he was getting in the States. That's how the two of them cooked up the idea of moving the operation offshore. But first they needed to run the plan by a Dominican lawyer. Walker consulted with Gustavo and Gustavo gave us the go-ahead. According to him, we're not violating any local laws. Technically, we're only giving out information over the phone. In fact, we're calling the new company Information Unlimited."

I had to admit it was a beautiful plan. As far as the players knew, nothing had changed. They had no idea their 1-800 calls were being answered in Santo Domingo. Ron would go on as usual, meeting with his agents and players in the States to do the paying and collecting.

It would be years before the federal government would learn that Ron Sacco had successfully launched the world's first offshore gambling operation.

■

TONY'S FIRST DAY OF work in Santo Domingo was a harbinger of what I could expect in the coming weeks. He was gone all day and didn't return to the hotel until ten in the evening. Back in L.A., our bookmaking days had been blissfully short: five hours a day Sunday through Friday, and eight on Saturday. In the Dominican Republic, that all changed.

The office opened at noon, local time, to take bets from the East Coast, and closed at 8 p.m. to accommodate the West Coast.

To compensate for the longer workdays, the clerks were given two days off a week instead of one. Six months out of the year, our opening hours would shift by an hour—the Dominicans did not adjust their clocks to daylight saving time like Americans did, so during that time we would open at 1:00 and close at 9:00. Grading was also no longer the clerks' responsibility. Now we had "graders," people whose sole job was to work nights correcting the tickets.

For Tony, the pressure increased dramatically. Without the need for secrecy, the size of Ron's operation doubled. Tony found himself running a mid-size company in a country whose language he didn't speak, with practically no day-to-day support from Ron.

When Tony left the following morning, I set out with Justine to explore our new home. I was determined to enjoy some of my newfound freedom. As I left the lobby, the concierge tried in vain to convince me to take a taxi. But I wanted to walk. I ventured down the road for twenty minutes before I gave up. The sidewalks were uneven and riddled with potholes, and navigating them with a stroller was impossible. I noticed several manhole covers missing, offering a direct view into the sewage system. All the while heavy traffic whizzed by us, spewing fumes into the air. Dejected, I headed back towards the hotel. On the way a sudden tropical downpour soaked us both to the skin.

My next attempt was by taxi that afternoon. I asked the driver to pull up outside what looked like a modern grocery store. Inside, though, it was dark and dingy. The metal shelves that lined the wall were rusted and barely stocked. On several tables were piles of fruit and vegetables, most of them still covered with mud, as if they had just been pulled from the ground. I saw none of the bright, inviting colors I was used to seeing back home—everything was brown and clumped with dirt. Even the eggs were smeared with chicken excrement, and many still had feathers sticking to the shells.

As I walked down the aisles checking out the local breakfast cereals, crackers, and cookies, a strange hush fell over the place. I realized that people were openly staring at me. I was the only foreigner there. I self-consciously carried on browsing, heading to the refrigerators at the back, which were stocked with a pungent selection of local cheeses, yogurt, milk, and butter. An overpowering stench came from packages of ground beef that were leaking blood all over the shelves. At the back of the store was a dusty stack of Coca-Cola cases. I was taken aback when I realized they were the old-style "ring-pull" cans. In the next aisle was a sparse selection of diapers, all of random size and in no particular order. The prices for these items were exorbitant. Next to the diapers were cans of formula and jars of Gerber baby food. I picked one up and examined it. It was months out of date.

When I arrived back at the Jaragua, I learned that the closest beach was forty minutes away. This area was hardly a tourist hotspot. The concierge explained that the hotel was booked with business travelers, and the only reason that tourists came to this part of the island was to visit the historic buildings of the colonial zone. Frustrated, I asked if he could help me find an apartment.

The concierge set up an appointment with an "English-speaking" real-estate agent for the following week. The agent showed up an hour late, without apology, and turned out not to speak a word of English. We rescheduled the appointment with a translator for the following day. When the time came, the translator didn't show up. I expressed my frustration to the concierge, who suggested that we try again, "*mañana.*" But nothing happened *mañana*, or the *mañana* after that. This was my introduction to the incomprehensible way that people did business in the Dominican Republic.

Two weeks later, we were still no closer to being in our own place. I longed to cook in my own kitchen and for Justine to have her own room. I complained to Tony, but he was too overwhelmed at the office to deal with house-hunting. Desperate to get out of the hotel, I went against my better instincts and called Gustavo, who cancelled on me twice.

Tony looked sour as I vented my frustrations one evening. "That's the problem with this country," he snapped. "Everyone promises to do things *mañana*, but *mañana* never comes."

■

ATLÁNTICO WAS THE HOTSPOT on the island. According to my father, five percent of the Dominican population held ninety-five percent of the wealth. As we pulled into Atlántico's parking lot—which was crammed with brand-new Jeep Cherokees, Porsche Carreras, and a slew of BMWs and Mercedes-Benzes—I could tell that this was one of the places where the five percent spent their free time.

The driver dropped Tony and me off in front of an ornate wrought-iron gate. The doormen looked us over before permitting us to pass. I was thrilled to have Tony to myself for the evening. We strolled hand-in-hand down a winding path toward the main entrance, past an exotic garden bar surrounded by bright tropical flowers.

A wide marble staircase led us up to a pair of imposing oak double doors. A uniformed attendant opened them and we stepped into a vast, crowded, and deliciously air-conditioned room. Beyond the long, well-stocked bar was a winding staircase that led down to a packed dance floor. Under the glimmering lights a crowd of people moved to the rhythm of American pop music. On the other side of a glass-walled DJ booth was a third staircase that led to the restaurant area. A fishpond, complete with ornate fountains, ran the entire length of the back wall. It was opulent, beautiful, and completely over-the-top.

I noticed that the majority of Atlántico's patrons were light-skinned. It was a young, glamorous, trendy crowd, and they were spending a lot of money. Darker-skinned waiters hovered over them, refilling water glasses and taking orders. The class divide, which ran so deep on the island, was laid bare for all to see. It wasn't a tourist bar—as far as I could see, we were the only foreigners in the place. A stunning hostess led us to a table.

Tony and I had not been out alone for months. "This feels just like old times," I said, squeezing his hand. Tony looked deep into my eyes, and smiled. "It's not L.A. But it'll do." When the waiter came over, he ordered a beer and a bottled water. "And tell the DJ to play some James Brown!"

The waiter returned a few moments later, shaking his head. Irritated, Tony pulled a five-hundred-peso note out of his wallet and pressed it into the waiter's hand. The waiter's eyes widened in disbelief. "James Brown, por favor!" Tony repeated.

I was chastising Tony for being so frivolous with his money when a tall, friendly-looking young man approached our table. I didn't know it then, but he was going to play a pivotal role in all of our lives in the upcoming years. With sad-looking gray eyes and brown wavy hair, he could have passed for one of the wealthy, light-skinned locals—until he opened his mouth.

"My name's Remo," he said with a broad Jersey accent. "I'm the general manager of the Atlántico. Welcome!" Tony and Remo shook hands as a James Brown track began to blare out over the sound system.

Tony and Remo hit it off immediately. Remo recounted some of his more unusual experiences managing one of the most exclusive clubs on the island, while Tony tried to match him story for story by recalling his hard-partying days in the hotspots of L.A. Neither of them reacted when I suppressed a yawn and excused myself to the ladies' room. As the only blond, blue-eyed woman in the club, I received plenty of appreciative stares from Atlántico's other male patrons as I walked across the floor.

In the bathroom I checked my reflection in the mirror. I smoothed down the little black Betsy Johnson dress I had chosen for what I'd assumed would be a special romantic evening. It hugged my curves and showed off my flat tummy. No one would guess that I'd given birth just four months ago. I fluffed my hair, fixed my makeup, and sashayed back to the table, determined to recapture my husband's attention.

Tony brightened when he saw me. "Babe!" he exclaimed like an excited child. "Remo can get me American milk!"

Tony usually drank milk by the gallon, but had a problem with the Dominican variety and never stopped complaining about the local brands. He had tried sheep and goat milk—had even bought a cow and had fresh milk delivered to him for a couple of weeks—but nothing came close to rivaling American milk.

"How?" I asked skeptically. Empty promises seemed to be a trademark of the country.

"Tell her!" Tony grinned.

"The American Airlines flight from Kennedy to Santo Domingo offers single-serving cartons of milk with breakfast," Remo explained. "I can get someone to bring me the unopened cartons a couple of days a week."

"That's great!" I said, certain that it would never happen.

Turning back to Tony, I reminded him that Justine would need feeding soon. I was hoping to lure him back to the hotel, but he suggested that I head back alone. He was going to hang out a while longer with his new buddy Remo.

"Tony, you have a flight first thing in the morning, remember?"

"I'll be back in an hour. Don't worry."

Tony rolled in around two in the morning, stinking drunk. He stumbled into bed and tried—unsuccessfully—to give me the "romantic evening" he'd promised earlier. The next morning, he slept through the alarm call and ignored my pokes and prods. Finally I shook him awake, reminding him that he had a plane to Las Vegas to catch and if he didn't hurry up he was going to miss his court appearance. At last he staggered out of bed and into the shower. Twenty minutes later he staggered out again, still unshaven and terribly hung over. "See you tonight, babe," he mumbled, leaving me a five-hundred-peso note on the dresser.

I was angry and determined to have it out with him when he returned later that evening. Except he didn't return.

When he didn't come back the following morning, I became sick with worry. Where was he? Why hadn't I heard from him? The court appearance in Las Vegas was a mere formality. Harold Fisher had told us that Tony and Ron's charges in Vegas would be dropped on the grounds of double jeopardy. Tony had already pled guilty and been convicted in Los Angeles, so legally he could not be sentenced for the same crime twice. Harold had assured us that the judge would have no choice but to dismiss the charges.

I called the office. Nobody seemed to know anything for certain, but Mathew told me something that made my stomach lurch. Rumors swirling around the West Coast said that Tony and Ron had been taken directly to jail from the court in Las Vegas.

The phone finally rang after midnight. I tensed up as I heard Joanna's voice on the other end. "What happened?"

Joanna sounded exhausted. "It's not good, Marisa. The judge deemed that separate prosecution is permissible under some sort of dual-sovereignty theory. Harold tried to explain it to me, but I don't really understand the ins and outs of it."

"But what does it mean for *us?*"

"Tony has to serve six months."

I sat there in stunned silence, clutching the phone. I opened my mouth, but no sound came out. *Six months?*

I hadn't even kissed Tony goodbye. What would I do here without him? My mind began to reel as I tried to imagine life on the island without Tony.

I took a deep breath. "And Ron?"

"He'll do a year," Joanna said with a heavy sadness. "We'll just have to cope until they get out. Harold is trying to appeal, but we have to prepare for the worst. In the meantime, I'll take over paying and collecting for Ron. Mathew's going to be in charge in the D.R. until Tony gets out."

I would receive Tony's salary for as long as he was away. Joanna assured me that I would not have to worry about money. "So will you go home?" she asked gently. "I mean, until Tony gets out?"

" I . . . " I caught my breath, tried to gather my thoughts.

I didn't know where home was anymore. There was no reason for me to go back to Canada. My father had just moved to Thailand, where he would be working for several years. My mother was still in Westchester, but I couldn't go back there—not under these circumstances. And there was no way I would ever go back to Red Bluff.

"I'm staying," I told Joanna determinedly. I would make sure that Tony had a real home to come back to. And for better or worse, this was home now.

13

WHEN TONY'S INCARCERATION WAS confirmed, morale at the office nosedived. Mathew was hit hardest. He found himself promoted to a job that he didn't want and was barely qualified to do. I got my first glimpse of just how out-of-his-depth Mathew was when I showed up at the office a few days after Tony had been imprisoned. "Pick up the fucking phones!" Mathew pleaded, but the clerks, especially the new guys, were barely reacting. It was like seeing a weak-willed substitute teacher confronting an unruly classroom. No one showed him any respect whatsoever.

The air of misery in the office was palpable. The clerks had flown down, seduced by Ron's fairy-tale promises of highly paid work on a beautiful tropical island, free of police hassles. The reality was very different from the sales pitch. They were marooned in a crumbling, chaotic city, miles from any beach. They were homesick and overworked—eating unfamiliar foods, getting eaten alive by bugs, and answering phones for eight hours a day in a hot, muggy office where no one seemed to be in charge. Tony had been able to hold the place together through sheer force of personality. Now that he was gone, the atmosphere was quickly turning rebellious. Even the guys I had known from L.A. barely mumbled hello to me.

I pulled Mathew aside one day and scolded him when we were out of earshot of the others. "You need to take control of this place! And you need to get someone in to clean up. It's a pigsty!"

The clutter and mess in the office only added to the sense of disarray. Mathew gave me a look filled with such hostility that it made me catch my breath. The gentle giant's mask had slipped, and it scared me. He stormed back into the office without another word.

I popped my head into the Small Office to see how they were coping, and was greeted by another sea of gloomy faces. At least the mess wasn't as bad here. Roger—whom I had first met at Dan Tana's—was running his office with markedly more success than Mathew. He looked dapper as he stood up to give me a hug.

"How are you bearing up, sweetheart?" he asked, his face lined with concern.

"As well as possible."

Justine squirmed in my arms and Roger's face melted. "Can I hold her for a minute?"

With Roger making goo-goo eyes at Justine, I took the opportunity to tear through the Big Office with a garbage bag, tossing in all of the candy wrappers, bottles of beer, and cigarette butts I could lay my hands on. Soon the call I'd been waiting for came in. "T-bone on four!" Ironically, the only way I could talk to Tony while he was in prison was on the 1-800 number that connected to the office.

"Watch what you say," Carmine warned. "The call will be monitored."

"I'm sorry," Tony said as soon as I picked up.

Just hearing his voice brought tears to my eyes. "We're fine," I assured him. "Don't worry about us. Just worry about you in there."

Tony assured me that he was okay and asked about Justine. There was nothing else for us to talk about. The clerks were listening on my end, and someone was listening in on his. Even saying "I love you" felt awkward.

I returned to the office a few days later for another scheduled call with Tony. Despite Mathew's angry reaction, my pep talk seemed to have had the desired effect. The office was spotless. The young Dominican girl responsible for this transformation was mopping the floors in the hallway. Her face lit up when she saw Justine. She shyly held out her arms to hold her.

"Justine," I said, gently passing my daughter over. "*Soy Marisa.*"

"*Soy Rosa,*" she smiled back.

■

WHEN I RETURNED TO the hotel, I was surprised to discover a cooler waiting at the front desk, addressed to Mr. Santino. The bellboy brought it up to the room and I flipped up the lid, curious.

"I'll be damned," I laughed. Inside, nestled in ice, were twenty tiny cartons of American milk, along with Remo's business card.

"Tony's been detained on a business matter," I told Remo, trying to keep the emotion out of my voice when I rang to thank him. I was touched at how disappointed he sounded, and chose the moment to ask my own favor. "I was wondering if you would help us find a place to live?" I knew Remo spoke fluent Spanish and understood the island and its customs. He also seemed to be the only person here capable of getting anything done.

"Okay," he said. "Let me see what I can do."

■

I TOOK A TAXI to Remo's studio apartment a week later, as arranged. He answered the door holding a file filled with newspaper clippings. Out in the bright sunlight and wearing his casual clothes, Remo seemed much younger than I'd first assumed. He looked like he was in his early twenties. He seemed shy, slightly awkward even—very different from the confident, witty man I'd met at Atlántico. The eyes, however, were exactly as I'd remembered them. They were soulful, almost melancholy, as if they belonged to someone decades older.

Remo gave the driver an address and we headed to Mirador Norte, a middle-class neighborhood. We turned off the main street and pulled up in front of a pale-pink apartment complex. The guard stationed outside was armed with a rifle. Remo told me that this was standard. Guards were cheap to hire, and held responsible in case of a robbery.

We went up to a third-floor apartment and were shown around by the landlord. The place was bright and clean, and the kitchen was adequate. Yet the dismal, windowless room beyond it was crammed with two beds and a toilet. I was shocked when Remo identified it as the servants' quarters. When the landlord produced the paperwork, Remo looked it over. His brow furrowed. After a tense conversation in Spanish, he turned to me.

"Time to go," he said.

"What's the rush?" I asked, hurrying after him.

"I'll tell you in the car."

As we drove to our next appointment, Remo told me that the landlord—who had advertised the apartment for three thousand, two hundred pesos a month—was now asking for six hundred U.S. dollars a month. This amounted to eighteen hundred pesos more than the original price. "It's going to be a problem for you," he said. "Most landlords are going to take one look at you and assume you're just another rich *gringo* they can take advantage of."

This was the first of many outings Remo and I would take in search of an apartment. By the third round I no longer questioned his motivations for turning down apartments that appeared to be perfectly acceptable. He knew all the right questions to ask, and was clearly looking out for my best interests. As our search unfolded, I began to understand exactly why Tony had taken such a shine to him. He was intelligent and easy to talk to, and had a wry sense of humor. On top of all this he was a fantastic guide to Santo Domingo, and I learned something new about the city every time we met up.

One day we pulled up outside a white apartment building bordering a lush courtyard. A distinguished gray-haired gentleman approached us as Remo apologized in Spanish for our lateness. Señor Torres introduced himself in perfect English. We followed him to the top-floor apartment. The moment I stepped inside, I fell in love with the place. It was bright and modern, with skylights and polished marble floors. The kitchen was brand-new, and the living and dining areas were spacious. A large covered balcony overlooked the courtyard below. The airy master bedroom had an *en suite* bathroom, accompanied by two further bedrooms and a guest bathroom where the shower was open to the sky above.

"It's beautiful," I said, walking awestruck from room to room. "It's *perfect*."

When Señor Torres inquired about my husband's business, I stuck to the familiar line about Tony selling sensitive information on high-risk ventures. Remo looked the paperwork over and told me that the price was fair. We were finally getting our own apartment. I knew Tony would be thrilled to come home to this place.

I was beaming by the time we got back in the taxi. "You'll need to have the contract notarized by a lawyer," Remo mentioned in the car. "I can recommend someone."

"I already have a lawyer," I said. I showed him Gustavo's card.

Remo looked it over, frowning. "Never heard of him."

"Well, apparently he's very well connected."

Remo shook his head. "No, he isn't. Marisa, if he were well connected, I'd have heard of him. What does he look like?"

"Short, chubby black guy."

Remo laughed. "What color black?"

This confused me. "I don't know. Just . . . black."

"There's no such thing as just black here. Race is a huge deal. You know how they say that the Eskimos have twenty-eight words for snow? Well, Dominicans have almost as many to describe skin color. It's not just about color—it's about class. Status. Black—real black—that's at the bottom of the pile. Haitians are black, and let's just say that the Dominicans don't treat them very well. They're exploited for cheap labor: construction, the sugar industry, whore-houses. If you call a Haitian black, they won't give a shit. But if you call a Dominican black, that's an insult."

At moments like this I realized how far away from home I was. "That's pretty unjust."

"It is. But the reason I'm bringing this up is that lawyers are rarely black here. So what color black is your lawyer?"

"Um . . . mulatto?"

"Hm. What kind of car does he drive?"

It seemed like a strange question, but I played along. "A Pinto. A '72 Pinto."

Remo burst out laughing. "You're kidding."

"No? What's so funny?"

"Trust me, Marisa. If your lawyer is driving a piece of crap like that, then I'll tell you, sight unseen, this guy doesn't have the kind of clout you think he has. If you're serious about starting up a business on the island, you need to find someone better, and do it quick. Your guy might have a brother or a cousin in the army, but basically, he's a nobody. Straight up, he wouldn't make it through the door at the Atlántico."

"That's harsh, Remo."

"I know. But believe me," Remo chuckled, "well connected, powerful lawyers in this country do not drive '72 Pintos."

As the taxi pulled up at the intersection, the usual crowd of beg-gars and peddlers swarmed the stationary cars. Remo rolled down his window and shook hands with a one-armed, one-legged man who greeted him by name. They chatted in Spanish for a while, and as they talked another peddler recognized Remo and came over to say hello. I was astonished. "They didn't even ask you for money!"

"Those guys gave up trying to hustle me years ago. They know I'm struggling to get by myself."

I was struck by how different Remo's attitude toward the street people was from Gustavo's. Remo saw them as human beings.

Gustavo, on the other hand, saw them as scum. At that moment I made a snap decision that I would not deal with Gustavo again if I could help it.

I asked Remo for the phone number of the lawyer he had recommended. As he got out of the taxi, I thanked him again for his help. "I owe you a drink," I said.

"Sorry," he grinned. "I don't drink."

"Me neither. Maybe dinner, then?"

"When your husband gets back, stop by Atlántico." The way he said it made it clear he had no intention of seeing me socially without Tony present. His reserve was slightly old-fashioned and charming. I suppose he thought that Tony would mind. On the other hand, there wasn't any attraction between us, and I would have liked to have a friend on the island. I knew I would miss our regular apartment-hunting sessions. As Remo walked away, I sensed a heavy undertow of sadness. He had integrated himself completely in the Dominican Republic, but it seemed obvious to me how much he missed America.

I set out early the next morning to buy a fridge, a stove, propane tanks, and ten meters of copper piping to hook them up. I bought the biggest mattress I could find, and ordered furniture from a factory that Remo had recommended. I carried bottles of water, groceries, toys, and suitcases up the stairs until my legs ached.

At seven that evening the lights in the new apartment winked off—and with them, the water. At eight I put Justine to bed. Left alone, I sat outside on the balcony. It was a pitch-black, breezeless evening. Waiting for the electricity to come back on, I experienced the profound silence of a power outage. I could hear the leaves rustling on the trees in the courtyard below. An animal skittered off somewhere in the bushes. From far away I heard the low drone of approaching cars.

The next morning I woke up to a rooster crowing. I was sticky with sweat, and discovered that my entire body was covered in angry, itchy red welts. Justine was in a similar state. We still had no electricity, and no water to shower. I grabbed a taxi, heading out to buy mosquito nets and lanterns. Within minutes, we found ourselves stuck in a seemingly endless traffic jam. The electricity was out everywhere.

Suddenly we heard the crash of metal on metal. The traffic around us ground to a complete halt. Our driver cursed and threw his hands up in frustration. For the time being, we were going nowhere. Moments later I heard the unmistakable sound of a gunshot. The silence that followed was eerie.

When the traffic began inching forward again, there was no honking, no yells of frustration. As we approached the accident I saw a light-skinned man dressed in a business suit, leaning against the hood of his slightly damaged Mercedes. In his hand—with no effort to conceal it—was a pistol.

Behind his car was a vehicle that looked like it had been welded together from parts of ten different cars. The windshield was splattered with blood. I caught a horrifying glimpse of the driver, a Haitian man. He was slumped forward over the steering wheel, his face slick with blood. With a shudder I looked away.

As we crawled past the macabre sight, the shooter remained leaning against his Mercedes. His face showed no remorse whatsoever. He looked mildly annoyed, as if he were running late for an appointment. He and everyone around him knew that killing a Haitian would have no consequence for him whatsoever.

14

ON NOVEMBER 7, JOANNA delivered the news I had been dreading. Tony's appeal had been denied. He would remain in prison until May.

The news sent shockwaves throughout Information Unlimited. The company was already struggling under Mathew's direction. When the clerks heard that Tony wouldn't be returning, three responded by walking off the job. Sick of the heat, the power outages, the constant chaos at the office, and frequent bouts of food poisoning, they fled the island that same night. In the following week, more clerks departed. Office morale hit an all-time low.

I was struggling as well. I was spending long days alone caring for Justine. I desperately missed having someone to talk to. The nights were worse. After one particularly long evening without electricity or running water, I made the decision to return to work. The following morning, I hauled Justine's playpen and toys down to the office and began taking bets again.

Rosa, the young Dominican girl who kept the office clean, began caring for Justine while I was working. Thanks to her, I was able to work full-time. In addition to keeping me sane, my return to work alleviated some of the pressure that the staff shortage was putting on the Big Office.

Unlike the rest of the clerks, I was enjoying life in the Dominican Republic. I had lived in Italy and Canada and traveled a lot before coming here, so being in a foreign country didn't seem so strange. I found the locals incredibly friendly, enjoyed their cuisine, and thought that their coffee was the best I'd ever tasted. A luxury hotel, El Embajador, was walking distance from my apartment, and Justine and I were welcome to use the facilities anytime. The island was covered with bright tropical flowers, and the sunsets were gorgeous.

Of course there were drawbacks. One evening as I was pushing Justine's stroller through a nearby park, I felt an insect bite my leg. I assumed it was a bee sting, but within twenty-four hours my leg had swollen up to the point where walking became painful. When I showed up for work, Carmine nearly spat his coffee all over the desk.

"Jesus Christ, Marisa, what happened to your face?"

I had no idea what he was talking about. I hobbled to the bathroom to look in the mirror. I gasped. My face was grotesquely swollen. Carmine immediately called a taxi to take me to a doctor. By the time I arrived at the dingy local hospital, I was having difficulty breathing.

A doctor arrived, inspected my leg, and called for assistance. He told me that the puncture marks indicated the bite of a spider called the *Tarantula Hispaniola.* It was a native arachnid too big to spin a web, so it lived in bushes or trees. It emerged at dusk to prey on beetles, moths, cockroaches, mice . . . and the occasional human. Its bite was not dangerous to humans, but unfortunately I was allergic to its venom.

Two men arrived and held my leg down. The doctor produced a scalpel and, without any anesthesia, stabbed it into my leg. He ignored my screams and cut a circle in my flesh around the area of the bite. He then removed the penny-sized chunk of skin and tossed it to the floor. I cried out in agony as he squeezed the open wound with his bare hands, presumably to force the poison out. When he was done, he rolled up a piece of gauze and stuffed it into the wound like a cork. He gave me a crooked smile and finished by delivering the understatement of the year: "This may take some time to heal."

The wound oozed for weeks and left a deep, ugly indentation in my leg that would put me off wearing skirts for years to come.

In Los Angeles, new clerks were usually recommended or vouched for by other clerks or agents. Since the bulk of our old staff had fled the island, we no longer had that luxury. So when a middle-aged man who called himself Crunch showed up, we thought we had lucked out. Crunch was a quick learner, quiet, and dependable. His respectable appearance made him the obvious choice to send to Miami to collect supplies and bring back the payroll, including Christmas bonuses. But Crunch never came back. He collected $250,000 in cash from Joanna, then vanished into thin air.

This betrayal was coupled with the overriding sense of dissatisfaction in the office. In January, three months after our arrival on the island, Joanna voiced suspicions that Mathew was ripping her off. Her fears had been aroused when Mathew had billed her for a second, nonexistent generator for the office. At first I didn't believe her. Mathew—the gentle giant, the longstanding employee? It seemed inconceivable. As the two of us investigated further, however, we discovered that Mathew was indeed embezzling. He was still collecting payroll and bonuses for employees who had left the company months before. I was heartbroken. Mathew had recently volunteered to fly back to Miami to collect supplies and pick up another $200,000 for the office. Joanna suspected he would disappear the same way Crunch had.

At the same time, our phone bill skyrocketed by twenty thousand dollars. Joanna sent me to talk to Edwin Walker—our contact at Codetel—to find out what was going on. I met with him in his comfortable, air-conditioned office. In his lilting Southern accent, Walker explained to me that the billing increments for our 1-800 numbers had been changed from fifteen to thirty seconds, resulting in the dramatic increase in price. Walker must have assumed that I would not challenge him. Just like Crunch and Mathew, Edwin Walker was trying to use the opportunity of Tony's absence to line his own pockets.

I sized him up from across the desk. Walker knew that no other phone company in Latin America could provide us with the services we required. Yet I knew that Information Unlimited was Codetel's biggest client. We earned them more money than American Airlines. Walker needed us just as much as we needed him.

I looked him straight in his steel-gray eyes and told him that we would not pay the bill until he changed the increments back. He smirked, rested his chin on his fingers, and purred, "Can't do that, I'm afraid."

"I think you can." A long silence followed as we coolly regarded each other.

"Why don't we meet for dinner tonight. Maybe you could try a little harder to . . . convince me."

I gave him a withering stare and rose to my feet. "How about you discuss this with my husband when he gets out of prison?"

The color drained from Walker's face. "But—but your last name is Lankester . . . I mean, I didn't know! I'm sorry!"

I stormed out of his office, fuming. Nobody would have the audacity to try to rip off Information Unlimited if Tony were around. He was respected, even feared. Edwin Walker followed me out, promising to resubmit the adjusted bill.

Joanna fired Mathew, and essentially promoted me to CFO. I left for Miami to pick up the two hundred thousand dollars, carefully concealing the money under loose-fitting clothing. I had arranged for Remo to collect me at the airport with an army officer whom he trusted implicitly. Even though I would be spared from going through customs and immigration, it was still an unnerving experience to smuggle that amount of currency into the country. When we disembarked, I was greeted once again by the merengue-and-rum crew welcoming tourists to the island. I bypassed them and headed straight for Remo.

Far from looking pleased to see me, Remo's expression was strained. He introduced me to a tall, uniformed man, by the name of Captain Miguel Garcia. We followed the captain through the terminal, out to his dilapidated car. I had to position my feet around a rusty hole in the backseat floor. When we were safely on our way, I turned to Remo. "What's going on?" I asked.

"I had Miguel here do a little checking up on your lawyer."

"And?"

"There are some things I think you need to know about Gustavo Flores."

15

Las Vegas, May, 1989

AFTER SIX LONG MONTHS, Tony was finally released from jail. I'd checked into a room at Caesar's Palace and was waiting for him to arrive.

"Where's Daddy?" I asked Justine brightly. She was sitting on the floor surrounded by new toys. I checked my watch. Where *was* he? He was an hour late. I checked my reflection in the bathroom mirror. My hair and makeup were perfect. I wore skinny jeans and a bright blue shirt that matched my eyes. Underneath, I was wearing a black lace-and-velvet underwear set that I'd bought especially for the occasion. I wanted today to be perfect. Romantic. All I needed now was Tony.

Finally, I was startled by an urgent knock at the door. With a squeal of anticipation I pulled it open. *At last!*

I barely had time to register how different Tony looked before his lips were crushed against mine. He pulled me into an embrace that was almost a bear hug. I was stunned, not so much by the ferocity of his embrace as at the dramatic transformation in his appearance. My husband was barely recognizable as the man who had been sentenced six months ago.

He broke off and I got a good look at him. His hair was scraggly and he had a full, untidy beard that tickled my face. He had put on a lot of weight. As he kissed me again, I felt his substantial belly pressing against me. In one smooth movement he kicked the door closed behind him and started tugging at my clothes.

"Hey. Hey, Tony!"

He stopped in confusion. He followed my gaze down to Justine. She was still sitting on the floor staring up, wide-eyed, at this bear of a man. She looked unsure whether to smile or cry. "Look, Justine," I said. "Daddy's home!"

With barely a grunt of acknowledgment to his daughter, Tony dragged me into the bathroom and locked the door behind us. He unzipped my jeans and before I knew what was happening he lifted me onto the sink and pulled my legs apart. This was nothing like the romantic coupling I had been fantasizing about for months. It was hard, crazed, and animalistic. Tony was completely absorbed in his own pleasure, and in moments it was over. He collapsed on me, gasping for breath.

"You have no idea," he panted, "how much I missed that."

■

BACK IN THE HOTEL room, Tony scooped Justine into his arms. She barely resembled the infant he'd left six months ago, yet his face was filled with painful longing. Justine whimpered and pulled away from him. She reached her arms out to me, frightened. Tony looked hurt as he passed her back. I assured him that she just needed time to get used to him again. As Justine reached for my breast, he said testily, "Jesus, you're still nursing her?"

"I was going to stop, but there was a typhoid epidemic on the island a few months ago, and . . . well, it's just safer this way."

He relaxed a little, showing a smile, and I saw a trace of the old

Tony. He came over and wrapped his arms around the two of us. "Sorry," he said. "I didn't think I'd still have to share those babies."

The next thing Tony wanted to do was eat. He had a whole list of comfort foods he was looking forward to having. Prison food was awful, he said—greasy and full of starch. That much is obvious, I mused as I eyed his bloated frame. I immediately felt guilty for thinking it.

Tony looked thirty pounds heavier. His face had filled out, an effect made worse by the Grizzly Adams beard he was sporting. His belly strained at the buttons of his shirt and pants. His skin was pasty. I felt an overpowering sadness as I saw him getting ready to go out. He had really let himself go. Worse than that, there was something different about *him*. I supposed that being locked up had left a deep mark on him.

Tony seemed oblivious to the change. In fact, he was happy to the point of euphoria. He bounded around the room like a child, looking out the window and talking excitedly about how liberating it was to be able to go wherever he pleased.

Later that day, we packed up our rental car and set out for Los Angeles. On the long drive he regaled me with prison stories, describing some of the characters he'd met inside. I did my best to fill him in on life in the Dominican Republic. I told him about the sugar, gas, and bread shortages that had crippled the country in the past months, the bombing at the American Institute, and the student riots sparked by soaring inflation.

"The island's two main generators are down, so we only have a couple of hours of electricity a day," I told him.

"What a mess," he said, shaking his head. "Out of one prison and straight back into another."

"It's not that bad, Tony. It's a pretty amazing place. Once you get used to it, I'm sure you'll fall in love."

"I doubt it," he sighed. "I'm surprised Carmine's still around. I figured he'd quit months ago."

I laughed. "Carmine's got a 23-year-old girlfriend. He isn't going anywhere. A lot of the clerks have girlfriends now."

Our staff had found themselves enthusiastically pursued by young, pretty local women. To them, an American boyfriend represented status and a possible way off the island.

"No wonder turnover's down."

"We lost a lot of guys in the beginning. Weird thing is, the tougher they looked, the faster they left."

The misfits and the oddballs had stayed. They were the ones who had nothing to gain by going back home. In the D.R. they were desirable in a way they could never be in the United States.

"I can't believe Mathew was ripping us off. Didn't see that coming," Tony said.

I hadn't planned on bringing up the Gustavo situation until we got back to the Dominican Republic. However, now seemed like a good time. Justine was fast asleep in the back seat. "Mathew wasn't the only person ripping us off. Gustavo's just as guilty."

Tony's eyebrows shot up. "Ripping us off? What do you mean? He didn't really have to do anything while I was gone. How could he rip us off?"

"I noticed a big discrepancy between the amounts of rent we were paying on the apartments Gustavo found for the clerks and the one I found for us. A big difference, Tony. We pay way less for a much nicer apartment."

"So what? You got lucky."

"I looked at a lot of properties before I found ours. There's something really off about the amount of rent our clerks are paying. Even the office! We're handing over eighteen hundred dollars a month for two small rooms, a hallway and a bathroom? In Santo Domingo? That's way too much." Tony looked like he was about to interrupt me, so I pressed on. "Also, did you know all of the rental agreements are in U.S. dollars? That's illegal under Dominican law. Gustavo must have known that. He is a lawyer, after all."

"I told Gustavo right off the bat I had no problem paying in dollars."

"I understand that . . . as long as the price is fair. I asked him for a copy of the office contract. He flat-out refused."

"So?"

"So he was hiding something."

Tony laughed in an irritatingly patronizing manner. "We pay more because of the zoning laws. We have no choice—we have to operate in that district. Gustavo told me all of this already."

"There is no such thing as a zoning law in the Dominican Republic. I checked into it. Look. Gustavo rented our office for nineteen hundred pesos a month. Then he turned around and re-rented it to us for eighteen hundred dollars a month. He's pocketing the difference!" Tony's face darkened and I saw his jaw tighten. I pressed on. "I can prove it, Tony. I have a copy of the original contract at home."

"Marisa . . . "

"*And* Remo put me in touch with another lawyer. Someone trustworthy—"

"*Will you shut up and listen?*" Tony hissed. "We can't do shit, okay? Information Unlimited is registered under Gustavo's name. We needed to have the company registered to a Dominican. Gustavo was our only choice at the time. Walker recommended him and that's good enough for me. Gustavo's well connected and anyway, it's not like we have another option."

I thought about Walker's attempts to rip off Information Unlimited while Tony was away. I was about to say something, but seeing the look on Tony's face, I backed off.

"What do Gustavo's connections have to do with anything if everything is legal and above-board?"

There was a long silence in the car. When Tony spoke again, it was in a low, dangerous voice. "Give me a fucking break, okay? I just got out of jail. I don't need this bullshit right now. I'm going to be back at that office tomorrow. Why don't you just worry about being a wife again. And a mother."

It took all of my self-control to bite my tongue. I reminded myself that he had just come out of prison. It would take time for things to get back to normal. Arguing would only make things worse.

Regaining his composure, Tony said, "We got more pressing

issues. They added two years onto my probation. I have to meet with Ruth Gordon in the morning. When we're done there, we can go shopping for supplies. Then we can take the red-eye to Santo Domingo."

I forced a smile. "Sounds great."

I watched as mile after mile of featureless desert zoomed past us. I had once loved it here, but now it seemed barren and inhospitable—like the surface of the moon.

■

THE PROBATION MEETING WENT off without a hitch. Afterward, we met Joanna for lunch. She kissed Tony on the cheek, then held him at arm's length, scrutinizing him.

"Darling," she said, "you are in dire need of a haircut and a shave." She turned to me and handed me a bag. "This is a little something to thank you for all the hard work you put in while Tony was away."

I opened the beautifully wrapped box. Inside was a taupe leather Chanel handbag, and tucked inside the purse were a pair of diamond earrings. I was speechless.

She hugged me tightly. "I don't know what we would have done without you."

After lunch, Tony led me across the street to a jewelry store. Joanna followed, carrying Justine. "I always regretted that I couldn't afford to buy you a nice ring when we got married," he said. "I thought about that a lot while I was away. But now I can." He saw the bewilderment on my face and smiled. "Anything you want. I want you to pick out something beautiful, okay?"

I looked around the store, slightly shell-shocked. I realized that Tony and Joanna must have been planning this for some time. I was incredibly touched.

"You don't have to," I whispered. I was perfectly happy with the plain gold wedding band Tony had bought for me in Red Bluff.

"No, get something beautiful. Six months in a place like that is enough to send a man crazy. The only thing that kept me going was that you were waiting for me on the outside. This ring is a thank-you, okay? A thank-you for being my wife. A thank-you for being faithful." He leaned forward and kissed me.

Thank you for being faithful? He could have thanked me for staying strong and keeping his daughter safe and healthy. He could have thanked me for going back to work and overseeing the office. Instead he chose to thank me for the one thing that had come as naturally as breathing.

The jeweler put a tray of rings on the counter. We leaned closer to examine them. They were beautiful—an array of sparkly stones in elegant settings. "I—I couldn't wear something like this on the island," I whispered. "It would be asking for trouble."

Joanna handed Justine to Tony. "Come over here," she said, taking me by the arm and leading me over to a second display case. "There's some more you should see."

When we were out of earshot she whispered urgently, "Sweetheart. Take my advice. You get yourself a great, big, fat diamond, and if you ever get into trouble you can sell it." She winked at me.

I knew I would never wear something so flamboyant, whether on or off the island, but the urgency in Joanna's tone suggested that she was giving sage advice. From what I had seen so far with the new Tony, I decided to take it.

16

TONY COULDN'T GET HOLD of Gustavo, so we couldn't return to the Dominican Republic that evening. It was too risky. Tony and I would be entering the country carrying $300,000 in cash. We needed the protection of an armed escort. I knew that if we couldn't reach Gustavo by morning, we would miss the next flight as well, so I suggested that Tony call Remo. His friend Miguel Garcia had collected me every time I returned to Santo Domingo with payroll.

Tony called Atlántico. I could hear Remo on the other end promising to take care of everything. Then Tony covered the mouthpiece and asked me how many people worked for us now. I told him twenty-three. "Hey Remo," Tony said. "Make a reservation for me for tomorrow night. Twenty-four people for dinner, at nine o'clock." As Tony hung up, I cringed at the thought of the guys from the office showing up at a formal place like Atlántico. With the exception of Roger and Tony, our clerks dressed appallingly. I was willing to bet that most of them didn't even own a pair of slacks.

The following day, we met Miguel Garcia at the Santo Domingo airport. He swept us through customs and immigration without a problem. Always eager to practice my elementary Spanish, I asked him a few questions as we went. Tony was surprised that I was bothering to learn the language. For him Santo Domingo was a temporary hitch, so why bother?

Miguel pulled into the courtyard and helped us carry everything upstairs. Tony took a quick tour around our new home, and I introduced him to Rosa, who was now Justine's live-in nanny. Tony barely had time to shower and change before heading to Atlántico. I unpacked and hid the diamond ring and earrings on the top shelf in the closet, where I imagined they would remain for years. Exhausted after all the traveling and high emotion of the past few days, I collapsed into bed and fell into a deep sleep.

Crash!

I blinked awake, utterly confused. I glanced at the bedside clock—it was 3:00 a.m. I reached across to the other side of the bed, but it was empty. The bedroom door flew open and Tony staggered in. He dumped his briefcase on the top of the dresser and slammed the door behind him. In no time he was naked and on top of me. He pulled my nightgown up, slurring, "I love you, babe . . . " I reminded myself that he'd been away for six long months and was trying to make up for lost time.

The next morning, I crept out of bed, closing the door softly behind me. Justine was just learning to walk and she tottered around the apartment, leading me by the hand. At ten o'clock, Tony finally appeared, looking hung over and angry. "Where's my briefcase?" he demanded.

"Isn't it on the dresser?"

I followed Tony into the bedroom. The briefcase was gone. He maniacally searched the apartment before collapsing on the couch. He cradled his head in pain. "I don't need this," he groaned. "This is bullshit. That *girl* must have stolen it . . . "

At first I didn't realize whom he meant. "Are you talking about Rosa? No way, Tony. You're wrong."

"Oh yeah? Well, the briefcase is gone. I doubt you or Justine took it, so that only leaves one other person."

Tony went upstairs to search Rosa's room. She burst into tears as she realized that she was being accused of theft. He stormed back downstairs.

"Call Remo," he snarled, "and tell him to get over here." He staggered off to the bedroom. A moment later I heard him yell, "Why is there no water? "

As I listened to him rant and rage, I realized that Tony was going to have a harder time than I'd assumed adjusting to life in the Dominican Republic. As a prisoner in the United States, he'd still been provided with uninterrupted water and electricity. This was a luxury the government in the D.R. still failed to deliver to its general population.

Soon there was an urgent knock at the door. Tony, still shirtless and unshaven, ushered Remo in.

"What's going on?" Remo asked. "What's the emergency?"

"The maid stole my briefcase."

"Oh, bullshit, Tony!" I yelled. I would have bet that Rosa hadn't stolen anything in her entire life.

"She must have snuck into our bedroom, took it, and threw it off the balcony to her boyfriend or something," Tony theorized as he paced furiously. "The only way in and out of here is that door, and I locked it."

"Are you sure you brought your briefcase home from Atlántico?"

"Yeah. I put it on the dresser. I've turned this place up and down, man. It's gone, and nobody else could have taken it. Look, Remo, talk to the girl. Tell her nothing will happen to her so long as I get the briefcase back."

Remo nodded and went upstairs. I angrily made another pot of coffee. While I didn't know what had happened to the briefcase, I knew one thing for certain: if Tony hadn't been drunk, none of this would have happened.

After ten tense minutes, Remo emerged again. "She didn't take it."

"Bullshit! She's lying!" Tony said.

Remo sighed and took the coffee I offered him. "She'd have no reason to take it. Your wife made sure that Rosa has everything she could possibly need. She has a big room, her own bathroom, new furniture, fresh linens, toiletries."

"So what?"

"Tony, back at home that girl probably shares a mattress with her sisters or a grandmother, and a toilet with half the village. Bottom line? She's never had it so good. Marisa, how much you paying her?"

"Five hundred pesos a month."

Remo nodded. "Days off?"

"Sundays and Mondays."

Remo smiled. "That's almost double the going rate, with an extra day off included. That girl has a dream job here. There's no way she'd risk losing it." Remo put the coffee cup down and looked at Tony sincerely. "Rosa did not steal your briefcase."

Tony's anger finally deflated. Remo suggested speaking with the security guard, or calling the police, but the look Tony gave him made it perfectly clear that getting the authorities involved was not an option. Tony wandered back into the bedroom miserably. Then we heard him call out, "Holy shit! Look at this!"

Tony was peering out of the window, resting his elbows on the windowpane. "Look!" We peered past him and saw several muddy footprints on the narrow ledge. It was a long drop down. Somebody had risked his life to steal Tony's briefcase. For a moment I felt vindicated. Then reality hit. Somebody had been in our room last night as we'd been sleeping. They could have murdered us in our beds. They could easily have gone into Justine's room.

My blood ran cold. I left to get Rosa while Tony and Remo debated the logistics of how the intruder might have made it across the ledge. I knocked on Rosa's door and apologized in halting Spanish. Then I took her downstairs to show her the footprints.

"Tony, this is a poor country," Remo was saying. "There are a lot of desperate people here. It's a small island. People notice when someone flashes a lot of money."

Rosa leaned forward. Her eyes widened when she saw the footprints.

"You need to be more discreet," Remo continued. "You spent thirteen thousand pesos on Dom Pérignon alone last night. That's more money than most people here earn in a year."

I frowned at Tony, and he squirmed uncomfortably. "It was a special occasion," he said lamely.

"Special occasion or not, people were staring at you," Remo said. "My boss gave me shit because your party was so loud and casually dressed. You guys were hammered when you left, so you wouldn't have noticed if someone followed you home."

I hoped Tony was getting the message. Maybe coming from Remo it would have more of an impact.

Tony was deep in thought. "Can you get me a couple of handguns?"

Remo looked as taken aback by this sudden change of direction as I was. "They're expensive. Difficult to come by."

Tony snorted derisively. "Right. You're telling me those suits at Atlántico last night weren't packing heat?"

"Most of our customers are armed," Remo conceded. "Wealthy people here tend to carry weapons."

"So can you get handguns, yes or no?"

Remo looked sheepish. "I guess cash won't be a problem?"

"What do you think?"

"Are you still on tourist visas?"

"Uh-huh. I'm working on getting residency permits for us."

Remo nodded thoughtfully. "Well, technically you're not allowed to carry a weapon unless you're a permanent resident . . . but that doesn't mean that it can't be worked out."

"Good." Tony slapped Remo on the back. "One for me and one for the little lady."

■

AFTER THAT, TONY TOOK extra precautions to protect his family and improve the quality of our lives. He supplemented the security guard's salary to motivate him to stay alert. He installed a safe in the walk-in closet, where we stashed my jewelry, our documents, and hundreds of thousands of dollars in cash. He bought a Mitsubishi truck for himself and a little blue Daihatsu for me. He had a five-hundred-gallon water tank installed on the roof of our apartment, and purchased a small generator. Theoretically, we would have a constant supply of water and electricity, no matter what.

Three months after Tony's return, the offices moved to a villa on Calle Salvador Sturla, in a quiet neighborhood called Plaza Naco. Remo found the house for us. It was less expensive than the old office, and three times the size. The Big Office was installed in the dining room, the Small Office in the living room, and the Baby Office in a converted bedroom. A second bedroom was dedicated to horse bets, and the last bedroom became Tony's office, complete with a safe the size of a fridge.

Tony promoted Gustavo to "corporate lawyer." At first I was incensed, but then I realized that Tony had installed Gustavo in the servants' quarters at the end of the property.

"I can keep an eye on him there," Tony said, with a steely glint in his eye. "That crooked bastard won't ever forget who the boss is again."

The new offices also boasted cutting-edge technology. Tony had a satellite brought over from the United States, and Edwin Walker—through Codetel—hooked Tony up with one of the first cell phones in the country. Sacco, at Tony's urging, invested in a company van, eliminating the need for the clerks to take taxis to the office. With Tony back in charge, the players lost the edge they'd gained, and soon the office was raking in more money than ever before. Tony's next trip to L.A. to meet with his probation officer was a breeze, and soon the company's future looked very bright indeed.

All of his industry had a downside, though. Tony would call just before leaving the office to check on the electricity. Our generator at home wasn't strong enough to run the TV, and Tony liked to relax at the end of the day by flipping through channels with a cold beer. If I told him the power was out, more often than not he'd skip coming home in favor of joining the clerks for a late dinner. It always felt like a slap in the face when he stayed out, as if watching TV was more important to him than being with us.

These frequent evening absences inspired my return to the office. I figured that if we were working under at the same roof, then at least I'd see my husband for a few hours a day. Justine was still taking long naps in the afternoons, and I hated sitting around the apartment doing nothing. One day I simply showed up at the office, took a seat in an empty cubicle and asked Carmine to read me the line.

Tony took a rare day off on June 11, when the three of us headed to the beach to celebrate Justine's first birthday. Remo had recommended the white sands and clear shallow waters of Boca Chica, as well as the excellent cuisine of Club St. Tropez. Once there, we were greeted by the owner, a lean, tanned, shirtless Frenchman called Jean-Michel who treated us like old friends the moment we mentioned Remo's name. We were set up with lounge chairs and umbrellas and café con leche. It was a perfect day. Justine played in the sand, squealing with delight when the water splashed her feet. It was wonderful to spend some time together as a family. I hoped that once the business was more settled, we would share more days like this.

By noon, the beach was packed. Sunburnt tourists walked along the shoreline sipping tropical drinks, or frolicked in the turquoise-blue waters. Local vendors descended on the strip, flogging inflatable rafts, balls, and floats. Others sold swimwear or Haitian artwork—wood sculptures, chunks of raw amber, or coral jewelry. Young Dominican girls offered manicures and massages, local children begged for pesos, scantily clad prostitutes trawled for clients, and Haitian women in vibrant outfits harassed people to get their hair braided.

As I played with Justine in the sand, Tony remained under the umbrella. As the afternoon progressed he barely moved, content to pound beer after beer. As soon as he drained one, a waitress came with another. His drinking had been getting out of hand lately. Not wanting to start an argument, I tried the subtle approach. "I'm ordering a water. Do you want one too?"

"Babe," he replied with an edge to his voice, "why don't you let me enjoy my first day off in seven weeks, huh?"

I left it alone. Jean-Michel summoned us for lunch, and we dined alongside European tourists and local businessmen, hidden away in the relative cool of a canvas awning. Everybody was served the same exquisitely prepared fish, caught fresh and served in a delicate cream sauce with grilled vegetables. It was the best meal I'd had since arriving on the island, and I told Jean-Michel so. He gave a little shrug of the shoulders and replied, "I know."

"So how do you know my good friend Remo?" he inquired next, sitting down next to us.

"From Atlántico."

"Ah yes," Jean-Michael sighed. "He is a manager, no? It is sad, seeing a natural talent like his wasted like that. He could have been a world-class chef like me," he said, with typical Gallic modesty.

"Remo can cook?" I asked, astonished at this piece of news.

Jean-Michel snorted. "I hired Remo years ago, after my wife left me to return to France. I taught him everything I know. It is a tragedy that he is not using his God-given talent."

"Why did he leave?" It seemed inconceivable to me that anyone would want to give up working in such a beautiful place to go work in the city.

Jean-Michael sat forward and gestured to a large, modern hotel at the far end of the beach. "I'll tell you why. The owners of that monstrosity were determined to clean up this beach. They paid the local police to drive away us small-business owners. We were terrorized. Told we needed permits that did not exist. Our power was cut. Our men were beaten, our women raped. They even shot my dogs." Jean-Michel's voice cracked with emotion. He looked out to the sea, seemingly lost in his own thoughts for a moment. "Those . . . bastards. They even blew up part of the coral reef with dynamite. They destroy nature . . . all so they can build up the beach in front of their ugly hotel!"

Jean-Michel sat back and sighed. "Remo, he is not a fighter. It was too much for him, this war. So he left. Abandoned me and broke the hearts of the girls of Boca Chica."

I laughed at this. Remo had never struck me as a ladies' man.

"What's so funny?" Tony asked. "Remo's a good-looking kid. Why wouldn't he have girls?"

I shrugged. "I don't know. I guess . . . I've never seen him show any interest in women before." I blushed when both Tony and Jean-Michel roared with laughter.

I'd made my assumption based on the fact that Remo had never looked at *me* like a woman. Their laughter indicated that my impression of Remo was far removed from reality.

Tony smirked. "The thing you don't know about Remo is that he likes his meat dark."

"Ah, *oui* . . . " Jean-Michel said, before lapsing into a pitch-perfect imitation of Remo's East Coast accent. "'The darker the berry, the sweeter the juice.'"

17

ONCE JEAN-MICHEL HAD FILLED us in on Remo's culinary talents, Tony set out to convince him to come work for Information Unlimited. Remo resisted at first. He was unwilling to give up his role as manager of Atlántico to be our in-house chef. But Tony was as charming, persistent, and persuasive as ever, and soon a compromise was reached. Remo was hired to provide food for the thirty-plus clerks during the hours of one to five, giving him plenty of time to make it to the club by seven. He was given carte blanche to renovate the kitchen, and told he could charge American prices for American meals. In the end, the lure of being back in the kitchen proved too much for him.

Because of Remo, staff morale went through the roof. The clerks loved being able to eat home-cooked meals. Five days a week Remo rustled up everything from grilled-cheese sandwiches to chicken Cordon Bleu.

A few weeks after the café had opened, we were out on the balcony enjoying lunch. Tony was polishing off a medium-rare Café de Paris steak.

"This is amazing, Remo."

"Thanks."

Tony took a long slug of his beer. "So what's up?" he asked Remo. "You look like you've got something on your mind."

"It's the general strike," Remo replied darkly. "I'm worried."

The country was teetering on the verge of a three-day general strike, to protest the government's inability to provide its citizens with even the most basic of services. The discontent had been simmering for a long time, and the walkout was expected to paralyze the country.

"I've seen this kind of thing happen here before," Remo added. "It's going to turn violent, no doubt about it. It's going to get dangerous."

"We stay open," Tony said coolly, preempting what he knew was coming next. "I have an obligation to my customers."

"For God's sake, Tony, everything will be closing. Restaurants, companies, shops—the lot. Any business that disrespects the strike by staying open will be a target. There are going to be riots. The only safe place to be during a strike like this is at home."

I knew that Remo was right, and hated how dismissive Tony was being. "You should listen to Remo," I told him. "I think for safety's sake we should—"

"The office is in a residential area." Tony addressed Remo directly, as if I weren't there. "We'll be fine."

"Tony, it doesn't matter where the business is," Remo replied. "You'll still have to get here. It'll be too dangerous—even for you."

"Hey, Domingo!" Tony yelled. Our company driver was napping under the shade of an umbrella. He shook himself awake and tottered over to us.

"You drive . . . when they strike?"

Domingo grinned cheerfully. "Drive strike, no problem!" He ambled back to his seat.

I scowled. "What do you expect him to say? You've already promised him an extra five hundred pesos a day to work through the strike. Of course he's going to say yes."

"We stay open. I don't give a shit about the strike. My job is to keep this business going. Remo, that means I need you here as well. My clerks need to eat. Get that kitchen stocked up, and let me worry about getting you here. And babe?"

"Hmm?"

"I don't tell you how to run the house. Don't tell me how to do my job."

I felt my cheeks redden. I stood up and stiffly thanked Remo for the food. Flinging open the terrace door, I stomped back to my cubicle. Ever since Tony had returned from prison, our relationship had been getting worse. I'd hoped that coming back to work might have brought us closer together, since I hardly saw him otherwise; but no such luck. He was still distant and dismissive of me; and on top of everything else, I realized just how much he was drinking throughout the day. The industrial-sized cooler out on the terrace was stocked with ice-cold Presidente beers. More often than not, he had one in his hand. He was never intoxicated at work. His decisions were sound. But by the time he came home, he was often drunk. I'd tried to talk to him about his drinking, without success. He always reacted defensively.

"Do you have any idea how much pressure I'm under? I have a couple of beers to take the edge off, and I have to deal with you freaking out—every single time."

"Remo works two jobs. He doesn't drink."

Tony scowled. "You think Remo's a saint. You should be grateful that I don't have the same addiction he does. If I did, our marriage would be over."

"What addiction?" The face that Remo presented certainly didn't suggest any secret vices. But Tony didn't bother to answer me.

After our confrontation on the terrace, I leaned over to Danny, who was in the cubicle next to mine. "Hey, Danny," I whispered. "If Remo had an addiction, what would it be?"

Danny raised his eyebrow and smiled. "Well . . . whorehouses, obviously." Noting my shocked expression, Danny went on with a kind of special delight. "And believe me, the kid is hooked. He loves black tail, and he ain't ashamed to pay for it."

"Really?" I recalled Jean-Michel's comments about the local girls. Clearly, I didn't know Remo as well as I'd thought.

■

TWO DAYS LATER, I set out to load up for the strike. The local supermarket looked as though it had been ransacked. Panic filled the air as customers waited on hour-long lines to pay for their stockpiled groceries. I drove to two other stores, but failed to find either bread or drinking water. Giving up, I headed to a local gas station to fill a five-gallon container for the generator. The line stretched off a mile down the road. Frustrated, I returned home empty-handed. On the way I noticed that shops had already started to close up. Shutters were down, and doors were padlocked. My unease over Tony's cavalier attitude toward the strike increased.

Domingo was supposed to pick up the clerks early in the morning during the strike. He hoped that by transporting people during the quietest part of the day, they could avoid trouble. On the first day, Tony tucked his gun into his belt and kissed me goodbye just as the sun was coming up. I sensed that he was getting a kick out of all of this subterfuge. He hadn't been in the country long, and he didn't understand how serious this situation was. I watched him from the balcony as he pulled back the heavy metal gate, slipped out, and closed it after him. An eerie silence lingered in the complex. Pino, the security guard, had—like Rosa—gone home the evening before the strike. They would not return until it was over. It was desolate. There were no cars, and not a soul in sight. Most of our neighbors had abandoned their apartments for the safety of the country, where they would remain for the strike's duration.

I had anticipated three long, quiet days alone in the apartment with Justine. Yet less than two hours after Tony left, I heard a vehicle rapidly approaching, furiously honking its horn. I ran to the balcony. The red company van screeched to a halt outside of the gate. Danny's panic-stricken face popped out of a side window, yelling for me to let them in.

By the time I'd raced downstairs, he and Domingo were lifting Remo's limp body out of the van. The first thing I noticed was his face covered in blood. The crude bandage wrapped around his head was bright crimson. My first reaction was a mix of terror and anger. This was Tony's fault!

I wrenched open the gate. "Is he conscious?"

"Just about," said Danny. Remo moaned as we struggled to get him up the stairs to the apartment.

"Lay him on the kitchen counter," I gasped. Once Remo was in place, I gently peeled back the bloody bandage. He had a deep, ugly gash above his ear.

"Oh, Jesus," Danny said when he saw it. "That's nasty. Dr. Badillo's on his way over."

I dropped the bloody dressing to the marble floor, where it landed with a splat. "Get me a towel!" I started applying pressure to the wound in an attempt to stanch the bleeding. I tried to reassure Remo, telling him that head wounds always looked worse than they were. "What happened?"

"The roads were deserted until we got onto Maximo Gomez," Danny said. "By the time we saw the smoke, it was too late. The whole street was on fire, and people started pelting us with rocks. Domingo started driving down the sidewalk trying to get away, but the rocks kept hitting us. They busted two windows, then Remo took a hit on the side of his head."

I turned my attention back to Remo. He was groaning in pain, which I took to be a good sign. At least he was conscious. We moved him to the couch, where he would be more comfortable. "Stay awake, Remo, don't fall asleep," I urged.

Ten minutes later, Dr. Badillo arrived. He was the company physician, an overweight man with a thinning thatch of gray hair. He was out of breath by the time he reached the apartment. He gave the ugly wound on Remo's head a cursory glance, and announced that Remo would need stitches. As he opened up his big black bag, the others started filing out of the apartment.

"Where are you going?"

"Work," Danny shrugged. "Tony told us to drop Remo off and get back to the office when Badillo showed up."

I cursed Tony silently as I clipped away some of the hair around Remo's wound. Badillo prepared a syringe full of local anesthetic. Why would Tony risk getting anyone else hurt? The doctor slid the needle into Remo's head, causing him to cry out in pain. Badillo began the grisly process of stitching the thick, ragged edges of Remo's scalp back together.

When Badillo was finished, he gave Remo a tetanus shot in the arm, a shot of antibiotics in the buttocks and another shot for pain. By the time he was done I felt awful for Remo, who looked miserable. The doctor checked Remo's pupils and seemed pleased with his condition. "The medication will make him sleepy," Badillo said in his thick accent. "He must rest."

■

BY AFTERNOON, GUNFIRE WAS erupting all around us. The street at the end of our block was ablaze with burning tires, belching thick black smoke into the air. Protestors darted between the piles of burning rubber, attempting to hurl rocks at soldiers. The soldiers responded by firing into the crowd indiscriminately. The country was descending into a state of feral anarchy.

By the time I put Justine to bed, the apartment was shrouded in shadows, and the noise on the street had lessened except for sporadic bursts of gunfire. Some fires were still burning, but the soldiers had beaten back the protestors. They patrolled the streets, sitting atop heavily armored military vehicles, shooting at anything that moved. An uneasy calm had taken hold.

Around ten, Remo stumbled out of the bedroom, looking unsteady. "What are you doing up?" I scolded.

"What's going on?"

"It's the first night of the strike. Things are quieting down."

"Where's Tony?"

"He checked everyone into the Plaza Naco. They'll sleep there until the strike is over."

Remo nodded, then winced. "It hurts," he groaned.

"I've got codeine."

I led him into my room, where I had stockpiled the drugs Dr. Badillo had left. The codeine was in an ampule and had to be administered via syringe. Remo watched in mounting horror as I drew up the liquid and flicked the needle to dislodge any air bubbles.

"Um, Marisa? What the hell is that?"

"Oh, come on," I grinned. "Don't be coy. Drop your pants. Doctor's orders!" Remo refused at first, but I eventually got him to unbutton his jeans, and shyly pull down enough of his underwear that a portion of his left buttock was exposed.

I swabbed the area with alcohol. Counted down. Then plunged the needle into his backside. He hissed as I unloaded the codeine into him. I had just given my first injection. I was wiping the site with alcohol when we heard the front door open. Tony's silhouette appeared in the hallway, gun in hand. I had to laugh as Remo struggled to cover himself up. He'd have to explain to a gun-toting Tony why he was with his wife, in their bedroom, with his pants down.

Just then we were startled by a deafening blast of gunfire that sounded as if it was coming from inside the apartment itself. With a crash, the skylight in the hall gave way, and Tony dove into the room to avoid shards of falling glass. We all stood there, frozen, as the glass rained down.

"You okay, buddy?" Tony asked, hurrying to Remo's side.

"I'll take a look upstairs," I said, darting out of the room.

"Get back here!"

At one time I would have obeyed Tony without question. Not anymore. My faith in his authority had been severely shaken of late.

I ran upstairs to Rosa's room. In the pitch black I crept over to the window and peered through the slats. A moment later, Tony was squatting down next to me.

"Holy shit," he breathed. On the roof of the building next to ours, soldiers were rounding up a group of men who'd been pelting them with rocks. We were close enough that I could see the terrified expression on the faces of the detainees.

"Let's get out of here," Tony said. "I don't want to risk anyone seeing us."

At sunrise, Tony left again. I tried to stop him, but he insisted that the back streets were perfectly safe. Remo stumbled out of bed, groggy and sore. "How on earth did you manage to get a doctor to make a house call with all of this going on?" he asked.

I shrugged. "Money. What else? Tony hired a company physician after he saw the way they treat spider bites here." Remo looked confused, so I showed him the ugly scar on my leg.

"It's funny, though . . . " I said, staring up at the ruined skylight. "Despite everything, the truth is I still love it here. I couldn't imagine living anywhere else."

Remo seemed lost in thought. "I miss the snow," he said quietly. "I think about it every day."

"When was the last time you were home?"

"Home?" Remo looked amused at the idea. "I don't have anything to go home to."

Remo told me that he'd grown up in the projects in New Jersey. His mother was an alcoholic. He had no idea who his father was. For the first time I was getting a glimpse into why Remo's eyes always seemed so full of melancholy.

"How did you end up here?" I asked.

"I always had a lot of uncles growing up. Not real uncles, just guys who were involved with my mom from time to time. One of them ended up moving to Cabarete, a place on the north shore of the island. He opened a little bar. I came to visit . . . and ended up staying."

And then you went to work for Jean-Michel?"

Remo looked as though he wanted to say something else, but then thought better of it. "Yeah. Jean-Michael taught me how to cook. He was a real mentor to me in the beginning."

"So how did Atlántico happen? That's a pretty big jump, isn't it? From a small place like Jean-Michel's to the most elite club on the island?"

Remo smiled, and then winced with pain. "You should have seen it when I took over," he said. "It was anything but elite."

Remo began reeling off the long list of improvements he'd made to the place.

"Well, I know Tony loves it there," As I said this, I saw something flicker in Remo's eyes.

"Remo—he *is* there most nights, isn't he?"

"Not so much," he admitted, "not anymore. It's the whole dress code, you know?"

"So where does he go with the clerks?"

Remo squirmed when he realized I wasn't going to let it lie. "Well . . . the Jaragua. Or the French place."

"The French place? You mean the Petit Chateau?"

I had often heard the clerks talking about the great food they served at the Petit Chateau, but when I suggested going, Tony was quick to change the subject. Now Remo was telling me that Tony was a regular there. Awful possibilities started whirling in my head. Is this why he'd been so distant? Was he involved with a waitress?

Suddenly the conversation I'd had with Danny about Remo's addiction popped into my head. "Remo," I said, trying to keep my voice under control. "The Petit Chateau is a whorehouse, isn't it?"

The expression on Remo's face told me all I needed to know. I jumped up as he went into full damage-control mode.

"No, listen! I don't want you to get the wrong impression, okay? It really is a restaurant. They serve excellent food. It's more like . . . a dinner theater."

"Dinner theater!" I said sarcastically.

"It is! The girls perform on stage. You can watch them . . . while you eat."

"And fuck them for dessert?" I spat.

"It's not like that, Marisa. I swear to you—on my life—that Tony has never, ever, taken a girl to one of the rooms. The others do, but not Tony. It's just stupid, harmless fun—I swear it. On my life, Tony has never cheated on you. I'd never let him do that."

So everybody knew that my husband was a regular at the local whorehouse—except me. I was livid. Not only had I been betrayed by Tony, but by everyone at the office. People I considered friends, colleagues. Even Remo.

"You know something?" I said. "I wake up at seven o'clock, every goddamned morning, with Justine. I work afternoons, come home, have dinner with my daughter, bathe her, read her stories, put her to bed, and then wait—wait for my husband to come home. But he doesn't. He's too busy watching naked girls dancing on stage in a whorehouse. How do you think that makes me feel?"

Remo dropped his voice to a hoarse whisper. "He's never cheated on you," he repeated.

I thought about how Tony would always paw at me for sex when he stumbled in at all hours of the night. Maybe Remo was telling the truth. It didn't make me feel any better.

"Just try and understand it from Tony's point of view for a second," he continued. "Tony's busting his ass for you and for his family back home. He's miserable here. The only reason he's staying is because he wants to make enough money for you to start over again in the States. He's trying to give you the kind of life you deserve."

"Oh, give me break! Why is he so unhappy here?"

Remo sighed. "Where do you want me to start? The heat. The humidity—"

"It's hot in California. He didn't have to visit whorehouses to cool off when we lived there."

"But he had air conditioning. He had his family. He could go to the movies, or a club. He misses home, Marisa. He misses hunting,

fishing, everyday stuff. He hates the food here. He doesn't understand the language."

"He hasn't even bothered to try! I'm learning, why can't he?"

"Tony misses watching his favorite TV shows. He misses electricity, for crissakes! What do you want me to say? He hates it here.
This shouldn't be a surprise to you. He's trying to make the best
of it, but he can't wait to go home again."

Despite my anger, Remo was right. He wasn't telling me anything I didn't know already. Tony was always complaining about
life in the Dominican Republic.

"Look, I know things are strained between you two at the
moment. But Tony loves you. He knows how uptight you are about
alcohol, and he hates that he can't unwind with a beer around you
without starting a fight. That's why he goes out. He just wants to
have a laugh. Relax. Be with the guys. I promise you, it's just harmless fun."

"There's nothing harmless about it, Remo. And it's not just me.
The other clerks have girlfriends too. It's not fair to them, either!"

Remo rolled his eyes. "God, Marisa, you're really sweet and all
. . . but look, have you ever stopped to think about why the clerks
have girlfriends? I mean, they're not exactly *GQ* material, are
they? But they all have these pretty young girls on their arms. It's
because they're American. Dominican girls see them as a ticket
off this island. Those girls are prostituting themselves just as much
as the girls onstage at Petit Chateau are."

We fell into a pensive silence while I tried to digest this. At last
Remo muttered bitterly, "At least with a whore you know where
you stand."

"Is that why you go? To whorehouses, I mean?"

Remo shifted around uncomfortably. "Well, when I first came
here, a lot of light-skinned girls hit on me, you know? They lost
interest as soon as they found out I didn't have any money. The
light-skinned girls here—they have a certain arrogance about
them. They know they're valued way more than darker-skinned
girls, and because of that, they have this attitude that they're

entitled to a better life. Darker-skinned girls, they have fewer expectations, you know? And whores—they have none at all. Even if I don't have anything to offer them, they're still nice to me."

I felt a profound sadness for Remo, and he must have seen the pity in my eyes. "It's okay," he said, forcing a smile. "No one's broken my heart yet. But it would really upset me if this were to come between you and Tony. I'm with him most of the time, and I promise you I would never stand by and let him do something I thought was wrong. I care about him too much. I care about the both of you. I haven't had a family in such a long time."

When he was done, he had tears in his eyes. I was touched. I'd had no idea he felt this way. I gave his arm a reassuring squeeze.

"Well, just promise me something, Remo. Send him home once in a while. Because I miss him. He might not be cheating on me, but I never see him anymore, and that's not the way a marriage works."

18

THE GENERAL STRIKE ENDED, Remo's wound healed, and life returned to some semblance of normalcy, at least for a while. This delicate peace was broken one afternoon while I was at Information Unlimited. The terrace door opened and a small, squat young Dominican man strolled inside. I leapt from my chair, shocked that someone would have the audacity to walk into our villa uninvited.

"Excuse me? This is a private establishment."

I was unnerved, but mostly angry. I didn't like this guy's manner one bit. He acted like he owned the place. And how on earth had he made it past the guard?

"I'm looking for Tony Santino," the man said. He smiled coolly at me, revealing a row of small, flat teeth with a prominent gap in the middle. He was short and ugly. There was something reptilian about him, toad-like.

"Please wait outside. I'll see if he's available." I stared the little man down.

He didn't budge. "I'll wait here," he replied, puffing out his chest. "Tell him it's Horacio Vargas."

Throughout the encounter I was intently aware of the phones ringing off the hooks as bets continued to stream in. I didn't have time to deal with this. Horacio's eyes were darting around the room, taking everything in, which only added to my unease. My gut told me that whoever this Horacio Vargas was, he was bad news.

"I'll see if Mr. Santino is available," I hissed. Vargas smiled at me, his eyes narrowed to slits.

■

"WHO IS HE?" I demanded as I followed Tony down the hallway. I couldn't recall ever disliking anyone so much on first sight. The man made my skin crawl.

Tony answered me in his typically offhand way. "Just some guy. I bought our appliances from him."

Horacio greeted Tony like he was an old friend. I watched for a moment before I had to turn and get back to my desk. As I continued to take bets, I glanced over my shoulder every so often to see the two men laughing and chatting under the shade of the awning. What could they be talking about for so long?

I noticed Remo beckoning me from the kitchen. I nodded to him. As soon as the calls tapered off, I headed over. Remo gestured to the window, where he had a clear view of Tony and Horacio sitting at the table, now slamming back beers. "What the hell's he doing here?" he asked.

"No idea. I don't even know who he is."

"Horacio Vargas. His family owns the store where we bought all my kitchen equipment. He's a leech. I specifically told Tony not to pay up-front for everything. Horacio knows my credit is good. But you know how Tony is . . . "

I did indeed. I could imagine Tony pulling out a thick wad of thousand-peso bills. Nobody threw money around like Tony, especially here, where the local currency had no more intrinsic value to him than Monopoly money. So that was it. Tony had flashed his money around Horacio and here he was, sucking up for more.

Horacio rose to his feet, and he and Tony shook hands. I hurried back to my desk, making it to my seat just as Tony came in. I followed him to his office and closed the door behind us.

"What did he want?"

Tony shrugged, nonchalant. "He just wanted to make sure that everything was running okay."

"And that's it?"

"Yeah. Oh, and he invited us to his house for a traditional Dominican Sunday dinner."

My face fell. "And?"

"And I said yes."

■

BY THE TIME SUNDAY rolled around, I had reconciled myself to the idea. I was hoping that my initial impression of Horacio had been wrong. After all, this was the first time we'd been invited to eat at the home of a Dominican family, and I was curious.

Almost as soon as Horacio opened the door to his modest home, I knew my original instincts had been correct. The tiny house was packed with the Vargas clan, and every single member of the family had been instructed to fawn over Tony. They treated my husband like a long-lost son, a visiting dignitary, a prince. While Justine and I were largely ignored, Tony was seated at the head of the table, served first, and given the biggest portions; and his every utterance—no matter how banal or inconsequential— was treated as it were witty and profound.

Horacio was the only one in the family who spoke English, which added another layer of ridiculousness to the whole spectacle.

Tony's jokes and comments would be translated by Horacio, and then the family would erupt into gales of forced laughter. Every time Tony finished a beer, another ice-cold one appeared in his hand. Soon he was well on the way to being smashed, while I was bored, irritable, and trying to soothe Justine, who was tired and squirming in my lap.

The hours dragged on further and further past Justine's bedtime. But Tony was in no hurry to leave—not as long as the beers kept appearing and his jokes were getting such a warm reception. I toyed with the idea of calling a taxi, but I was afraid to leave Tony alone. He might well attempt to drive home, intoxicated as he was. I was trying to get his attention when Horacio turned his gaze to me. Justine was busy trying to grab one of my hoop earrings.

"She's very tired," I said coolly. "It's past her bedtime."

Horacio nodded. "Why don't you take your daughter and go sit on the couch?"

"Yeah, babe," Tony slurred. "Put her on the couch. She'll probably fall asleep."

I clenched my jaw and flopped down on the sofa to watch the performance from there. Tony was oblivious, lapping up the attention. It didn't occur to him that this was all being orchestrated. Tony was usually very perceptive about people, but he was falling for this charade.

Tony began boasting about Information Unlimited. I cringed as he went into details about the company. We had all been given specific instructions about what we could and could not say about the firm, but Tony—his tongue well lubricated by the beer—blathered on and on.

As his mother returned from the kitchen with more beers, Horacio began offering Tony business advice. He tried to hook Tony up with a local printer and a new lawyer, and when Horacio's mother asked—in Spanish—if we had someone trustworthy to clean the house, I blurted out "Si!" before Horacio could translate. I could see how determined this man was to worm his way into our lives. In the end, this painful dinner drove home to me just how far apart Tony and I had drifted over the last few months.

Commerciales Vargas, like all Dominican businesses, closed during siesta, giving Horacio the perfect excuse to show up regularly at Information Unlimited for beers with his new best friend. We were invited to dinner again, and I struggled through yet another endless evening of dealing with the Vargas clan, this time vowing it would be my last. The next time we were invited I claimed I wasn't feeling well. To my dismay, Tony went without me.

A few weeks later, Tony casually asked me for the registration papers to my car. "What for?"

"I'm going to register it in Horacio's name."

Alarm bells started ringing immediately. "Why would you do that?"

Tony scowled at me. "You're the one who told me not to trust Gustavo. So I'm taking all the vehicles out of his name and putting them under Horacio's. You got a problem with that too?"

I knew that until our residency permits came through, we couldn't have the vehicles registered in our names. But while I didn't trust Gustavo, he was definitely the lesser of two evils.

■

A FEW NIGHTS LATER, I awoke from a deep sleep with Tony pawing at me for sex. He had been out earlier with Horacio. The two of them were supposedly to meet Jose Rijo, a star pitcher for the Cincinnati Reds.

"Stop it," I snapped at Tony, but he ignored me, ripping at my nightgown in a frenzied stupor. I managed to clamber out of bed, but he came after me, blocking my escape.

"Get away from me," I spat. "It's four in the morning and you're drunk . . . *again.*"

He fixed me in a bleary-eyed gaze. Then a look of such intense malice came over him that I flinched.

"Fuck you!" he bellowed. He punched the solid concrete wall, inches from my head.

By the time he woke up, Justine and I were gone.

Remo tracked us down the next day. I saw him making his way through the lush grounds of the Hotel El Embajador toward us. "I thought Tony hit you," he said, "but that bikini isn't big enough to hide a bruise."

"He hit the wall. I think he might have broken his hand."

Remo grabbed a nearby deck chair and sat down next to me. "So what happened?"

"Same dumb-ass shit as always," I said, trying to hold back my tears. Justine, who had been kicking a ball around, came running over when she noticed Remo, and jumped into his lap. I smiled sadly as Remo tickled her.

"Justine doesn't even go to her own father like that," I said. "He's a stranger to her."

"Tony works hard." Remo always had the same old excuses for Tony.

"So what?" I snapped. "You work hard. I work hard. We don't have to get shitfaced every night. I've had it. He's gone too far. I was afraid he was going to hit me."

Remo's expression was grim. "What are you going to do?"

"I don't know. I really don't know."

I knew Tony had sent Remo to broker a peace deal. I wondered how the morning had played out in the apartment. Did Tony even remember what he'd done? Did he wake up sick and hung over, notice his bloody knuckles and missing family and realize that he scared us away? I imagined him showing up at the office, frantic, barging into the kitchen, no doubt shoving a handful of hundred-peso bills into Remo's hand and ordering him to find us.

"Marisa . . . Tony feels terrible. I've never seen him so upset. He's practically suicidal."

I rolled my eyes. "Hung over, you mean."

Remo was about to continue pleading Tony's case when I removed my sunglasses and looked him straight in the eye. "I need a few days to myself, Remo. I would really appreciate you not telling him where I am."

Remo told me that Tony had Captain Garcia check with immigration, so he knew I had not left the island. This information startled me. After the way Tony had been treating me the past few months, I was shocked he'd gone to that trouble.

"Tony loves you," Remo said. "He knows he fucked up. Believe me, he's suffering."

■

FOUR DAYS LATER, I stood outside the apartment rehearsing the scathing lecture I planned to give my errant husband. He might have grown up watching Sophia take his father back again and again, but there was no way I was going to emulate that unhealthy dynamic. Tony had a sixteen-month-old daughter, and he needed to start behaving like a husband and father.

As soon as I turned the key in the door, Tony came flying out of the bedroom. He looked clean-shaven, alert, and awake. We regarded each other warily.

"Didn't expect to see you out of bed so early," I drawled.

"I quit drinking," he blurted out before I could say another word. "I haven't had a drink since you left."

I didn't see any of the bloated, bleary-eyed messiness that I had come to expect from him in the early hours. This announcement did change the picture. Alcohol was at the root of all the problems Tony and I were going through.

"Marisa . . . I am so, so sorry."

His voice quavered and his brown eyes were filled with sadness. For the first time in as long as I could remember I saw the old Tony standing before me. I had no doubt his regret was genuine. I hugged him. I wanted so desperately to believe him. I wanted us to be a real family again.

19

THE RAINY SEASON ARRIVED. The clear blue skies clouded over, turned an ominous gray. The atmosphere at the office turned equally grim. Tony kept his word. He no longer drank to make it through the workday. At night he came straight home to be with Justine and me. Yet this newfound sobriety came at a price. He was short-tempered and irritable. I felt that he resented me. I had been cast in the role of the castrating mother figure. When he growled, I bit my tongue. I told myself that his post-drinking sourness was temporary. Soon he would be back to his old self.

As Christmas approached, the clerks became restless. Nobody wanted to spend the holidays so far away from home. Some quit, others demanded time off. The bowl season was approaching, and we desperately needed more manpower. One day Tony flashed a rare smile and announced that he'd just hired an experienced clerk. His name was Paulie and he would be bringing his girlfriend along. I was excited at the prospect of having another woman around. I hoped that maybe we would become friends.

When Paulie and Leslie showed up at the office, I had to stop myself from laughing out loud. Paulie's look was pure *Miami Vice*. His dark hair was slicked back tight against his skull. He was wearing a shiny white suit with a colorful silk shirt unbuttoned halfway down to his navel. Leslie's thick brown hair was heavily teased and sprayed. She wore a bright-pink halter-top dress with a wide black patent-leather belt cinching her tiny waist. She was tottering on top of a pair of sky-high pumps. On first glance she looked to be in her mid-twenties, but she had so much makeup smeared on her face it was hard to tell. Danny leaned in to me and whispered, "Three weeks."

"Ten days," I whispered back. I figured as soon as this girl couldn't use her curling iron because of a power outage, she'd be on the first flight home.

On the upside, Paulie was a seasoned professional. As soon as Leslie headed back to their apartment, he went straight to work taking bets. As his appearance suggested, he was loud, brash, and cocky. At first he kept the office entertained with jokes and stories. He was clearly used to being the center of attention. But it wasn't long before his attitude started to change. By day three he was complaining about the weather, the food, the locals, and the conditions. I felt bad for his girlfriend. Leslie had no doubt been promised that she would be living in an island paradise, spending her days lounging around on the beach. Instead she was trapped in an apartment, due to the rainy season. I decided to call her and offer to show her around Santo Domingo.

Leslie met me at my apartment a couple of days later. She looked completely different than when I'd first met her. She was dressed casually, with her hair tied back in a ponytail and her makeup toned down. Instead of the garish eyeshadow, I noticed her beautiful green eyes. I suggested visiting the colonial zone, but she had already been. She had also visited every other touristy site I recommended.

"You know what I'd love to do?" Leslie said. "Go shopping. I need some things for the apartment. Is there, like, a mall here?"

I had completely misjudged her. I was impressed that she had already ventured out so much on her own. Most of the other clerks had zero interest in exploring the island. For Leslie, everything in Santo Domingo was new and exciting. I knew then that we were going to be great friends.

As Leslie piled bedsheets, pillows, and towels into a shopping cart, she asked me how long it had taken me to learn Spanish. I invited her along to my next lesson. Judging from the items she was purchasing, Leslie intended to stay for a while.

It was exciting to see the city through her fresh eyes. There was something innocent and open about her—she was not jaded in the slightest, and lots of fun to be around. Over the next two weeks we spent more and more time together. Soon she was holding Justine on her hip as naturally as if Justine were her own child. Leslie practiced Spanish with every local she encountered. No matter where we went or what we did, she always made it fun. Suddenly Justine had a brand-new auntie, and I had my first girl-friend in years.

It was through Leslie that I landed an extra role in the Robert Redford movie *Havana,* which was being filmed on the island. She noticed the flyer calling for light-skinned extras while in Atlán-tico. In her typically breezy way she persuaded me to come along with her. Leslie was convinced we'd be "discovered," and sure enough, we were cast as a pair of high-class call girls. "We're going to be prostitutes in Havana!" I exclaimed, and we laughed until our sides ached. Life had not been this much fun in a long time.

The following day, Paulie didn't show up at the office. When I asked Carmine, he confirmed my fears. Paulie had quit. Danny had called it right—just over three weeks. As the day dragged on, I felt myself growing sadder and sadder. I had barely gotten to know Leslie, and now she was gone.

I was floored to see Leslie appear at the patio doors. She marched straight into Tony's office, winking at me as she waltzed past my cubicle. Twenty minutes later, she sat down next to me and told me that she had broken up with Paulie. He was preparing to fly home, while Leslie would start clerking at the office tomorrow.

As she left, Danny whistled to himself and said, "Didn't see that coming!"

"Me neither," I said. For the rest of the day I couldn't stop smiling.

■

TONY'S LAST PROBATION MEETING of 1989 was scheduled for December 7. This time, Justine and I were accompanying him back to Los Angeles. Ron had recently been released from Nevada State Penitentiary, and Tony was spending a few days with him before the three of us headed to Red Bluff for the holidays. We were taking our first vacation as a family. I hoped that two weeks away from the office would do us all good.

Before we left, Rosa helped me clear the fridge of anything that might spoil. When I saw how overjoyed Rosa was with the bags of food to take back home, I decided to go through the rest of our belongings, looking for clothes and shoes that we no longer wore. Tony helped us haul the bags downstairs and load them into the car. I had no clue where Rosa lived, only that it was forty minutes away and close to a river.

I followed her directions as we headed out of the city. Nothing but open land showed on either side of the road, and the farther we went, the bumpier the road became. The road ended at a concrete pier, where several moored fishing boats bobbed gently in the water. Rosa directed me down a tiny dirty road toward a neighborhood that was poorer than any I had ever seen. Pedestrians walking along this winding dirt lane did a double take when they saw the car. People stared openly at the new vehicle and my white face. Scores of barefoot children followed the Daihatsu as I navigated the potholes. After a short way, the road became utterly impassable. I parked and left the car where it was. We walked the rest of the way, helped along by a gaggle of children who shyly offered to help carry the bags I had given Rosa.

Once we reached Rosa's barrio, the neighbors started emerging from their homes. They goggled at the strange procession heading toward Rosa's tiny concrete house. We ducked under several rows of washing lines and past a pig tied to a mango tree. Rosa ran ahead, calling excitedly for her grandmother. An old lady appeared in the doorway, her face weather-beaten and ancient, her gray hair tied back in a neat bun.

I was profoundly sad to see the impoverished conditions in which Rosa and her family survived. The roof was corrugated tin and the floors were dirt. A small black-and-white television sat atop a rickety pine bookshelf. A wooden bench and table took up the rest of the space in the room. I spotted a power cord plugged into an extension cable strung along the entire length of the wall via an elaborate series of hooks. Rosa explained that although they lacked both running water and a phone, they occasionally had electricity—which, as in every other shack in the barrio, was hooked up illegally. Rosa's grandmother served sweet, thick coffee that she prepared on a propane hot plate while the rest of the village observed us through the slats in the window. Later, remembering Remo's words when defending Rosa against Tony's charges of theft, I learned that Rosa did indeed share a bed with her grandmother, and a toilet with half the village.

"You know," I said to Tony as we made our way to the airport that afternoon, "Rosa's family has nothing, but they still seem so happy."

Tony just stared out of the windshield at the wild, untamed country before him, and said nothing.

20

"WHAT'S UP, LOBSTER FACE?"

Ron was burnt to a crisp, having fallen asleep in the sun.

As Tony roared with laughter Ron grinned. "Kiss my ass, fatso."

Unlike the drastic change jail had wrought in Tony, the time Ron had spent in prison had not altered him one bit. The two men discussed business while Justine and I relaxed with Joanna. It felt good to be back in California with the two of them.

We left L.A. on Saturday and began the long drive north. I didn't mind the upcoming visit to Red Bluff—I knew our stay was only temporary. Sophia greeted us as we pulled up. We followed her into the kitchen, where she instantly pulled two cold Budweisers from the fridge and held one out to Tony. Tony looked at me, then declined. "No, thanks, Ma."

Sophia was affronted that her son was refusing a beer at eight in the evening. "Whaddaya mean, no thanks? Why can't you have a beer with your own mother?" She scowled in my direction, as if to say, *Back off.*

Tony turned to me and pleaded his case. "It *is* vacation . . . "

Without waiting for a reply Sophia pulled the tab back and pushed the beer across the counter to her son, muttering under her breath. Tony was waiting for my response. I was let down that he couldn't even stand up to his own mother and honor the commitment he had made to me.

"American beer has way less alcohol content than the stuff back in the D.R.," he said.

"Do what you want," I sighed. Sophia was triumphant.

Later, over dinner, Tony complained endlessly about life in the Dominican Republic. Angela and her husband had joined us, and every inquiry they made about our new home was met with a whining monologue about blackouts, awful food, unbearable temperatures, and the lack of home comforts. If I'd been given the chance I could have waxed lyrical about the colonial zone, with its quaint restaurants and bars, or the deep-blue waters of the Los Tres Ojos, or the Galeria de Arte Nader and all of the other wonderful art galleries dotted around Santo Domingo like hidden treasures. I could have told them about the country's rich history and culture, or the warm, friendly locals, whose resilience in the face of so much hardship I admired greatly. I could have— but nobody was interested in what I thought.

Tony spent time with his family in Red Bluff, watched TV, shopped at the Redding mall, went fishing, and gorged himself on American food. Our time there did nothing to bring the two of us closer together. It only reminded me of how different our outlook on the world was.

Back in Santo Domingo, the countdown to my acting debut in *Havana* was under way. I marked the day in my calendar, giddy with excitement about the upcoming experience. Tony didn't share my enthusiasm. The biggest betting event of the year—the Super Bowl—was scheduled to kick off on the evening of January 28. At six o'clock the following morning I had to be at the

Jaragua Hotel, where I would be bused to the set along with the other extras. I begged Tony for Sunday off, but he refused; it wouldn't be fair to the other clerks. We eventually compromised that I'd be able to leave as soon as the game kicked off. This arrangement wasn't perfect, but at least I'd be guaranteed an early night that way.

Only one line was read on Super Bowl Sunday: "San Francisco minus 12, over/under 15." As soon as we put the line out, the calls were fast and furious. The pace was relentless as we struggled to record thousands of bets on the biggest sporting event of the year. The second the game started, I flew out the door.

By the time I made it home, Jerry Rice had already caught a twenty-yard pass, scoring the first touchdown. While I was deep-conditioning my hair, the 49ers scored two more touchdowns. By the time I painted my nails bright red—as requested by the makeup artist—Jerry Rice had scored yet another touchdown, bringing the score to 42–3. The 49ers slaughtered the Broncos 55–10, in one of the most lopsided Super Bowl games in history. Not a great day to be a Broncos fan—but a very good day for Ron Sacco and Information Unlimited.

Sometime in the middle of the night I was awoken from a deep sleep by the insistent ringing of the phone. I stumbled out of bed and picked up the receiver. As soon as I heard Ron's voice on the other end I was wide-awake. "Put Tony on."

But the bed was empty. "He's not here. What's going on?"

"Ruth Gordon. She left two messages on Tony's phone at Bimini, and another over at Decorator's Choice. She's called an unscheduled meeting with Tony tomorrow morning. Joanna's booked him a flight through LAX. She'll pick him up and drive him to Crenshaw."

"Okay, okay. I'll call him right now."

I tried Tony's cell phone, but it was out of range. Bleary-eyed, I crawled back into bed. It was almost midnight. Surely he'd be home soon. He hadn't been out drinking for months. He wouldn't start now.

Twelve-thirty rolled by, then one. I got out of bed, cursing under my breath. I got dressed and headed over to the Jaragua, hoping to find Tony with the rest of the clerks finishing a post–Super Bowl celebration dinner. Yet the restaurant was closed, as were the bar and the casino. Where *was* he?

I was due back at this very same location in four-and-a-half hours. Thanks to Tony I would show up tired, puffy-eyed, and exhausted. I'd been looking forward to this day for months. Why wasn't he answering his phone?

Everything was closed. In desperation I headed to Remo's apartment. I woke him up and explained the situation.

"He's got an unscheduled probation meeting first thing tomorrow morning in L.A. If he doesn't make the 6:30 flight to Miami, they'll toss him back in jail for five years!"

Remo leapt into action. He pulled on his clothes, asking me where I had looked already. Moments later we were in the car and I was following his directions south. "So all those business trips to the States—?"

"Meetings with his probation officer," I confirmed.

"Jesus Christ," Remo said with admiration, "that takes balls."

First we tried a place called Lapsus, then other places that might be open on Sunday. Finding everything shut down, we drove by Horacio's house. There was no sign of Tony's or Horacio's cars, which confirmed my worst fear: they were together. All we could do was head home and wait.

As Remo and I headed upstairs, I heard a car approaching. We sprinted back downstairs. Tony emerged from his car without a care in the world. He caught sight of Remo and me. "What's going on?" he asked cheerfully.

"Jesus Christ, Tony! I tried calling you! You have to fly to California in two-and-a-half hours!"

I could smell booze on him, but he seemed remarkably alert. "Ruth Gordon needs to see you," I explained. "Where were you? We looked for you everywhere!"

"You didn't look at Cayacoa, did ya?" Tony grinned.

"Where's that?"

"A resort, right off the Duarte," Tony babbled. "They're building an eighteen-hole golf course there. I just bought two lots." Something about Tony's manner was odd.

"You were at a business meeting?"

"Uh-huh."

"At three in the morning?"

Tony kissed me exaggeratedly on the cheek. "Not exactly. The business meeting finished at one. Then we celebrated."

21

"Mr. Redford plays a gambler who's traveled to Cuba to take part in a high-stakes card game in the days leading up to the revolution."

The assistant director looked frazzled, and it wasn't even lunchtime yet. All around us the set was a blur of activity as cameras, lights, and sets were wheeled into place. Someone was screaming into the poor man's headpiece, but he ignored it and continued explaining the setup. "You," he gestured to me and two beautiful local girls standing next to me, "are high-class call girls present at the big game. You'll be standing by this couch, talking to Alan."

Alan Arkin, looking dapper in a dark suit and silk tie, raised his hand and pointed playfully at himself. One of the lovely Dominican girls looked puzzled. *"Que esta pasando?"*

The assistant director's face fell. "Please tell me she speaks English," he said.

I shook my head. It just wasn't his day.

"Tell them to look over there when they hear the machine-gun fire." He pointed at a black X marked on the wall. "Okay? You should look startled for a moment. But when the gunfire stops, you go back to chatting with Mr. Arkin."

I translated while the makeup artists touched us up. Someone snapped Polaroids for continuity purposes. Behind the camera was the director, Sydney Pollack. A few yards away Robert Redford was seated at a card table with a handful of other familiar-looking actors.

Soon we were ready for a take. When Mr. Pollack yelled "action," Alan smiled at me and said, "You can say anything now. We're off camera."

I smiled awkwardly. "I never imagined I'd be a prostitute one day," I said.

"Darling, we are all prostitutes."

Just then machine-gun fire erupted and we turned our heads toward the X—an imaginary window—as the camera zoomed in on us.

As the scene continued, I kept thinking about the events of the night before. Over the course of the morning, I became convinced that Tony had been high on cocaine. He had been blinking in an exaggerated way, a behavior I recalled seeing back in Los Angeles when he'd been a regular user. Plus, he'd been so alert and energized, despite reeking of booze.

"Cut!"

Much to their disappointment, the Dominican girls were sent home while I was asked to stay. Two hours later, I was leaning against a faux-marble pillar several feet from the card table where Robert Redford was playing. The shooting was in a lull while the lighting was adjusted for the next shot. As the technicians set everything up, the big-name actors left the set. Now the scene was peopled with stand-ins, dressed identically to their big-screen counterparts. A handsome, light-skinned Dominican in a dark suit stood facing me; the other stand-ins sat around the table, happily chatting, except for the younger, well-rested version of Robert Redford, who kept apart from the group. He leaned back in his chair with his arms folded, apparently too important to mingle with the others. I wondered if a hierarchy existed among the stand-ins. Maybe the A-list stand-ins wouldn't be caught dead hanging out with the plain old extras.

As the technicians continued to tweak the lights, I was careful not to move from my marked position. I was exhausted after my long, frantic night searching for Tony. I wondered if he had made his all-important meeting with Ruth Gordon. The U.S. authorities were clamping down anew on bookmaking. A few days earlier we had learned that members of the Computer Group had been arrested. This caused shockwaves in the bookmaking community. It was almost unheard-of for gamblers to be prosecuted. Law enforcement usually focused on bookmakers. I wondered if someone from the Computer Group had ratted Tony out. If that was the case, Tony might not be coming home for a long while. I stifled a yawn. Our marriage had deteriorated to the point that the prospect of him not coming back barely fazed me.

The set once again came alive. The real actors filed in to replace their stand-ins. I straightened up, ready for a take. As Robert Redford sat down at the table near me, I caught a close-up glimpse of him. He didn't look like a glowing, charismatic star. He seemed a little sad and world-weary.

A tall, lean man who had been playing cards with Redford in the previous scene approached me. "Richard Portnow," he said, reaching out to shake my hand.

"Marisa."

I knew I had seen this handsome, balding man before. The answer came to me in a bolt of inspiration. "You were in *Tin Men.*"

He responded self-effacingly. "Yes. And *Twins, Kindergarten Cop* . . . " He shrugged and gave me a cheeky smile. I felt immediately at ease.

As Sydney Pollack went over the scene with the actors at the card table, Richard leaned in and quietly explained our roles. "In this scene I'm out of the poker game, though I do still have some lines with Robert. You and I should talk . . . I might run my hand up your arm, or whisper something in your ear. The camera won't pick up what we're saying, but it should be clear to the audience that you'll be accompanying me to my room later."

Sydney Pollack yelled "action," and the scene was under way. As the others delivered their lines during the card game, Richard and I flirted for all we were worth. "Remember," he said dryly as he ran his hand gently up my arm, "this is just acting." Right on cue, he turned and delivered his line to Robert Redford before turning his attention back to me.

We repeated the scene several times. He whispered in my ear continuously, touching my waist and moving me closer to him. "Your eyes are an amazing color blue," he said. I wondered if this was the middle-aged actor with the receding hairline talking, or Mike MacClaney, the gambler he was portraying. After several hours and countless takes, I didn't care. I was having a blast flirting with Richard. He was suave and fun. He made me feel desirable, a sensation I hadn't felt in a long time.

We would share two more days of pillar antics. If Sydney Pollack noticed that Richard and I were pushing the boundaries, he didn't mind. As the takes went on, he planted soft kisses along the nape of my neck. His hands traveled around my waist and down to my hips. He encouraged me to trail my fingers over his abdomen. They were rock-hard, a product of his daily boxing workouts.

In addition to being an outrageous flirt, he was witty and smart. The time flew by. We discussed anything and everything. His mischievous brown eyes melted when he talked about his beloved pet dogs. When the assistant director announced that it was a wrap, my heart sank. The actors got up from the table and technicians came to cart equipment away. I stood there, next to Richard, unwilling to believe it was over.

Ignoring the commotion all around us, Richard looked deeply into my eyes. He gently peeled the long white glove from my right arm. He then pressed a carefully folded piece of paper into my hand.

"I leave tomorrow," he said. "But I would love to see you tonight."

At home, I showered and scrubbed the makeup off my face. While I was in my robe the phone rang. Tony reported that everything had gone well in California, and he would be back the following afternoon. I flopped back on the bed and unfolded the piece of paper with Richard's room number at the Jaragua written on it. No one would ever know if I joined him there tonight. I was surprised at how easy the idea of breaking my wedding vows seemed. Even more shocking was how much I wanted to. I gazed at the phone, recalling Richard's hard, flat stomach, his muscular arms. The temptation to call was powerful.

I hadn't felt that kind of intoxicating desire for Tony in a long time. We were still having sex regularly, but the passion, the tenderness that had once been all-pervading, had gone. Our passion had never really been the same since he got out of prison. But despite our problems I still believed that Tony was faithful.

I tore up the number and tossed it in the trash. I lay back on the bed, confused and upset. I had come so close to doing something I was sure I would have regretted for the rest of my life.

While *Havana* had been an extraordinary experience, I had fully expected the film experience to be a one-off. However, in late February one of the movie's makeup artists called, asking if I'd be interested in doing a local commercial. I agreed, and a week later I was heading up into the mountainous La Vega province southwest of Santo Domingo, on my way to Constanza. This was a picturesque town where apples, strawberries, and raspberries grew against a lush backdrop of rivers, waterfalls, and jungle. The commercial was for Constanza menthol cigarettes, and although I was not a smoker, I was warned I'd be expected to smoke on camera.

I arrived with a crew of makeup artists, hairdressers, cameramen, and technicians, as well as my co-star, a Spanish male model named Pedro. Filming the commercial was chaotic. Tropical downpours constantly interrupted the shoot, and the cast and crew would have to take shelter from the rain, where they would listen to merengue music on an old transistor radio and spiritedly argue about politics. Whenever the sun poked through, we'd all run down to the water's edge, where Pedro and I would have our makeup touched up before climbing into the white boat where the action took place. The setup was simple—Pedro rowed while I reclined on a nest of plush green pillows, smoking Constanza cigarettes as seductively as possible.

That job led me to Veronica Chavez, who ran the only casting agency on the island. She was a strikingly beautiful woman of indeterminate age who called everyone "*Darrrrling.*" I signed on with her Agencia de Modelos and was promptly dispatched to Bavaro Beach—a virtually deserted stretch of pure white sand framed by tall, graceful coconut trees and calm blue waters. For three days I played tennis, swam, and dined in beautiful restaurants, while a photographer snapped pictures of me for the Bavaro Beach Resort brochure.

I modeled in Puerto Plata, Sosua, and Cabarete on the north shore, and in Juan Dolio to the south. Life was idyllic. Modeling took me to every corner of the island. It was a wonderful time in my life. I had a beautiful daughter, a fantastic girlfriend in Leslie, a dear friend in Remo, and a caring nanny to help out at home. With everything else so perfect, it was easy for me to overlook the fact that my marriage to Tony was in such a shambles.

Leslie had really come out of her shell. Gone was the tacky Jersey-girl look she'd been rocking when she first showed up at the office. She was so lighthearted these days, so comfortable in her own skin. Her green eyes sparkled with happiness, and according to Remo, a string of eligible bachelors in Atlántico were vying for the attention of the petite beauty. Clearly, leaving Paulie was the best move she'd ever made.

I wondered how I would feel if I were single again. I dwelled on the thought more and more. However, I refused to take it any further. Tony and I were just going through a rough patch, I told myself. We'd been together for five years, and all marriages had their highs and lows.

The first time I saw the Constanza commercial air, I was at the office. I'd been taking my lunch break on the terrace with Leslie when Danny came bursting out to announce that I was on TV. When Leslie and I hurried inside, it was being simultaneously broadcast on all of the televisions in the Big Office. Seeing myself on the screen was a surreal experience. While my memories of the shoot had been mostly of mud and tropical downpours, none of those problems were visible in the finished product. The editor had spliced all the footage together, added music, and expertly created a stunning commercial. It ran practically all day on all three of the local channels, and as a result I became an instantly recognizable face on the island. At first the notoriety was fun, a novelty. That soon wore off, though. Instead, I had to deal with an uncomfortable new reality. Everyone on the island suddenly knew my face.

At the time, the Dominican Republic was about to enter another phase of dramatic instability. The country was preparing for general elections, and Remo was already muttering darkly about the need to stockpile food, water, and fuel in preparation for the riots that would inevitably follow. Santo Domingo quickly became engulfed in election fever. Brightly colored billboards went up all over the city, screaming their support for either President Balaguer or his rival, Juan Bosch. Cars and motorcycles were decorated with flags representing their candidate of choice. Many ordinary Dominicans saw this election as a once-in-a-lifetime opportunity to finally rid themselves of their 84-year-old president. Balaguer had been in power for decades, and the marginally younger Bosch carried the promise of change and hope for a better future for this deeply troubled and impoverished country.

Yet after the election, local TV and radio stations announced that Balaguer had "won" the election by a 1.2% margin. The outcry from Bosch's supporters was immediate. A general strike was planned, and Balaguer had the military flood the streets to squash any dissent. August was a hot, humid, and violent month. Five thousand people were arrested in protests, and dozens were shot down in the street like animals as the army went on a bloody offensive against their own people. The same day that the local newspapers announced plans for additional protests, seven of our clerks resigned on the spot, fearful for their safety.

In November, a thousand strikers were detained by police, two thousand more were tossed in jail, and several were shot dead during anti-Balaguer demonstrations. In December, four more clerks handed in their notice and caught the next plane out of town.

As the political situation continued to deteriorate, so did my marriage. Football season had begun, and Information Unlimited went into it critically short-staffed. Tony was charting during the day and grading during the night. I had no doubt that he was using cocaine to stay awake. I barely saw him, and when I did he was edgy and paranoid, a drugged-out shell of the man I had once fallen in love with.

By mid-December, the locals eased up on protests to prepare for the upcoming holidays. I took the opportunity to slip away to Miami with the excuse of doing Christmas shopping. Instead, I headed straight for the cinema. *Havana* had just been released, and I was eager to see the finished product.

I sat alone in a half-empty theater. My eyes were glued to the screen as the movie began. I laughed to myself when I spotted Leslie. My heart skipped when Richard Portnow came on-screen for the first time. I remembered his smile, his laugh, and his expressive brown eyes. I remembered the way he made me feel. Then I appeared next to the two Dominican girls, reacting to the sound of machine-gun fire. A moment later Richard and I were talking by the pillar. A quick cut, and I was walking out of the room with him. It was jarring to see three days of filming reduced down to mere seconds on-screen.

I had declined Richard's offer to join him in his room at the Jaragua because I felt that I would regret it later. However, as Tony sank further into a morass of cocaine and booze, I spent most of my time regretting that I had not gone. A heavy sadness came over me. Tony seemed unwilling to forgo any kind of temptation in pursuit of his own selfish pleasures. I had taken the high road and denied myself the opportunity to feel special for one mad night. I knew I'd never be able to enjoy the movie, because those few seconds of screen time with Richard would always remind me of something I might never feel again.

22

GETTING ANYTHING DONE QUICKLY in the Dominican Republic
was nearly impossible. It was a poor country with barely any infra-
structure, mired in corruption and red tape. Strangely, though,
filing for divorce was easy. A change in local laws in the 1970s
enabled foreigners to obtain legal, uncontested divorces, free of
the hassle and expense of doing it at home. As a result, the island
became a divorce hotspot.

Dr. Manuel G. Espinoza was the king of the quickie Dominican
divorce. He made the big leagues when Barbra Streisand and
Elliott Gould sought his help to go their separate ways. Soon big-
name couples were flying in from all over the United States to
have their marriages dissolved. The wood-paneled waiting area
outside his office at the El Embajador was decorated with framed
newspaper clippings, showing the celebrity marriages he'd had a
hand in dismantling. As I waited to see him, I found myself faced

with a picture of Mike Tyson's recent Valentine's Day divorce. I was nervous but determined. My marriage to Tony was over.

Under California law I would have been entitled to half of everything Tony owned, but I had no intention of delaying the process any more than necessary. Espinoza promised me I could be divorced in twenty-four hours if I met the criteria, and after what Tony had put Justine and me through, a single day sounded long enough.

Espinoza ushered me into his office and got down to business without any formalities. He asked me if I was seeking spousal support, and I answered in the negative. I had already spoken to Ron about my plans to divorce Tony. He assured me that I had a job at Information Unlimited for as long as I wanted. I knew I could support myself. I didn't want or need Tony's money. The only property to divide was the land that Tony had bought at the golf course, and he was welcome to that. The sole issue was child custody. Espinoza explained that uncontested divorces usually meant that the parents would have joint custody. Yet I knew I would be the one taking care of Justine. I already was. Why would anything change once we were divorced?

Espinoza gave me a list of documents he would need to start the process, and I raced home to get them. Stepping into the bedroom, I wrinkled my nose at the rank odor of sweat and stale booze. Tony was asleep on top of the bedsheets, fully clothed. I went to the closet, opened the safe, gathered the papers, and took the eight-hundred-dollar divorce fee from my savings.

I opened the blinds and stared at his grimy, bloated body in disgust. His shoes were still on. His zipper was down. His shirt was covered with blood and his nose caked with white powder.

"Wake up!" I shook him roughly. His bloodshot eyes opened a crack. He moaned, shielding his eyes from the sunlight that streamed in through the windows.

"Sign this." I shoved the papers toward him.

"Huh?"

"Sign this. I'm starting divorce proceedings, Tony. You have to sign this."

He was coming around now. A look of intense pain filled his face. "Huh? Babe . . . what? Why?"

"Why?" I laughed without any humor. "I'll tell you why. Because your daughter is terrified of you. Because she doesn't want to come home until you're gone."

He sat up with difficulty, then staggered to his feet and hobbled toward the bathroom.

I followed him, jabbing the papers toward him. "Sign!"

In the bathroom he caught sight of his reflection. He stared in confusion at the three-day beard, swollen eyes, and bloodstained shirt. "What the fuck happened?" he groaned.

"Do you even know what day it is?"

He ran unsteady fingers through his hair. "Wednesday?"

"It's Friday. You've been missing for three days. Half the office was out looking for you. I had no idea if you were dead or alive. Your car's out in Boca Chica with the front smashed in."

"Babe . . . "

"Justine woke up this morning to find the complete stranger you brought home in her bedroom. He was vomiting on her carpet. I woke up when he wandered into our bedroom. You didn't even notice. You were too busy ransacking the kitchen trying to find more booze. At seven o'clock in the morning."

Tony was completely stunned by this. He obviously had no recollection of any of it.

"You want to know what happened next?"

Justine, hysterical, had watched her bloody, disheveled father, his face twisted in rage, pushing me up against the wall and screaming at me. She had run, terrified, from the room.

I looked at Tony with a mixture of anger and pity. He was a pathetic shadow of the man I had once loved. He shook his head, wincing. "I don't remember . . . anything," he said.

I handed him the paper and a pen. "Sign it," I said. "Then . . . get out."

Dr. Espinoza was true to his word. The following Monday, Tony and I were legally divorced. When I returned to the apartment,

Tony was gone. His drawers were empty; every last trace of him had been removed. Only then did I breathe a sigh of relief. Only then did I allow myself to grieve for the end of my marriage.

■

THE DIVORCE DECREE ARRIVED by messenger twenty-four hours later. I dropped one set of copies on Tony's desk that same afternoon. He snorted when he saw the fat Manila envelope. His response to the divorce was denial. He simply sulked and tried to ignore what had happened. "I can't believe you're still mad at me for something I don't even remember doing," he said.

The divorce made me a pariah at the office. Tony was constantly in a foul mood and he took it out on the clerks, who in turn blamed me for their misery. For Remo, the break-up was personal. He'd celebrated the previous two Christmases and Easters, as well as various birthdays, with us. Justine called him "Uncle Remo." He reacted as if his own parents had just gotten divorced.

"Marisa—" he began.

"I know what you're going to say. Tony loves me. That's not the issue here. He's completely out of control."

"He never cheated on you."

Hearing the same old excuses was maddening. Why did everyone always stick up for him?

"This is worse," I snapped. "You have no idea what it's like to lie awake at night wondering which Tony is going to come home: drunk Tony, horny Tony, or the Tony who doesn't take no for an answer. Everybody thinks he's such a great guy because all they see is the side he wants them to see. You have no idea how brutal he can be. Neither does he, for that matter, because he blacks out. He wakes up with no recollection of what he's done, then acts as if I'm the asshole because I won't talk to him! He turns into a monster and thinks he doesn't have to take responsibility for it. You think I deserve that?"

Remo looked uncomfortable and dodged the question. "He's under a lot of pressure."

"Big deal. So am I. My concern is Justine's future, and frankly, I don't think Tony should be part of it. Not when he values drinking and getting high more than us!"

Remo's entire demeanor changed with this revelation. "What do you mean, getting high?"

"He's doing cocaine."

Remo blanched. "Jesus Christ. You can get away with a lot of shit in the D.R., but not drugs. You can't even buy your way out of that kinda trouble. If Tony gets caught with coke, he can kiss his ass goodbye."

"Yeah, well, maybe someone should tell him that."

Remo looked terrified at the idea of Tony being involved in a drug bust. "They'll lock him up and throw away the key. Tony's money won't mean anything. You know where he's getting it from?"

I had my suspicions. "Horacio. Who else?"

"No. He wouldn't risk it, not even for Tony. He probably hooked him up with someone, though. Marisa, you have to talk to Tony. I know you're mad right now, but unless you want to see him serving twenty years—"

"I'm done talking. He doesn't listen to me anyway."

"Then let me try."

∎

WHAT FOLLOWED WAS A war of attrition, waged by Tony, in an effort to punish me for leaving him. He took away all the perks I'd enjoyed when I'd been the boss's wife. I was given a fixed schedule along with everyone else, and asked to hand over half the rent since it exceeded the allotted living allowance for a clerk. I accepted these conditions without complaint. As far as I was concerned, they were a small price to pay for my newfound freedom.

Tony found adjusting to single life difficult. I would notice his car parked outside the apartment building at odd hours of the evening, presumably checking to see that I was home. Then the late-night phone calls started. I knew it was Tony calling, though he'd hang up as soon as I'd pick up. Tony, who had never kept tabs on me when we were married, who'd never cared about where I was as long as it didn't interrupt his hard-partying ways, was now playing the role of the jealous lover.

Leslie invited me to go out with her, but I declined. I didn't want to inflame the situation. But when Tony left for a routine probation meeting in California, I no longer had an excuse. Leslie twisted my arm and I reluctantly agreed to accompany her to Atlántico. I was still at the height of my "Constanza girl" fame, and felt all eyes turn to me as I entered the club. Suddenly the idea of rejoining the world of single people filled me with anxiety. Several men made a beeline for us. They chatted to Leslie in perfect English while I glanced awkwardly around at the packed club.

A man approached. To my relief it was Remo.

"I need a word," he said.

"Sure."

"Not here." He took me by the arm and led me to the relative quiet outside. "Please don't go back in there," he said gravely.

I was stunned. "Why?"

"Coming here alone sends a very bad message, Marisa."

"I'm not alone," I laughed, "I'm with Leslie."

"That's worse. Leslie's . . . friendly. People will automatically assume that because you're with her, you're friendly, too."

I didn't know whether I should be angry or amused. "What is this, the 1950s? You're being absurd."

"Marisa, please. I know what I'm talking about. Those men in there want nothing more than to—to fuck the Constanza girl. Okay? They want to get in your pants so they can brag about it to their friends!"

I stared at Remo, utterly appalled.

Leslie came out and found us. "What's going on?"

"Nothing!" Remo barked.

"Tony put you up to this, didn't he?" Leslie said. Remo reached out for my arm, but I shrugged him away.

"No one you meet in there will ever love you the way Tony loves you!" he said.

"Grow up, Remo!" Leslie laughed. "She's not looking for love! She's just here to dance and have a good time!"

"Marisa, please!"

As angry as I was at Remo, I knew that he had my best interests at heart.

"Come on," Leslie pleaded. My best friend was worried about me shutting myself away in the aftermath of the breakup. All she wanted was for me to have fun. "Demetrio's inside. I want you to meet him!"

Remo started bickering. "Leslie, Demetrio's married!"

Suddenly I spotted a vaguely familiar face. He was standing behind Leslie, chatting with two young, beautiful women. As if he'd felt me staring at him, he looked over and our eyes locked.

In a flash, I realized who he was. The last time I'd seen him he'd been leaning back against his Mercedes, holding his gun. It was the man who'd shot a Haitian in cold blood because he'd dented his precious car. Everything stopped dead, all the sound faded away, and I was suddenly awash in the eerie silence that had followed the shooting.

Leslie grabbed my arm, pulling me back to the present. Now tonight didn't seem so fun anymore. The idea of meeting some divorced guy on the prowl seemed tawdry and cheap. And the fact that I was a stone's throw away from a cold-blooded murderer wasn't helping my fragile emotional state.

"Let's go somewhere else," I said.

■

IN THE WEEKS THAT followed, Tony tried everything to get me to reconcile with him, but I refused. When he realized that I wouldn't budge, he tried the next best thing—he focused on Justine. He began to slowly build up his relationship with her. He began stopping by the apartment to read her a bedtime story, or taking her down to the courtyard to ride her tricycle. Soon she was looking forward to his visits, and he started spending whole days off with her. I was happy to see Justine finally enjoying time with her father, but this turn of events also saddened me. Why did a crisis have to happen for Tony to decide to get to know his daughter?

It wasn't an easy time for me. My emotions swung up and down. Some days I felt strong, while others were a real struggle. The fact that my marriage was over broke my heart. Tony kept up the pressure, but I refused to give him another chance until he confessed to using cocaine. He dug in and denied, causing a stalemate.

He was so adamant that I started to doubt the evidence of my own eyes. Had I really seen the traces of white powder around his nose? Was his weird blinking and hyper behavior really the result of cocaine use, or was I jumping to conclusions? I was scared of the prospect of ending up like Tony's mother, constantly forgiving her husband and taking him back no matter what he did. But now that Tony's drinking was back under control, I became conflicted. On one hand, I felt that I would never love anyone the way I had loved him. On the other, I remembered his drunken rages and those long, worry-filled nights he wouldn't come home.

The situation came to a head when my sister called and announced that she would be coming to visit. The political situation had stabilized, and Heather was determined to come down while things were relatively calm. She and her boyfriend Joel would be here in August.

This posed a problem. Nobody in my family knew that Tony and I had divorced. I'd spent three years convincing them that I was happy and safe in the Dominican Republic. If my family learned that Tony and I weren't together, they'd pressure me relentlessly to leave the island.

While Heather continued talking, I desperately tried to think of a way around this awkward situation. Should I lie and say that Tony was out of the country? Or confess and swear Heather to secrecy? I knew that wouldn't be fair to her. I jotted down the dates and hung up the phone.

Tony moved back into the apartment the day before Heather and Joel arrived. The deal was that he would only stay for the week. Once my sister left, Tony would move out again. I made it clear that sex was not going to happen and he agreed—albeit with a cheeky smile. Heather's arrival gave Tony an unexpected second chance. He planned on making the most of it.

Tony surprised us all by renting a beautiful villa at Casa de Campo, the premier resort in the Dominican Republic. We spent five blissful days there, sailing, waterskiing, and exploring the beautiful Altos de Chavon, a replica of a 16th-century European village. We dined outdoors and strolled the cobblestones hand-in-hand. In the mornings Tony and Joel played golf, while Heather and I hit the beach with Justine.

"You're so lucky," Heather told me one morning. "After all the years you've been together, I can still see how much Tony loves you. "

At first our being together was a charade, but after a few days the atmosphere infected me. Being around Heather and Joel, who were still in the early flush of love, certainly helped. Plus, the idyllic setting removed us from the stress of our real lives. Whatever the reason, I started letting my guard down. My life had been so sad and strained before this visit. Under the circumstances, not having sex seemed pointless. One night as we lay intertwined, a full, clear moon streaming through the bedroom window, I wondered why our relationship couldn't be like this all the time. As if reading my mind, Tony kissed me and said, "I want it to stay like this, Marisa. This is the way things should be."

When Heather and Joel returned to Canada, Tony stayed at the apartment. I started to believe that the divorce was the best thing that ever happened to us. It kept us both on our toes. We learned not to take the relationship for granted. It seemed our relationship had just weathered another huge storm.

But every time I thought things were getting better, it seemed that bad news came knocking. This time it announced itself with the furious ringing of the front doorbell.

NOBODY EVER USED THE front door at Information Unlimited. I joined Roger at the door and peered through the peephole. A middle-aged blond woman stood next to our guard. She looked like she was crying.

"Can I help you?"

When I stepped outside I got a better look at her. Her eyes were puffy and her cheeks wet. She was wringing a Kleenex between her trembling hands. "I need to speak to Tony Santino," she blubbered. "I'm Isabel Walker. Edwin's wife."

As I led her around the side of the house, she rambled on about how Edwin hadn't been home in days and nobody had a clue where he was. She'd trawled the city's hospitals and morgues, to no avail. Even his car had vanished. I left her pacing nervously on the terrace and went to get Tony. As soon as she saw him, she burst into tears.

"I don't know who else to turn to," she wailed. "Codetel won't help me!"

Tony nodded sympathetically and asked Remo to call Captain Garcia. He did his best to comfort Mrs. Walker, and promised he'd do whatever he could to find her husband. As I led her back to her driver, I felt that something was amiss. I sensed from the way Tony had reacted to the news that he knew something.

When I returned to Tony's office, he was pacing the floor in a rage. "That son of a bitch!" he said.

I closed the door behind me. "What?"

Tony took a deep breath. "Walker. I gave that cocksucker over a hundred and eighty thousand dollars on Monday morning to settle the phone bill. And now he's gone. Vanished into thin air."

"You're not suggesting . . . ?"

"I sure am. He took off with our money."

I told him he was being ridiculous. "Walker probably earns twice that working for Codetel," I reasoned, but my words did nothing to soothe him. Not until the following afternoon did

Captain Garcia discover what had happened to Edwin Walker. He had been arrested in a sting operation, changing dollars on the black market.

Although illegal, changing dollars on the street was a common practice because the black market gave a higher rate than the banks. Walker was in the habit of changing Information Unlimited's money on the black market and then pocketing the difference. This time he'd waltzed right into a police setup. He was being held at a police station in Sabana Perdida, a poor barrio forty minutes outside the city. According to Garcia, it was the perfect place for someone to "disappear." So far the captain's attempts to see Walker had been denied. Tony feared that the police might kill Walker, take his car, and pocket the cash.

Walker showed up at our office three days later. He was pale and unshaven, and looked like he'd aged ten years. The police had confiscated the money, as well as his company car. As the money had not been declared when it came into the country, Gustavo was unable to recover it. He warned Tony to simply let it go, or run the risk of having the police broaden their investigation. Nobody wanted the authorities looking into the financial dealings at our office. Tony, unsurprisingly, was spitting blood.

"You useless prick! You ripped me off, lost my money, and brought me to the attention of the police!"

Everybody in the office heard the merciless dressing-down Tony gave him. By the time he left Tony's office, he looked like a broken man. He was immediately fired from Codetel, a huge blow to Information Unlimited. Despite his money changing, Edwin had been a key player. That night when Tony stormed out of the office, he didn't come home.

For the next two days the atmosphere at Information Unlimited was one of quiet sadness. The clerks were all painfully nice to me as we anxiously awaited news of where Tony was. He resurfaced two days later. He never said a word. He went straight to his office and stayed there. When I went home that evening, I saw that he'd already stopped by to clear his things out. I'd warned Tony that if he ever disappeared on another binge again, the truce was over. This time he didn't try to justify or defend his actions. I had opened my heart to him, and once again he had chosen drugs and alcohol over his family.

Devastated, I took time off work, unable to face the holiday festivities alone. Leslie tried to get me to join the rest of the gang in ushering in 1992, but I stayed home. I spent a quiet New Year's Eve in sober self-reflection. I would be thirty years old soon. I needed to take charge of my life. I needed to start planning for my future.

While Tony had failed me, to his credit his commitment to Justine never wavered. On the morning of January 8, he arrived at the apartment just as I was leaving. Neither of us felt any animosity now. The final disintegration of our marriage had sapped us of all the bitterness and anger we had for each other. We shared nothing more than a resigned sadness these days. He asked me where I was going so early.

"Picking up a check," I told him. I had completed a modeling job months earlier, and was finally getting paid for it. Then I would head over to the office. I was in the courtyard when I realized I had forgotten my passport. The accounting department had insisted on seeing official ID before releasing a check for that much money to me.

I ran back upstairs to get it. Before I left, I glanced back into the living room. Justine was sitting on Tony's lap as he read to her. Her left arm was draped over his neck, and she was absentmindedly toying with his earlobe, just as she did with me when I read to her. They were so engrossed in the story, they had no idea I was watching them. I felt a pang deep inside, a bittersweet sadness. I realized I was crying.

23

Santo Domingo, January 8, 1992

I KEPT MY EYES tightly closed and tried to ignore the incessant wail of sirens as the police convoy sped through the city. I tried not to think about the awful moment when the heavily armed soldiers had stormed our office, or the sight of Gustavo, our "well connected" lawyer, lying on the floor in a heap, weeping from the blow to his belly. I tried not to think about the expression of sheer terror on Remo's face during the raid, or how detrimental this awful situation might be for Roger and Carmine. Both were elderly; both had health issues.

Instead, I tried to focus on the positives. Clearly Tony had intercepted the company van, which meant that the rest of our clerks were safe. Ron surely knew by now that his office had been raided. Perhaps he had already learned that the FBI was involved. Either way, I knew that he and Tony were working together to secure our release. I tried to comfort myself by thinking about Tony, but my mind flashed back to the yellow crime-scene tape and I shuddered. The feds must have been planning this for a while. Did Tony stand a chance of helping us?

The van finally stopped and we were ushered out at gunpoint. We found ourselves standing in the middle of a vast, dusty court-yard. A huge concrete building dominated the cheerless square. Bordering it were several other dreary structures. The entire complex was surrounded by high, sun-bleached cinder block walls, except for the heavily guarded chain-link entrance. The constant rumble of traffic told me that we were somewhere near the center of the city, though I had never seen this foreboding place before.

We were led into a small one-story building. Inside, the ceiling fan battled uselessly against the humid fug permeating the room. At the front desk a guard ordered us to enter our names, birth-dates, and nationalities in the ledger.

"What did he say?" Roger, like many of my colleagues, had never bothered to learn Spanish.

I translated the guard's words and we were released from our handcuffs. After entering our information in the thick book, we were marched to a holding cell. The dank room was furnished with a single metal bunk bed corroded with rust. A tiny window and a bare bulb provided the only illumination.

As soon as the barred gate slammed shut, we began to furiously compare notes. All of us agreed that the FBI was responsible for the raid.

"But the FBI has no jurisdiction here!"

"Unless—"

"Unless what, Remo?" Carmine asked.

"Unless drugs or murder are involved."

I laughed nervously. "Well, we're not killing people. Or dealing drugs."

I looked over to Roger, desperate for him to back me up. Even in the half-light of the cell I could see the worry etched on his face.

"I wouldn't put it past Agent Peterson to lie to the Dominicans. Not if it meant he had a shot at taking us down."

The FBI were frustrated by the success of our offshore gambling operation. Information Unlimited was raking in millions of dollars, tax free, and the American authorities couldn't do a thing about it. Would they go so far as to mislead another country's government about our activities? Judging by the look of disgust on the commanding officer's face when he realized that we were "only a *banca*," he'd clearly been deceived.

Trying to ignore the icy feeling in my gut, I said, "So what if Peterson lied to the Dominicans? As soon as they figure out that we have nothing to do with drugs or murder they'll have to let us go!"

"Wake up, Marisa. This isn't America!" I cringed at the hard edge in Remo's voice. "It's not 'innocent until proven guilty' here. We're guilty until we can prove that we're innocent. That could take forever."

I looked around the bleak holding cell. The prospect of staying here more than a few hours hit me hard. When would I see Justine again?

"Tony will get us out," I said. But Remo wasn't listening. He sulked off to the other side of the cell.

Of all of us, Remo had the least to fear. He was just a cook. The three of us watched wordlessly as he grabbed hold of the metal bunk bed and started to drag it noisily across the concrete floor. He positioned it under the tiny window and scrambled up to peer out.

Suddenly a large black shape shot out of the hole in the wall that Remo had unintentionally exposed. "Rat!" Carmine shrieked. It darted across the floor with its long pink tail flailing behind, squeezing itself under the bars. The soldier standing guard outside went after it, stomping it repeatedly with his heavy boots until it was a mass of blood and fur. He kicked the carcass to the corner, lit a cigarette and walked off, leaving bloody footprints behind.

"Tony will get us out," I repeated, trying to wipe the sordid scene from my mind.

"I know he will," Roger said softly, putting his arm around me.

■

POVERTY RIDDEN. POLITICALLY UNSTABLE. Riddled with corruption. My father had done his best to dissuade me from moving to the island. Looking around this filthy cell, I started to wonder if I should have listened to him. I'd spent the better part of my life not taking advice from the two people who loved me most in the world. "Why can't you behave more like a girl?" was a favorite expression of my mother's. I heard it every time I came home covered in dirt and mud, or sporting a bloody knee or torn clothes. I'd always preferred climbing trees and exploring the roofs of neighbors' houses to my ballet and piano lessons. "DO NOT ENTER" and "NO TRESPASSING" signs only served to arouse my curiosity, and beckoned me to investigate. I'd always had a thirst for adventure, and the lure of establishing the world's first offshore gambling operation had proved too much of an adventure to resist.

"Listen!" Remo hissed.

More vehicles were arriving. We heard car doors slammed and orders barked. The sound of footsteps filled the corridor. We jumped down from the bed and joined Roger and Carmine by the door. My heart sank as I saw our clerks dejectedly tramping toward us. The gate opened and they filed in. I scanned their faces desperately—if Tony was among them, we were in deep trouble.

Thankfully, he wasn't. But Leslie was. "What's going on?" she cried. She was wearing tiny white denim shorts and a midriff top that left her flat, tanned stomach exposed. The soldiers were already pressing their faces against the bars of the door, openly leering at the petite green-eyed beauty.

I ushered her to the far end of the cell. "How did they get you?"

Bruce, another of our clerks, explained how Tony had flagged down the company van and sent everyone home to await further instructions. The driver had been dispatched to notify the rest of the staff to stay away from the office.

"So what happened?"

Leslie wiped her tears with the back of her hand. "Gustavo happened!"

Our lawyer had the addresses of all the clerks in a company file. The soldiers had dragged him from apartment to apartment. Our unsuspecting employees had answered the door, only to be pounced on by soldiers.

"I thought Information Unlimited was legit!" Bruce cried. His outburst brought a few mutters of discontent from the others.

"It is!" I protested. "Gustavo set everything up—"

"That prick's the reason we're in here!"

As the clerks adjusted to the shock of being in prison, I sensed the mood turning mutinous. I was the closest person to Tony, and in his absence they looked to me for answers. Except I had none. All I could do was try to assure them that Tony would fix the situation. They were scared. We all were. And Leslie, in her skimpy shorts and shirt, was in real danger here.

Roger tried his best to calm everyone down. Some time later he joined Leslie and me by the bunk bed. He dropped his voice. "Listen, we decided it's best to keep you girls out of this, completely. Marisa, you were at the office to visit your friend here." He gestured to Remo, who gave a faint nod. "Leslie, you're here on vacation. Neither of you has anything to do with the office. You never worked there. You don't know anything about Information Unlimited. Got it?"

Remo laughed sadly and shook his head. "They'll keep interrogating us until we tell them what they want to hear."

Leslie started to cry. "Thanks, Remo," I snapped.

While I was annoyed with Remo for speaking so frankly, I also suspected that he was right. Nobody knew the ins and outs of the island like he did. He had been living here for years before we had arrived.

Rush hour had long since ended. The streets were quiet, and we could hear sirens approaching from miles away. More prisoners were being brought to the cell. We nervously anticipated the last of our clerks joining us. Instead, six strangers entered the cell, led by a huge thug. His shoulders were broad and muscular, and his nose looked like it had been broken several times. His close-set eyes darted around the room. Without acknowledging us, he led his entourage to the far corner of the cell.

"Who are they?" Carmine muttered, eyeing them suspiciously.

"The big guy is Sonny LoBue," Roger whispered. "Based out of San Francisco. At least he was."

"Did you know there was another operation here?" I asked, glancing over at LoBue's men.

Roger shook his head. "No. But let's just say that LoBue isn't exclusively into bookmaking."

"Maybe that's what this is about," I whispered hopefully. "The feds are probably after them."

Two police officers appeared, with the guard in tow. He began to read off a list of names. Three of our clerks stepped forward, and my heart leapt as the door was unlocked and they were escorted out. The murmuring in the cell grew to a fever pitch. A few minutes later the guard and the officers reappeared, and the procedure was repeated. This time we exchanged cheers and high-fives as the clerks were led out, presumably to freedom.

Sonny and his men sourly watched the proceedings. I was right—they really were after Sonny's gang. Seeing that Remo was still perched up on the bunk bed, staring miserably out of the window, I waved for him to join us, but he shook his head. I scrambled up to join him.

"What's wrong?"

He nodded mutely toward the window. Our clerks were being marched toward the far end of the compound. They were in handcuffs again. The building they were approaching was a huge concrete slab with bars on the windows. Our clerks weren't being released. They were being imprisoned.

Inside, people were still smiling and chattering excitedly. I said nothing. There was no point in taking away this fleeting moment of happiness from them. I rested my head on Remo's shoulders, fighting back the tears that were pricking my eyes. It had been a long, terrible day, and I was beginning to lose hope altogether.

"LoBue, Anthony."

Sonny broke away from his pack and headed for the door. As he passed the bunk bed he turned to face me.

"RB," he grunted. I was startled to hear him address me by my nickname; I had never met him before. "Tell Tony to watch his back," he said, "cuz Sacco's going to fuck him."

Before I could reply, Sonny made his way out of the cell.

Remo looked alarmed. "You know that guy?"

"No! I've never even seen him before!"

"Well, he knows who you are. Who's Sacco?"

I took a deep breath. I was still trying to process why a mobster would say that to me. "Our boss."

Remo's brow crinkled. "I thought Tony was the boss."

"He is," I said. "But Sacco is Tony's boss."

Remo resumed staring out of the barred window, looking even more worried than before. I wanted to say more, but I didn't know how Sonny LoBue knew my name or anything else. I did know that Ron would never betray Tony.

The cell continued to empty until only Leslie, Remo, and I were left. I faintly hoped this might mean we'd be released after all. Leslie and I were the only women in the group, and Remo was merely the cook.

"Grayson, Remo."

Remo slid off his sentry post on the bunk bed and choked out the word, "Goodbye," as though he would never see us again. I hugged him, but he just stood limply in my arms. He slouched off like a condemned man, and the door slammed back into place with a heavy clang.

The guards pressed their faces against the bars. One of them rapped on the bars with his keys. "*Ven acá, pequeñita,*" he called, and the others laughed. Leslie glanced up at them, her wide eyes trembling. We were alone, and utterly defenseless.

I pulled her closer. "Just ignore them," I whispered.

"Constanza girl," one of them cooed at me in broken English, "you wan' suck my cock?"

I pulled my baseball cap further down over my face. Leslie

began to cry softly, which only seemed to encourage them. We sat in that empty cell for what seemed like hours, listening as the guards yelled obscenities at us.

The insults stopped abruptly with the arrival of two plain-clothesmen. Loud salutes were exchanged, and the guards quickly dispersed.

Leslie and I were escorted toward the oppressive multi-story building. We climbed a narrow outside staircase and, once inside, walked down a concrete corridor lit with flickering lights. Turning a corner, we found ourselves in a bright, open area. Two men were sitting behind a desk, poring over a chaotic pile of papers. The place was a mess—Manila folders were stacked waist-high along the floor. It occurred to me just how easily I could go missing in an archaic system like this.

Yet the way the men were methodically filing papers was almost comforting. It seemed dull, routine. Plus, we hadn't been hand-cuffed, which I took as a good sign. I started to hope that we would be discharged. We were told to sit on a wooden bench.

"I think they're going to let us go," Leslie whispered, reading my thoughts.

"*Silence!*" the man behind the desk shouted sternly. I averted my eyes and stared at the floor.

Leslie nudged me and pointed to a sign hung above a feature-less brown door. In Spanish it read, *"Everything that goes on here is secret, and stays within these walls."* At the sight of this, my heart began to pound. Although the Dominican Republic was now a democracy, it had a recent and bloody history of authoritarian rule. Among the widespread human rights abuses, it was not uncommon for people to simply "disappear."

As the minutes dragged by, I slumped farther down on the bench. I had not eaten or had a sip of water in the nine hours since we'd been arrested. Suddenly a shrill ring split the air, and I jolted upright again. An old rotary phone was quickly answered, then wordlessly hung up. The young man stood up and approached me. He had a gun casually tucked into his belt.

"Get up," he ordered, ushering me toward the brown door. I looked back at Leslie. The color drained from her face as she realized that we were being separated.

The door slammed behind me. The room was devoid of windows. The single naked bulb suspended from the ceiling made me think of those Nazi interrogation scenes in old black-and-white movies. The walls were painted a dreary gray, the floor lined with linoleum tiles. Chairs flanked a bare desk, and a metal filing cabinet stood nearby. Above it was a sign identical to the one outside, insisting on the need for secrecy. Above the desk was a small, square mirror. Something about the way it reflected the light struck me as odd. I sensed that it was a two-way mirror. I sat down and waited in the profound, heavy silence, certain that I was being observed.

The police had my purse, and it contained a wealth of information about me. My Canadian passport was inside, so they knew that I frequently traveled in and out of the country. Also in my purse was a Manila envelope, which contained a check, and a brochure of the most luxurious hotel on the island. The check was payment for a modeling job I had recently done. The brochure was the result of that work—a glossy booklet full of photographs of me enjoying all the amenities the five-star hotel had to offer.

I cursed the unexpected consequences of collecting my pay earlier this morning. By the time I received the check, it was too late to go home, so I'd gone to the office early.

I tried to focus on the positives. The check was evidence enough for them to release me. And everyone on the island knew my face from that ubiquitous Constanza commercial. All of my papers were in order. I had every right to live and work in the Dominican Republic. I would simply play the dumb blonde who happened to be in the wrong place at the wrong time.

An hour passed. By then I had traced every crack in the ceiling and every chip in the linoleum floor, and had noted the dried bloodstain on the wall, reddish-brown against the pale gray paint. I had a suspicion it had been left there intentionally, a reminder to detainees that the secret police were not to be taken lightly. As time dragged on, I felt my eyelids growing heavier. The silence compounded my exhaustion, and I leaned forward on the desk, resting my head in my hands. My last thought, as I drifted into a fitful sleep, was that Tony would get me out of here.

A noise behind me made me bolt upright. The door had burst open.

"You're not here to take a nap!"

I sat up, startled and confused. A man went around to the other side of the desk, carrying an ancient typewriter. He placed it on the desk and took the seat across from me. He pulled a sheet of paper from the desk, expertly loaded it, and sat there ready to go. I tried to clear my head. How long had I been asleep?

Another man wearing an officer's uniform entered, slamming the door behind him. The man behind the desk rose to his feet and hastily saluted. The officer glared at me and ordered me to remove my L.A. Lakers cap. I had taken to wearing it ever since the Constanza commercial had aired. With my long blond hair in a ponytail and a pair of sunglasses to cover my blue eyes, I could wander around Santo Domingo unrecognized. Now as I removed the cap, I felt vulnerable and exposed. I glanced up at that strange mirror above the desk, and wondered how many pairs of eyes were watching me from the other side.

Pacing furiously, the officer rattled off a series of questions. "Name? Date of birth? Nationality?"

I answered as quickly as I could, though my mouth was dry as sawdust. The rattle of the typewriter filled the room. Then he asked me a question that took me by surprise. "What is your relationship to Mr. LoBue?"

I was stumped. I had been rehearsing my answers silently all afternoon, anticipating any question I assumed they would ask. I was prepared to tell them about Remo, Leslie, my modeling, or anything else I thought might help create the impression that I was only peripherally involved in the company. But Sonny LoBue?

I heard a scream. It was faint, distant, but I knew I hadn't imagined it. It sounded like a woman. It sounded like Leslie.

"What is your relationship to LoBue?" the man demanded again.

"I—I don't know him!"

"Liar! We know you're married to him!"

I turned to face him. The officer's face was flushed with fury.

What on earth was happening? "I—I don't even know the man," I protested. "I just met him today, for the first time."

The officer slammed his fist into the desk, and I jumped back. He put his face inches from mine. "You are his wife!" he bellowed.

I shook my head. "No! No, I'm not!" What kind of nightmare was this? My eyes darted to the mirror and the faceless people on the other side, watching my every move. Yet the interrogation had only begun.

24

I WAS SO TIRED, I was slurring my words. "I'm telling you the truth. I'm not married to Sonny LoBue!"

The interrogation had gone on for hours now. Still, the officer, who had asked me for what seemed like the tenth time about my "husband" Sonny LoBue, wasn't buying it. He put his face close to mine. "We know he is your husband."

Turning my head away, I looked directly into the two-way mirror. I lifted my left hand and wiggled my fingers so whoever was on the other side could get a good look. "No ring!" I yelled. "See? No ring, no husband!"

The officer slammed his fist on the desk. "Look at me!" he bellowed.

My eyes were bleary. My lips were cracked and dry, and I felt faint. Fourteen hours had elapsed since the raid and I hadn't had a drop of water. I wondered absently how much longer this would go on.

"I need something to drink," I croaked. It wasn't the first time I had asked, and I didn't hold out much hope that anyone would care.

At that point during the endless interrogation a memory came to me. When I'd been in the holding cell with the others and the guard had called for LoBue, he'd called him *Anthony* LoBue, not Sonny. Maybe that was the source of the confusion. Had one of the clerks, under duress, told the interrogators that I was "Tony's wife?" Even though we were divorced, the clerks—and Tony himself—had never stopped referring to me that way. Since the police had Anthony LoBue in custody, did they assume that he was the Tony in question?

Even as I became increasingly sure that this was what had happened, I had no idea what I could do with this information. I couldn't say anything that would send the authorities looking for the real Tony. After all, he was our only hope of getting out of this place.

As my exhausted mind wrestled with this puzzle, the officer leaned in to me. He watched me carefully, his jaw clenching and unclenching. Before he could yell at me again, the door to the interrogation room swung open.

Two guards entered. The officer greeted them with a scowl. Striding over to the two-way mirror, he gestured to whoever was on the other side, clearly pleading his case for a little more time to work on me. His request was denied. He had failed to get his confession. The guards hoisted me out of my chair. My relief that the interrogation was over was short-lived, however. It occurred to me that they were simply taking me to someone else. Someone who might prove a little more persuasive.

I was frog-marched down the corridor. When I stumbled, exhausted and disorientated, the guards shoved me forward. I was pushed into a bright, spacious office where I was unceremoniously dumped into the nearest chair. The guards saluted the occupants of the room, then left without a word.

I found four men staring at me. Seated at the desk was an officer in full military uniform. A brass plaque identified him as Colonel Eduardo E. Rivera Munoz. Two men wearing similar though less elaborate uniforms flanked him. The fourth man was a tall, dark-skinned Dominican wearing a mustard-colored suit and Ray-Bans. He was rail-thin, with sharp, bony features. He casually leaned against the wall behind the uniformed men.

The colonel reached into a drawer of his desk, pulled out an Uzi, and pointed it at me. I presumed this was an attempt to intimidate me. All of the men were armed. If they had wanted to kill me, a single bullet from a handgun would have been sufficient. The idea that they would spray me with submachine-gun fire was laughable.

Disappointed by my lack of reaction, he placed the Uzi on the desk. He turned his attention to a Manila file. As he perused it, I noticed with annoyance that the contents of my purse were splayed out across his desk. My heart began to race in anticipation of the questions that would inevitably follow.

The colonel picked up the check issued to me for seven thousand pesos and scrutinized it carefully. He passed it to the others to examine. The man in the mustard-colored suit picked up the accompanying brochure and began flipping through it. He stopped, interested in one picture in particular. I felt a prickle of dread that he was staring at the image of me in a bikini sitting by the pool. I suddenly felt very exposed, as if I were sitting in front of him naked. I sensed he was enjoying my discomfort. As the interrogation got under way, I found myself stumbling over my answers. It was a combination of my exhaustion and the continuous, unnerving gaze of the man in the sunglasses.

Following a soft knock at the door, someone entered bearing a large tray piled high with food for the colonel. Two lackeys busied themselves clearing the desk to provide space for his generous meal. I glanced at my watch. 1:40 a.m. My stomach growled as the aroma of chicken and fried plantains filled the office. I was forced to watch while the colonel ate hungrily, every so often pausing to ask me a question with his mouth stuffed with food. Once in a while the man in the mustard-colored suit would lean forward to pluck a plantain chip from the colonel's plate without asking, which told me straightaway that he outranked everyone else in the room.

Once the colonel had polished off his meal, the man in the suit leaned forward and removed his sunglasses. For the first time I got a proper look at his face. Up close I could see the sharp angles of his skull poking through his skin. My breath caught in my throat when I saw his eyes. They looked sickly, diseased. The irises were cloudy and the whites of his eyes were tinged yellow. For the first time he addressed me. "Do you want to go home?" he asked in Spanish.

In a voice that was barely a whisper I said, "Yes."

He nodded. His face remained expressionless. "Do you want to go home with me?"

I knew that I had to be wary in my reply. The only reason he could afford to be so cavalier, I realized, was because of his rank. In Spanish, I thanked him for his generous offer but politely declined. He said nothing for what felt like a long time. Then he began to chuckle. Following his lead, the others began to nervously laugh as well. Soon all four were laughing, briefly puncturing the tension in the room.

In the commotion I thought I heard something. Leslie's voice! I strained to listen over the sound of the men's braying laughter. I was so tired, I wondered if my mind was playing tricks on me. But as their laughter subsided I heard her again, and I knew it wasn't my imagination this time. I glanced toward the door, which hadn't been fully closed when the food was brought in. Leslie was whimpering outside, pleading with someone in the hallway behind me. Taking advantage of the momentary distraction, I lunged for the door and wrenched it open.

When Leslie saw me burst out of the office, she broke free from her startled guard and reached for me. I grabbed her with every ounce of strength I had and dragged her into the room. I sat back down and pulled her firmly onto my lap. The laughter stopped immediately. A pensive silence settled over the office.

The confused guard hurried into the room, apologizing profusely to the man in the mustard-colored suit, whom he addressed as General Hernandez. The general regarded me with a steely glint in his strange eyes. "Let her go," he said.

I clasped my arms around Leslie and shook my head. I wouldn't allow her out of my sight again.

"Be careful," the general purred. "You are about to be sent home. She, however, is to remain here." He snapped his fingers and the guard tried to drag Leslie free of my grasp. She hung onto me for dear life.

"No!" I insisted. "She comes with me, or I stay with her! I'm not leaving her alone!"

The only reason that I was being freed was that somebody—most likely Tony—had negotiated my release. The general wouldn't get his bribe money until I was safely out of prison. If my instinct was correct, then I had some bargaining power. If I was wrong, I knew I would pay heavily for this transgression.

In the tense silence, the men looked to the general for his response. He dismissed the guards, and I allowed myself to relax a little. "Someone has vouched for you," he said in an expressionless monotone. "You'll be entrusted to his company until tomorrow morning at six-thirty, when you will both report back here for further questioning."

My passport lay on the desk, among the other items from my purse. I silently screamed with frustration as the general picked it up and pocketed it. On any other day it would have been tucked away in the safe at home. But because of simple bad luck, it was now in the possession of a corrupt general who had just effectively trapped me on the island. Colonel Rivera scooped up the rest of my belongings and dumped them back into my purse. He handed it to one of the officers behind him. He summoned some guards, and Leslie and I were led away.

We dared not speak, or hope that it was really over, as we were escorted through a maze of hallways and corridors. We paused in front of a door and then—gloriously—I felt a breeze on my face as the guard opened it. We stepped outside and were led down the same narrow concrete staircase that we had climbed all those hours ago. We walked past the holding cell where I had seen Sonny LoBue for the first time. Across the compound was the building where Remo and the clerks had been taken.

We passed Roger's impounded red Cherokee, which was parked next to a couple of black sedans. In the middle of the courtyard was a familiar, battered old AMC Pacer. As we approached, it flashed its lights and the engine turned over. My heart sank.

"I can't believe Tony sent *him* to pick us up," I said.

I was almost too tired to be mad as Leslie and I both climbed unsteadily into the back seat. The guard pulled open the heavy chain-link fence, allowing Horacio Vargas to drive us away.

25

"THANKS FOR COLLECTING US," I said, breaking the awkward silence.

The last person on the island I wanted involved in whatever was happening was Horacio. Yet here we were, sitting in the back seat of his car. My gut feeling told me that if Horacio could find a way to take advantage of our misfortune, he would. Why hadn't Tony sent Captain Garcia instead? I assumed that he was the one responsible for getting us out of police custody in the dead of night.

"Did Miguel have anything to do with us getting released?" I asked.

"Miguel Garcia is only a captain," Horacio said loftily. "He doesn't have the kind of connections to get people out of custody. I vouched for you, on Tony's behalf."

I bit my tongue. *He* vouched for us? The man couldn't even get past the bouncers at Atlántico. Our eyes met in the rearview mirror, neither of us making an effort to hide our dislike for the other.

"If it was so easy, what took you so long?" Leslie asked.

"That's not important," he replied smoothly.

"Yes, it is!" she said. "In another few minutes I would have been gang-raped by a bunch of prison guards! So yes, it is fucking important!" Sobs racked her body as she slumped back in the seat.

"Nothing's going to happen to you," Horacio said.

"Then why do we have to go back in the morning?" I asked.

"I can't go back there!" Leslie cried. But we had to go back. Leslie's apartment would have been ransacked along with all the others, and the police most likely had her passport as well. We didn't have a choice.

The electricity was out, but the moon was bright enough to make out the tiny corrugated-tin-roofed houses and small businesses lining the potholed Avenida San Martin. Soon he pulled up outside Commerciales Vargas, and we followed Horacio inside the small appliance store. Tony's unmistakable silhouette rushed toward us, holding a lantern, and he pulled me tightly into his arms.

"Are you okay?" he asked, studying my face. "Where's Justine?"

"With Rosa. She's safe."

Before I could say another word, he told me that he was about to leave for a scheduled meeting with Ruth Gordon. Postponing was not an option, but the thought of him taking off at such a critical time was devastating.

"You're leaving now?" Leslie sounded panic-stricken.

"I'll be back in a couple of days with our lawyer," he said, trying to placate us. "I'm leaving for Puerto Plata with Miguel. I'll fly out from there." The tiny airport was a four-hour drive away on a dangerous two-lane highway, but since it was used almost exclusively by tourists visiting resorts on the north shore, security checks were lax there.

"What about us?" I asked, as flickering headlights illuminated the street outside.

"It's Miguel," Horacio confirmed, peering out of the window. He unlocked the door and let the captain in. Tony shook Miguel's hand warmly.

Miguel turned to me. *"Señora,"* he said, looking at me intently. *"Todo bien?"*

I nodded mutely.

"Listen, you and Leslie will stay at Horacio's tonight," Tony told us. "He'll drive you to the police station in the morning. If things go according to plan, everyone will get out later today."

"And if things don't go according to plan?"

He smiled. "Luckily, Horacio knows someone in the Secret Service, which is why you're here now and not in custody. The police will make a statement in the morning, and then everyone will be released."

I glanced over at Horacio. The light from the lantern distorted his features and gave him a sinister look. "I need to see Justine," I said. "Leslie can stay with me, and we'll take a taxi to the police station in the morning."

"No, Marisa," Tony said. But I persisted, and within minutes we were having a full-blown argument.

"You'll sleep at Horacio's tonight. It's safer!" he insisted.

"No! The police don't have my address, so it's just as safe at home. I need to see Justine!" I wouldn't be able to sleep anyway. It was two-thirty in the morning. We had to be back at the police station in four hours.

"Horacio, take my wife home," Tony snapped, heading outside with Miguel to the Mitsubishi. Horacio quickly locked up the shop and hurried after them. "If the girls are going home, then why don't I drive you off to the airport?" he suggested. "They'll be safe with Miguel."

This infuriated rather than placated me. I knew full well why Horacio had volunteered to go to the North Shore with Tony: if for any reason Tony did not return from the States, Horacio would simply keep the Mitsubishi, which was conveniently registered in his name. I also knew that raising my suspicions with Tony was completely pointless. The switch in drivers was made, and as Miguel was pulling out of the parking lot, I remembered Sonny LoBue's warning.

"Wait, stop the car!"

I wanted to pass on Sonny's message to Tony, but Horacio's plot had distracted me. I watched the Mitsubishi roar away, spewing pebbles until it disappeared into the darkness.

I pondered what Sonny had told me in the holding cell. What were his exact words? *"RB . . . tell Tony Ron's going to fuck him."* How had he known my nickname?

By the time we were back in the city, Leslie was half-asleep with her head slumped against the window. I was wide-awake. It struck me that if the police wanted to impound my car, they would try to get hold of the keys before resorting to more drastic and costly measures. I pushed my hand into my pocket and pulled them out. "Miguel, can you please go by the office?" I asked quietly, so as not to wake Leslie.

Miguel turned off the headlights and we crawled along slowly until we reached the villa. The Information Unlimited sign had been removed, but there was little else to show for the raid—just some tire marks on the lawn and a few shreds of yellow police tape blowing softly in the early-morning breeze. I spotted my Daihatsu parked in the driveway, exactly where I had left it.

"I don't see anyone guarding the house," I whispered.

"Someone should be watching it," Miguel assured me.

He parked a few houses away but kept the engine running. I saw no sign of a policeman. I focused on the driveway, noting the slight incline. If my Daihatsu were in neutral, it would roll backward into the street.

Putting aside the fact that it was my only form of transportation, new cars were worth a fortune in the Dominican Republic. "Wait here." I opened the door and sprinted silently across the street.

Miguel jumped out after me. *"Señora! Señora!"* he hissed angrily.

I crouched down and crept toward my car. There wasn't a soul in sight. Unlocking the driver's door, I slid into the seat, released the hand brake and depressed the clutch. The Daihatsu rolled backward into the street. I turned the wheel and let the momentum take me forward, coasting past Miguel toward the end of the block. Only then did I turn the key in the ignition and pull over to the curb, where I waited for the captain.

Miguel shook his head at me in disbelief. Leslie sat up, confused and groggy, and I beckoned her into my car. I thanked Miguel and said goodbye.

I sped west on Avenida Sarasota past the elaborate entrance to the Hotel Embajador, a mere mile from home. Soon I was at the gate, waiting for Pino to pull it open. I made a sharp left past the lush courtyard and pulled into my parking spot, relieved to be home at last.

I took the stairs two-by-two up to the apartment and unlocked the door. Everything was blissfully normal. I tiptoed into Justine's room and found her sleeping peacefully. Fighting the temptation to wake her up, I stroked her cheek as I gazed at her.

"We should get some rest," Leslie yawned behind me. I gave her some clothes and she staggered to the guest room to shower and sleep. I spun the dials on the safe, took out five hundred-dollar bills and Justine's passport, then shut the door again. I jotted down my mother's number for Rosa to call in case of an emergency, and slipped the five hundred dollars into an envelope with the passport.

I took a quick shower, set the alarm clock for five-thirty and collapsed into bed. My hair was still wet when the buzzer went off two hours later. I stumbled to the kitchen and prepared a pot of coffee, hoping the strong Dominican brew would clear my head. I pulled on jeans and a T-shirt, stuffed a few pesos into my pocket and wrapped a cardigan around my waist. I heard the hiss of steam and poured three mugs, adding milk and sugar. "Wake up," I said to Leslie gently.

I crept into Justine's room and kissed the top of her head, fighting to keep my emotions in check. I didn't have time for tears—Leslie and I had to leave in a few minutes. I closed the door softly and went upstairs to wake up Rosa. She joined me down-stairs a minute later, rubbing the sleep from her eyes. I handed her a mug of coffee and told her what had taken place the previous day. I passed Rosa the envelope and keys and explained what needed to be done in the event things did not go as planned.

Leslie came into the kitchen wearing one of my T-shirts and a pair of jeans she had rolled up and cinched with a belt. I dialed the Hotel Embajador for a taxi, and we said goodbye to Rosa and went downstairs to wait. It was a clear morning and the sky was just hinting at dawn.

The little *colmado* half a block away was just opening up, so I ran over to buy a newspaper. "There's nothing here," I called to Leslie as I flipped through the pages. Surely it was big news that the Dominican Army, Secret Service and FBI had coordinated the raid of an American-based, billion-dollar gambling operation in Santo Domingo? I was worried that nothing had been printed about it. Twenty-five Americans had just disappeared, and no one knew anything about it.

26

By day, the headquarters of the secret police looked completely different. The ominous silence was replaced by the bustle and chatter of a government office in full work mode. People streamed in and out of the waiting area, dropping off papers, picking up files, and barking orders. Couriers arrived with envelopes. Phones rang incessantly. A group of men ran down the hallway, their police radios crackling. It looked no scarier than a DMV or county clerk's office.

Leslie and I waited on the same hard wooden bench where we'd been stuck the previous night. Despite our lack of sleep, we were wide-awake. I strained my ears for any mention of Information Unlimited, but heard nothing. Seeing how busy the office was, and how preoccupied with other operations, was reassuring. Surely we were insignificant in the bigger scheme of things.

As the morning dragged on, anxiety was replaced by boredom. Eventually a young Dominican in slacks and a button-down shirt approached us and introduced himself as Delgado, a lawyer for the Policia Nacional. "Leslie Tomei," he said, "Señor Vargas is waiting for you downstairs."

Leslie's face flushed with relief as he called a guard over to escort her out of the building. I was getting to my feet in anticipation of being released also, when Delgado shook his head.

"Marisa Lankester, you are to come with me." Panic gripped me. I did me best to keep my voice neutral, unconcerned.

"I was told I would also be released, Mr. Delgado."

"The FBI is waiting to interview you."

My mouth suddenly went dry. Mustering the best smile I could, I told Leslie that I would be home soon. We walked together in tense silence until the corridor split in two. We hugged. Then Leslie and her guard turned left—toward freedom—and Delgado and I turned in the opposite direction.

"I'm confused, Mr. Delgado," I said as we walked on. "I was led to believe that the FBI has no jurisdiction in the Dominican Republic."

"Jurisdiction?" he said, with a trace of bitterness in his voice. "The FBI doesn't need jurisdiction. They are the most powerful agency in the world. If they want something, they get it."

My heart sank. The ominous feeling in my gut deepened when we came to a stop outside Colonel Rivera's door. Delgado rapped on it and we were told to enter. I was bracing myself for a room full of federal agents. Instead I found just Colonel Rivera and General Hernandez. Delgado saluted them and left.

"Have a seat," Rivera said. He leaned back in his chair, his medals gleaming. Hernandez was once again lurking behind him, Ray-Bans hiding his diseased eyes. My heart froze when I saw a tape recorder and a familiar yellow ticket in front of me.

Our office had been raided before opening hours, so technically all of the tapes should have been blank. Tapes were collected at the end of each workday and stored at another location. That way, if Information Unlimited burned to the ground, we could duplicate all of the tickets. Seeing a claim ticket, I knew that had to mean the corresponding tape was in the recorder. My heart began to pound in earnest. Somehow the police had managed to open Tony's safe, where claims were stored. This was evidence of the most damning kind.

Rivera's steely eyes bored into mine. Without breaking his gaze he pressed the play button. I heard my voice fill the room. "RB," it said.

"7802," said a player. "What do you have on the Steelers?"

"Four and a half."

"Give me the dog for ten."

"7802, I've got San Fran plus four and half for ten dimes."

The tape went on for several minutes in a similar vein, my voice reading the lines and taking one bet after another. I didn't try to deny that the voice was mine, and the colonel didn't ask me to. In less than five minutes all of those denials of being involved with Information Unlimited were rendered useless. Rivera clicked the tape off.

I tried another tack. "Gambling is legal in the Dominican Republic, isn't it?"

Rivera ignored the question. A cold smile spread across his face. "What is the value of ten dimes?" he asked.

I looked between Colonel Rivera and the still-expressionless General Hernandez. Ignoring the question for the moment, I began to unknot the sweater tied around my waist. The air-conditioning in the office was on full blast and I was freezing.

I had one arm in my cardigan when Hernandez walked over and wrenched it off me. The viciousness of his anger shocked me. He flung the sweater into the corner before calmly returning to lean against the wall once more. My hands began to tremble.

"Ten thousand dollars," I admitted. Both men barely suppressed their triumph at hearing this. Rivera leaned closer to me.

"Edwin Walker. He worked for Information Unlimited?"

"No. He was our contact at Codetel. At least before he was fired."

Clearly Hernandez and Rivera knew Walker from the sting operation that netted their department our hundred and eighty thousand U.S. dollars. The fact that the money went unclaimed had made it evident to the officers just how lucrative Information Unlimited's business must be. The questions that followed concerned the day-to-day business at Information Unlimited, focusing in particular on how we managed the money.

The interrogation continued until we heard voices in the hallway outside. Rivera stopped talking mid-sentence, and Hernandez sprang into action. With unexpected strength and speed he dove across the room, pulled me from my chair, and dragged me into a corner. He clamped his hand over my mouth and held me there while Rivera casually went to the door to answer the knock that followed.

I realized then that this interview was happening off the record. Clearly, Rivera and Hernandez were exploring how they could profit from allowing the company to continue operating. When Rivera answered the door, I recognized Agent Peterson's voice as the colonel greeted the FBI agents outside. I was only a few feet away, but they had no clue. Rivera casually flipped off the light and closed the door behind him, leaving Hernandez and me shrouded in darkness. The general kept me pinned to the wall until the men's voices had disappeared down the corridor.

Hernandez put his lips to my ear. "Not one word," he said before removing his hand from my mouth. He took me by the arm and led me from the dark office. We headed in the opposite direction from Rivera and the federal agents, down a series of hallways to a key pass–operated elevator. We descended three floors in silence.

Exiting the elevator, we walked briskly down another series of hallways until we came to a vast room. The doors and hallways outside were heavily guarded, as was the elaborate marble and wrought-iron staircase leading to a second floor. It was a chaotic scene. In the center of the room, two women sat behind a desk doing their best to accommodate a bustling crowd of people all vying for their attention. Hernandez led me past them toward a set of heavy doors. Unexpectedly, we stepped outside into the blinding sunshine. I raised my hand to shield my eyes and realized that the building was the same one I'd seen in the movie *Havana*. Lena Olin had walked down these very same stairs, having just been tortured there, to find Robert Redford waiting patiently for her at the bottom.

Sadly, I found Horacio waiting for me. He was leaning against a wall next to Tony's parked Jeep. I noticed, with growing irritation, that he was not only using Tony's car but he was also cradling his cell phone.

He hurried eagerly over to Hernandez.

"Compadre!" he said.

Hernandez barely acknowledged him. "Take her home," he said, releasing my arm.

■

"LESLIE IS AT YOUR apartment," Horacio said as we approached my building. "The two of you will have to organize getting food to the clerks until I can get them released."

"Why?"

"This isn't America," he sniffed. "In the Dominican Republic, the prisoners' families are responsible for taking care of them."

"Fine." I got out of the car without another word.

"Marisa!"

I stopped and turned. "Don't try to leave your apartment and don't make any phone calls," he said. "Your line is tapped." Horacio lowered his sunglasses and looked at me over the rim. "Stay inside until you hear from me."

"So how am I supposed to get food to the clerks?"

"You'll figure it out."

I walked away, muttering under my breath. Lopez, our day guard, pulled back the gate to let me in.

My next-door neighbor greeted me gaily on the way to her chauffeur-driven car, just as she would on any other day. The gardener was tending the plants in the courtyard—someone else was mopping the marble staircase—everything seemed blissfully normal. I climbed the steps to my apartment and rang the bell. Rosa's face flooded with relief as she opened the door. Justine rushed into my arms. *"Café, por favor,"* I begged Rosa, hoping that my pounding headache would ease once I had a cup.

"The phones are tapped," Leslie told me, two coffees later. "You can practically hear people breathing on the other end." Justine was sitting on my lap while Leslie and I worked on a shopping list for dinner. "Did Horacio give you any idea how long the guys will be locked up?"

"Nope."

"He told me to stay here until we heard from him," she said with a wry grin.

"That's what he told me too." I tossed her a baseball cap. "Let's get going."

Leslie followed me downstairs and we climbed into my Daihatsu. Lopez opened the gate and I pulled out, inching forward to check for oncoming traffic. Suddenly, with a screech of brakes, a car pulled up in front of me, cutting us off.

"What the hell?"

A man jumped out and ran over to the driver's side, pulling my door open. I recognized him straightaway. I'd seen him in the secret police headquarters.

"Back up!" he yelled. Lopez came running through the gate, ready to come to my aid. He hadn't taken more than three steps when a second officer jumped out of the car and pointed his gun at the horrified security guard.

"Okay, okay!" I slowly backed up.

The man followed me into the courtyard. He opened he door again and said, *"Dame la llave!"* I pretended not to understand.

"Give him the fucking keys!" Leslie cried, and I reluctantly handed them over.

He shook his head at me as he pocketed them. "You cannot leave," he said simply, before turning and walking away.

Lopez closed the gate again, looking shaken and confused. "I thought they didn't know where you lived," Leslie moaned.

"They didn't. That bastard Horacio led them straight here!"

We were prisoners now. Everything outside the gate was off limits. The thought put ice in my belly. Yesterday, when General Hernandez took my passport, I had been alarmed by the idea that I was no longer free to leave the country. Now I was no longer free to leave my apartment.

27

NINE LONG DAYS HAD passed since the raid, and Rosa, Leslie, and I were trapped in a monotonous cycle of cooking and cleaning as we struggled to feed our clerks. The three of us jostled for space in the kitchen, churning out pasta and rice dishes, sandwiches and desserts for twenty-five men. The place was a mess. The floor was strewn with bags of food and cartons of vegetables. The cupboards were overflowing. Every inch of space in the refrigerator was packed with food, every bit of counter space taken.

"We need to get more organized," I said, rummaging around in the chaos for a packet of lasagna noodles.

Leslie swore, "Shit!" and dropped the knife. She'd cut herself dicing onions. She lifted the bleeding finger to her mouth and hissed, "I *hate* this!" She stormed off to find a Band-Aid.

Rosa took over slicing the onions while I checked on the cakes. As I opened the oven door, the smell of warm chocolate spilled into the room, colliding with the aroma of garlic and butter. It was stifling in the kitchen. All four burners were on, and not even a hint of a breeze was coming through the window.

Leslie was taking our confinement the hardest. Her life outside the office consisted of dressing up, going out to dinner, then dancing into the early hours. Now she was trapped in an apartment and forced into a seemingly neverending routine of thankless domesticity. She returned to the kitchen, freshly bandaged, and asked the same question she asked every day.

"How much longer do we have to do this?"

But I didn't know the answer. All I knew was that the police were stationed outside the gate twenty-four hours a day. The phones were tapped, and if we didn't provide food, the clerks wouldn't eat.

Two days after the bust, Information Unlimited was front-page news. *Listin Diario* and *El Sieglo* both reported that Information Unlimited had been smuggling arms into the country and drugs into the United States, using a *banca*—a gambling establishment—as a front. These scandalous fabrications had clearly originated with the FBI, and had the desired effect; the Dominican authorities had no option but to close us down.

Our neighbors quickly made the connection between the news reports and the presence of plainclothes officers outside the gate. Their once-cheerful greetings ceased, and their children no longer came to play with Justine. Soon I stopped bringing her downstairs to ride her tricycle—the silent, downcast looks from my neighbors became too much for me to bear. I couldn't blame them. They were scared. The secret police were notorious for taking in everyone associated with a criminal for questioning. Even acknowledging us threatened their safety.

Leslie began angrily chopping onions again. "It's been over a week already." She slammed the knife down. "I thought Tony was supposed to come back with a lawyer."

"He will!" I snapped. "I'm sure he's doing everything he can."

Actually, I had no clue what had happened to Tony. He was supposed to return after his meeting with Ruth Gordon, but I hadn't heard from him since. I couldn't call anyone, not with the secret police eavesdropping on every conversation. I was desperately worried.

"Do you even know if he's on the island?"

"I have no idea where he is, Leslie. None at all."

Feeding twenty-five men three times a day was turning out to be incredibly expensive. Rosa was taking several taxi trips a day to pick up groceries and supplies, and we had already gone through three propane tanks for the stove, plus gallons of gas for the generator. Then we had to pay for the daily taxi runs to the prison to deliver the food. The drivers were inflating their fares to compensate for the risk of associating with us. The stack of cash in the safe was dwindling rapidly.

That night, the phone rang for the first time since this ordeal began. I was frozen. Should I answer it? The secret police would be listening in. Leslie and Rosa appeared at my side as the phone continued to ring. "Whoever it is knows we're here," Leslie said.

I tentatively raised the receiver to my ear.

"Get ready for company!" Tony blurted out. The line went dead.

Leslie was about to ask who it was, but I shushed her. The unmistakable sound of approaching footsteps was faint but grew steadily louder. I had left the front door wide open to cool down the apartment, so all that separated us from whoever was approaching was the iron gate. Rosa bolted, locking herself in Justine's room. Leslie gripped my arm. One by one, General Hernandez, Colonel Rivera, Delgado the lawyer, and two other officers appeared at the gate. All were in uniform, and all were armed.

As Rivera tried the handle of the gate, the color drained from Leslie's face. More people were stomping up the stairs. The next person who came into view was Horacio Vargas. Why had he brought them here? I was furious. The colonel tried the handle again. I didn't budge.

"Open the door!" I heard Tony's voice say, then he appeared at the gate. I tried to read his expression, but I couldn't. It was simply a mask of exhaustion. Cautiously, I stepped forward and unlocked it.

Tony gave me a weak smile. Up close, he looked haggard. I would later learn that Tony had returned to the island without our lawyer, Harold Fisher, who'd refused to have anything to do with the spiraling mess in the Dominican Republic. Instead Horacio had taken Tony to meet with General Hernandez, who promised to negotiate the release of the clerks—for a price. Tony had to return to the United States for more money.

The men filed in and followed Tony to the terrace. Leslie and I hung back, but Rivera beckoned us to join them. Tony was busily arranging chairs around one of the coffee tables outside. When he was done, he leaned over the balcony and called to Pino, floated a hundred-peso bill down to him, and sent him to the *colmado* for beers.

Tony did his best to play the genial host. It was a strange scene. Belying the forced smiles was a heavy undercurrent of tension. He made small talk in English, but few of his guests understood what he was saying. When Pino returned with the beers, Rivera suggested that Tony should arrange for something for them to eat. Horacio used Tony's cell phone to call the Chinese restaurant at the Hotel Embajador.

Delgado said in Spanish, "It is a pity that your *banca* is not licensed." Horacio translated for Tony, who cursed Gustavo for this pivotal blunder. Tony studiously avoided my gaze, no doubt aware of the I-told-you-so expression I was wearing. "Normally this situation would be resolved with a simple fine. However, this oversight, coupled with the fact that many of your employees are here on tourist visas . . . and some have criminal records . . . " Delgado gave a shrug of the shoulders. "The FBI is insisting that we deport them."

"I had a team of lawyers working with me on this, and they all assured me that the FBI has no jurisdiction here."

"Except when drugs or murder are involved," Delgado replied.

"I'm not involved with either, so how can you and how can they justify raiding my office?"

"When the FBI informed us that LoBue was dealing in weapons

and drugs, we agreed to cooperate. Our investigation into LoBue's operation led us to your office at Salvador Sturla."

Tony leaned forward in his chair. "I have no knowledge of Sonny LoBue, or anyone involved with him," he insisted.

I recalled Sonny's warning again, but knew better than to mention it now.

"Local phone records linked his office to yours."

Hernandez leaned back with a little smile after dropping this bombshell. Tony was just as baffled by this revelation as I was. Players accessed us from the States via our 1-800 numbers. We did have a local phone number, but only a handful of people knew it.

Tony sent Pino to get another round of beers, and the atmosphere began to lighten up. At least it seemed that we were all on the same side.

"Our objective is to make a clear separation between your operation and LoBue's," Rivera continued. "We found no drugs or weapons at your establishment, and it is clear now that we were deceived by the FBI. LoBue and some of his men are facing serious charges in San Francisco, and will be deported as soon as we complete our investigation. We can release your men once the FBI has left the island."

While Tony listened intently, the colonel laid out the new scheme. Information Unlimited would reopen . . . under Colonel Rivera's direction. Further inquiries by the FBI would be dealt with by General Hernandez, who—like the other officers present—would be generously compensated for his cooperation. Horacio would find a new office space, far from our current location in the upper-middle-class enclave of Esanche Naco, and closer to Avenida 30 de Marzo, an area crammed with *bancas*. In addition, Horacio would apply to the Ministry of Sports for a standard gambling license, which Gustavo Flores had failed to do.

Tony's cell phone rang. The food was ready for pickup. He took a thousand-peso bill from his wallet and handed it to Horacio.

As Horacio stood to leave, General Hernandez casually suggested that Tony go along to help him. My breath caught in my throat. Tony did not take orders from anyone. He gave orders; he had people run errands for *him*. The two men locked eyes. An uneasy silence fell over the balcony. I knew that Tony would never willingly leave Leslie and me alone with the secret police. When Tony stood up and followed Horacio outside, it became frighteningly clear who was calling the shots now.

No one said a word after they left. The only sound came from Hernandez's creaking chair as he rocked back and forth. Then he leaned forward and placed one of his empty beer bottles on the coffee table. He laid it on its side and then flicked it into a spin. It spun around twice and stopped with the bottleneck pointing at Rivera. Hernandez leaned forward and spun the bottle again. It slowed to a stop between Delgado and the other officer. He spun it once more, and it slowly came to rest pointing at Leslie. The men snickered.

Hernandez grinned at Leslie. Without breaking eye contact with her, he reached for the bottle again and turned it until it pointed directly at me. I stood up abruptly, disgusted by his attempts to intimidate us with a juvenile game of spin-the-bottle. I marched to the kitchen, ignoring his calls for me to come back and sit down. Tony and Horacio would be back shortly, I told myself. The Embajador was only minutes away.

I took a handful of knives and forks and dumped them on a tray. As I reached for the plates, I sensed movement behind me. I knew without looking that it was Hernandez. My breath became shallow as I counted out napkins and plates, desperately trying to appear absorbed in what I was doing. I sensed him slowly coming around the counter, creeping toward me, blocking my means of escape like some predatory animal.

"How is your daughter?" he purred, moving ever nearer. The space between us was closing fast and I backed into the corner, trying to conceal my alarm. He plucked a lock of hair from my shoulders and began to roll it playfully between his fingers. I winced, repulsed by his proximity. I could smell his breath, feel the heat from his body. I wanted to push him away, but my instincts told me not to. Laughter drifted in from the balcony as Hernandez went on toying with my hair.

Floating up the stairway was Tony's voice. He was chatting to Horacio. There was a terrible, forced brightness to his conversation, as if he was at great pains to make it clear that picking up the food had been no big deal. I heard the metal gate open. Surely Hernandez would back off now. The smell of Chinese food wafted through the apartment. I heard Tony and Horacio deposit the food on the balcony and then Tony asked, over the commotion, where I was.

Hernandez pinned me against the counter and brought his face toward mine. I turned my head and tried to push him away, but he had a thick strand of my hair in his hand and he used it to pull my face toward his. The gold cross around his neck swung toward me as he pulled me closer.

Tony was walking towards the kitchen. He would kill the general with his bare hands when he saw what was happening. Then, just as Tony was rounding the corner, Hernandez stepped away from me, scooped the tray from the counter, and calmly walked past him toward the terrace.

"What's wrong, babe?" Tony gave me a long, hard look as I struggled to control my emotions. "Was he bothering you?" he demanded, raising his voice. "Was that son of a bitch bothering you?" When I didn't answer he hissed, "I'll blow a hole in his fucking head!" He stormed out of the kitchen and toward our bedroom, heading for the safe where my gun was.

I ran after Tony, pleading with him to stop. "Nothing's wrong. I'm just tired." I knew the five heavily armed senior officers of the Policia Nacional wouldn't deter Tony if he thought one of them was bothering me. He would calmly step outside and start emptying bullets into them, starting with Hernandez. He would probably manage to shoot two or three of them before getting shot himself. Leslie and I would end up in prison, where we would doubtless be gang-raped by the rest of the Dominican police force.

"Don't!" I begged, tugging his arm, trying to pry his fingers from the dial. "Please!" I threw my arms around him, but his body was rigid, his face determined. He pushed me away and continued twirling the dial on the safe. I heard the group outside, laughing at a shared joke, and Horacio's voice calling for us.

"Think about Justine! Think about what will happen to her!"

This finally got through to him. He stopped, took a deep breath. "If any of them even tries to lay a finger on you, they're dead."

When we returned to the balcony, the officers were feeding like pigs at a trough, plates piled high, shoving down the food Tony had bought. Rivera smacked his greasy lips on a piece of duck. My stomach was in knots, and I could only push the food around on my plate. As Tony nursed a beer, I could sense his dangerous anger simmering just beneath the surface. He was used to being in charge. His resentment at this new arrangement was palpable.

"There are local police legitimately working with the FBI, and they will continue to cooperate with them as long as they are here," Hernandez warned. "That cannot be helped. As long as the FBI is on the island, our people will remain outside your door"— he paused to look at Leslie and me—"for your protection."

Hernandez then addressed Tony. "Under the circumstances, it is too dangerous for you to remain in the city. We cannot help you if you are detained by the FBI."

"I know someplace safe you can stay," Horacio interjected eagerly.

Hernandez nodded his approval. "Good. We will notify you when the FBI has left the island." The general raised his beer to Tony, smiled warmly and cheerfully toasted his new "compadre." Hernandez radioed the car outside and was given the all-clear to leave.

Tony met my eye and I saw the apprehension in his face. He squeezed my hand but said nothing as he followed the others out. I locked the gate behind them, and Leslie and I breathed a sigh of relief.

We went back outside to the balcony to clean up. "Why did they come here?" Leslie pondered aloud.

I shrugged. At first I'd blamed Horacio, but now I suspected that Hernandez had orchestrated the meeting. I had a feeling that Tony hadn't known they were coming, which would explain his hurried warning.

We washed and dried the dishes and tidied up until no trace of the officers remained. "Leslie," I said, giving the counter a final wipe, "I need a favor."

"Anything."

I took a pair of kitchen scissors out of a drawer. "You said you'd been a hairdresser back home," I said, handing them to her. She nodded. "Will you cut my hair?"

28

JUSTINE PEDALED PAST US at high speed on her tricycle through the dining room and living room and toward the balcony, disappearing through one of the French doors and reappearing through the other. She whizzed past the kitchen and began the second leg of her journey, heading toward my bedroom, where she turned around and started towards us again. She repeated each lap with an expression of intense concentration, and pedaled on unendingly.

I wistfully eyed her newly cropped hair. She had woken up, seen my pixie cut, and insisted on having hers done the same way, despite our best efforts to dissuade her. So once again Leslie had deftly wielded the kitchen scissors, and Justine's beautiful red curls had dropped to the floor.

Her determined little expression suddenly changed. Behind the locked iron gate was a stranger with a police radio in his hand and a gun tucked into his belt. He was one of several men who passed his days parked outside the property. "You must come with me. *Ahora mismo,*" he said to me curtly, in a voice that forbade contradiction.

"*Momento,*" I pleaded, taking a step toward the bedroom to change out of the shorts I was wearing.

"Now!"

Justine abandoned her tricycle and flung herself against me. Rosa hurried over to comfort her. I tried to assure them that I would be back soon, but my voice quavered, and Justine burst into tears. Rosa pried her away so I could untie my apron and grab my flip-flops. I opened the gate with trembling hands and followed the policeman downstairs.

The usual vendors were working the intersections, flogging fruits and vegetables. A deaf and mute beggar grinned, recognizing me. I always slipped him some pesos, but today I stared straight ahead. Apart from the fact that I had no change, I was consumed with dread. What was awaiting me this time at the offices of the secret police?

When the car passed the main station, I nervously asked the driver where we were going. My question was ignored. Soon we pulled up in front of an imposing building, patrolled by uniformed guards. Inscribed on the top were the words: *Palacio de Justicia.* I was being brought to the courthouse on a Sunday evening. We exited the car, and I uneasily followed the officers up a broad marble staircase.

This once-grand building was now in a state of significant disrepair. I followed the officers out to a dilapidated garden courtyard lined with marble benches. Along the perimeter were a series of vacant offices. The men led me down a long corridor toward a crowded cell at the far end of the building. As we approached, I realized with horror that the cell's occupants were female.

It was a scene out of the Middle Ages. Sick, desperate women filled every inch of the cell's filthy concrete floor. Some were lying on the bare cement amongst piles of empty bottles, plastic bags, and discarded clothing. Most were sitting with their backs against the walls, staring blankly at us as we approached.

I stopped abruptly. The idea that I was about to be tossed into this awful pen froze me in my tracks. The police urged me forward. I continued to walk toward the cell, each step feeling heavier than the last. Then at the final moment the officers made a left. Instead of unlocking the cell and ordering me inside, they led me past it.

I was brought to another cell instead. This one was full of men. A grimy, bedraggled figure was leaning against the bars, his head drooping, with dirty, unkempt hair covering his face. As he heard us approach, he looked up. It was Danny.

His jaw dropped when he saw me. "Jesus Christ!" He leapt to his feet and pressed his face against the bars. "RB?"

As I stared back in shock, two more figures hurried out of the shadows behind him and shuffled toward the bars. I realized they were Carmine and Roger. "What are you doing here?"

I hardly recognized my workmates. Carmine and Roger both had scraggly beards and were utterly disheveled. The rest of the clerks quickly followed, separating themselves from the other prisoners and crowding around the bars. Their clothes were filthy and hung from their bodies. An overpowering stench of body odor wafted out of the cell. I could not believe the conditions they were being held in. What had happened to the clean clothes I sent them? And to the shampoo, soap, and razors?

"We were transferred here a few days ago," Danny said. "They told us we were going to be fined and released. But we haven't heard anything since."

"But I—I sent soap and clothes, and underwear—"

"Nobody's given us anything."

"What about food?"

Carmine, looking ill and shriveled up without his dentures, muttered, "We're getting a little . . . "

I felt like screaming. I thought of Rosa, Leslie, and myself slaving away in that hot kitchen day after day, sending in huge parcels of food—all so we could feed a bunch of corrupt guards and their families. All our work, for nothing. All our money wasted.

My heart broke to think that the guys were being held under such deplorable conditions. They must have felt totally abandoned.

"When are we getting out?" Danny asked, his voice trembling with desperation.

"Soon! Tony's working with the local police. We've been sending you everything you'd need! I can't believe this—none of it got to you? Nothing at all?"

"You have to include money for the guards." Roger, who was always so meticulous about his appearance, now looked like one of the beggars who swarmed the cars on Maximo Gomez. "If you don't include the money, they won't pass it on to us."

My eyes darted around the desperate faces pressed up against the bars. "Where's Remo?"

Roger shook his head sadly. "Nobody knows. He freaked out when he saw the cells at the main police station. I guess he's claustrophobic. It took four guards to take him down. He only stopped struggling after the injection—"

"Injection?"

"Big fucking needle, right through his pants," Carmine continued. "He went down like a stone, and they dragged him off. We haven't seen him since."

The officers, having decided I'd seen enough, took me by the arm and started to drag me away from the bars. Carmine reached out with shaking fingers and grabbed my hand. I could feel layers of grease and dirt on his skin.

"Please," he begged, "you got to get us out. We're going crazy in here!"

The officers led me back to their car. My fear was fading rapidly. Instead, I was filling up with a righteous fury. How could they get away with this blatant abuse of power? Our clerks were being brutally persecuted, and for what? And Remo? He had done nothing to warrant this cruel fate. As we drove away, the officers chatted casually in the front, completely unaffected by the horror we had just witnessed.

I knew where we were heading now. A guard opened the gate and we pulled into the awful dusty courtyard at the main police station. They parked next to Roger's impounded Cherokee. The men led me up the stairs, through a maze of corridors and to a small waiting area outside an office. One of the men knocked on the door. I heard the unmistakable sound of General Hernandez's voice on the other side.

"*Adelante!*"

He was leaning back in his chair, chatting casually on the phone, feet up on the desk. Dressed in his street clothes, he had the air of a man without a worry in the world. He indicated to a chair and I sat down. Hernandez waved the officers away, leaving me alone with him.

Hernandez ignored me and continued to chat. His office was bigger and better furnished than that of his colleague, Colonel Rivera. Several framed diplomas hung next to a well-stocked bookcase; a set of crystal glasses and several bottles of expensive liquor stood on a polished mahogany cabinet behind his leather chair. Above that was a matching shelf with two FBI baseball caps on it.

I couldn't decide whom I hated more—the FBI, with their lies and trumped-up charges, or the Dominican police, who were working the situation to their own advantage with complete disregard to the human cost. I watched with mounting anger as Hernandez sipped his coffee and chuckled into the phone at some amusing anecdote.

I laid into him before the receiver was even fully down. "Your men have been stealing thousands of pesos of supplies and food from us!" I spat. "Our cook, Remo Grayson, was beaten and drugged by your men!" His complete lack of reaction only served to egg me on. I reeled off the catalogue of injustices I had witnessed, sparing no detail. I finished with what was supposed to be my coup de grace. "I will get the American Embassy involved if this situation does not improve . . . immediately!"

The general took his feet off his desk, opened a drawer and pulled out a tape recorder. He placed it on the desk between us and pressed play. The room filled with the familiar sound of me taking bets. Was he trying to remind me of my involvement in the operation, or that I could be sharing the same fate as my colleagues?

Regardless, my anger quickly evaporated and once again, fear took its place.

Hernandez clicked off the machine. "One of your friends must have told the FBI that you work for Information Unlimited, because they are adamant about interviewing you," he said smoothly. "I assured them that you are only a model, but they still insist on seeing you."

Suddenly my chest felt tight. He stood up and poured two glasses of Johnny Walker Black Label, placing one in front of me. "Prisons are difficult places for women in the Dominican Republic, especially foreign women," he said gravely. "They are repeatedly raped, and even forced into prostitution. Once the guards have tired of them, they are taken to the male prisoners, and offered to the highest bidder. I'm astonished that the FBI is so anxious to have you detained, when they know how difficult it would be for you to prove your innocence under our laws."

I stared at him dumbly. He was threatening me with gang rape. Hernandez removed the cassette from the recorder. "Know your friends, Marisa. Keep them close," he said, dangling the incriminating tape in front of me. "I have kept this from the FBI. Your anger should be directed at them, not at me. They are responsible for the incarceration of your friends."

He slid the tape into a drawer and produced another. A jarringly cheerful and upbeat merengue song filled the room. Walking around his desk to my chair, he pulled me to my feet. I could smell his cologne, heavy and sweet. He trailed his fingers across the nape of my neck.

"I like your hair short," he said. "It shows off your beautiful blue eyes."

I felt my body go rigid. One of the general's hands slipped to the base of my back and he pulled me closer. He slid his other hand into mine as if initiating a dance. He began to swivel his hips to the music, while I stood limply opposite him. I felt his body moving against mine while I just stood there, acutely conscious of the threat that hung in the air.

"Why so sad?" he asked gaily. "I thought it would make you happy to see your friends." The song ended and he let go of me abruptly and took a seat on the edge of his desk. I slid limply into the chair. Hernandez reached for the phone and called for a guard.

"It's Sunday night," he said. "You should be home with your daughter."

■

"LESLIE'S GONE," ROSA SAID as soon as I walked in the door. She had taken her chance, fleeing as soon as the secret police had driven off with me. Rosa had given her some money. Of course I was sad. I would miss Leslie terribly, but it was the right thing for her to do. Now that she was free, perhaps she might find a way to help us.

Rosa and I sank back into our tiring routine, but instead of elaborate meals we stuck to simple sandwiches, sent along with generous "tips" for the guards. On January 19, I baked a cake for Danny, as I always did for the clerks on their birthdays. That evening I sent along thirty slices of chocolate cake to the Palacio de Justicia—plenty for the guards and our clerks—with enough money to ensure it got through.

I was still putting things away in the kitchen when the doorbell rang. I glanced at the clock. It was almost eleven at night, and I had no intention of answering it. Rosa had gone to bed long ago, and I was exhausted. The bell rang again. And again. I crept to the balcony and peered over the edge to the courtyard below.

I couldn't believe what I saw. Roger's red Cherokee was parked downstairs next to my Daihatsu. They'd let him go. I ran to the door, elated at this unexpected breakthrough. I wrenched open the door and my stomach flipped.

General Hernandez was standing on the other side of the gate. "Open up."

I remained rooted to the spot, paralyzed with fear. He took his gun out of its holster and pointed it at me through the wrought-iron bars.

"Open the door, Marisa."

29

THE MARBLE FLOOR FELT cool against the side of my face and on my bare legs and arms. I focused on the tiny flecks of dust I could see on the ground, amazed that I could distinguish individual grains from each other.

I felt a drop of sweat hit my cheek. Revolted, I craned my neck as far away as I could. Above me Hernandez was moving rhythmically, thrusting into me with a kind of detached aggression. His breath came in short, rasping gasps.

How long had he known that he was going to rape me? I thought of how he had sent Tony away "for his own protection." That must have been a part of his scheme.

He grunted and I felt his body relax. His full weight pinned me down until he pushed himself away. I heard the wet slap of rubber as he pulled the condom off his penis and tossed it to the floor. I heard rustling sounds as he adjusted his clothing, then his footsteps walking away . . . the click of the door, the squeak of the gate.

■

THE DOORBELL RANG AGAIN, several nights later. I had convinced myself that Hernandez would not come back. *No*, I thought, *I can't go through it again. I've learned my lesson.* My hands began to tremble uncontrollably. When I didn't answer the door, he began to tap on the gate with his gun.

Hernandez had the power to banish me to prison with a snap of his fingers. In there, my situation would be infinitely worse. He would separate me from Justine without a moment's hesitation.

I learned to cope. I forced my mind to drift, and let my eyes wander. As I lay pinned to the floor on one of those awful nights, I spotted an intricate spider's web in the corner and made a mental note to sweep it away in the morning.

Later, as I stood under an ice-cold shower, trying to scrub all traces of him from me, I recalled the first time I had encountered Hernandez. I remembered the casual way he had plucked plantains from Colonel Rivera's plate without asking. Now he was driving around Santo Domingo in a Jeep that didn't belong to him. Clearly, the general was used to having what he wanted. So was he punishing me? Or was he just doing as he pleased because he could get away with it?

Rosa knew nothing of the general's late-night visits. I suppose it was odd that she didn't notice anything was wrong, or seemed different about me. But then again, we were working endless hours full of stress and sadness. Forced smiles had long been necessary, so as not to cause Justine any more upset. I had worn this mask for weeks, so why should she realize it was hiding some fresh trauma? Anyway, I was glad not to talk about it. I was deeply humiliated by what was happening to me. Having someone else know would only have compounded the profound shame I felt. I was grateful for the continuous cycle of preparing meals for the clerks, cleaning up, and caring for Justine. During the day, at least, I had little time to dwell on what was lying in wait for me when the sun went down.

■

MY RESIGNATION TO MY situation was such that when the doorbell rang one afternoon, I simply untied my apron, grabbed my shoes and walked to the door. I expected that the police were coming to take me somewhere, and I knew that protesting was pointless. To my surprise, Domingo, the company driver, was standing at the gate.

"Hello, lady," he said cheerfully. He handed me a plastic bag full of pesos and a scribbled note from Tony. Domingo would be at my beck and call so long as the clerks remained in jail.

Not being at the mercy of taxi drivers was a relief, and we needed the extra pair of hands to help us during the day. Domingo lightened the gloomy atmosphere with his happy-go-lucky demeanor. He was overjoyed to have a job again, and an opportunity to practice his rudimentary English. Via Domingo I learned that the clerks had been moved back to the main police station from the Palacio de Justicia. He didn't know the reason for the transfer, but assured me that they were more comfortable there. He told me that they were being detained in a "very roomy" cell.

"Only *Americanos* there," he said.

"And Remo?"

Domingo shook his head. "No more Remo," he said, and I felt as though my heart would split in two.

With a driver, unlimited funds, and a van at our disposal, we were able to ensure that the clerks had everything they needed. We sent gallons of drinking water, mats, pillows, clothing, cigarettes, and toiletries. We did their laundry and took requests for meals. They asked for electric fans, books, magazines, and alcohol. One evening Domingo pulled me aside and said that some of the clerks were asking for prostitutes. "You give Domingo pesos . . . Domingo get lady for Americans."

"No—no way!" I was horrified. He was reminding me of the threat I felt hanging over my own head.

I managed to get through most days by pretending that everything was fine. As soon as the sun set, however, my anxiety would build. By the time Justine and Rosa turned in for bed, my chest felt so tight I could hardly breathe. It was worse during the frequent blackouts. Sitting alone in the stifling darkness, listening for the general's footsteps coming up the staircase, I felt like I was counting down the minutes to my own execution.

I tried to tell myself I was being dramatic. What was the big deal? Someone was fucking me against my will—so what? How many times had Tony come home and forced himself on me when he was drunk? I would berate myself—*Stop being so melodramatic! Grow up! Get over it! Don't be such a goddamned baby.*

In my darker moments, the word "whore" would bubble up from the depths of my psyche. I knew that the only reason the clerks had been moved, the only reason that they were getting everything we sent to them, was because of Hernandez. How could it be rape if I was getting something in exchange?

Whore. Whore. Whore.

One night after Hernandez left, I unplugged the TV and VCR. I put every movie we owned into a bag and sent Domingo to take the items to our imprisoned clerks. The voice in my head piped up again. *See? You're a whore.*

At times I even felt that I owed Hernandez something. That I should be grateful to him. After all, he was withholding evidence from the FBI. Sometimes I wondered if things would have gone differently if I'd treated him with more respect in the beginning. The thoughts made my head spin. Sometimes I'd be doing something ordinary, like making a sandwich or folding Justine's clothes, and I'd stop—paralyzed by a fury so intense it made me shake. How could this be happening to me?

■

"REMO! REMO!"

I put down the knife I was holding. Justine was excitedly tugging my apron and pointing toward the door. It couldn't be Remo, but I smiled indulgently and followed her anyway. And there he was.

I pulled him inside and threw my arms around him in a crushing hug. "I didn't know if you were alive or dead!" I whispered, holding him tight.

Remo stepped back and looked at me, aghast. "What happened to your hair?" He eyed me up and down. "Jesus Christ, you're skinny."

I ignored his remarks. "How did you get past the police?"

Remo pulled a laminated card out of his pocket and handed it to me. "Take a look."

It was the business card of the *sub-jefe* of the Policia Nacional, someone named Sanchez-Castillo. "I don't understand."

"He's tipped to be the next chief of police. He was educated and trained in the States, and he's a reformer. This guy is determined to root out corruption in the police force."

"I don't get it."

"Turn it over."

On the reverse side it said in neat, typed letters: *The bearer of this card, Remo M. Grayson, is hereby granted protection under the highest military and police authority.* It was stamped, dated, and personally signed by Sanchez-Castillo.

Remo grinned. "I'm practically bulletproof. I showed it to the cops downstairs and they saluted me."

"But the last I heard, you were fighting a bunch of guards and had to be sedated. What happened to you? How did you get out?"

Remo sighed heavily and took a seat in the dining room. "I woke up in a cell with a bunch of Dominicans. Two days later, the guards came for me. I thought they were taking me back to the clerks, but they took me to the main building instead."

"To the secret police?"

"No. To a big comfortable room where I heard my boss, Demetrio, laughing with someone in the adjoining office.

"The next thing I knew, the fourth-most powerful man in the country was apologizing to me for everything I went through." Noting the confused look on my face, Remo pressed on. "Demetrio figured something was wrong when I didn't show up at

Atlántico. I've always been reliable. When he read the newspapers, he put two and two together. He knew I wasn't involved in a drug-and-gun-smuggling operation. He guessed that I was the wrong nationality, in the wrong place, at the wrong time. He wasn't happy to find out that I'd been moonlighting, but that's hardly a crime." Once he'd recounted his story, he asked if I knew what was found in Tony's safe.

"Yeah." I recalled my last visit to Hernandez's office. "Claim tapes."

"All the receipts for the kitchen equipment were in there as well, and they were all in my name. I told Sanchez-Castillo that I had been hired to open up a cafeteria for a company, but that I knew nothing about their activities. The clerks told the police the same story. But that wasn't enough to convince them to let me go. The only reason I'm free now is because Demetrio has no clue how to run his own nightclub," he laughed. "That's why he called Sanchez-Castillo. They were roommates at the University of Texas El Paso. Demetrio asked him to look into my situation. Demetrio's testimony and those kitchen receipts saved me. Sanchez-Castillo gave me this card," Remo smiled, cradling it gently in his hand, "so I don't ever get arrested by accident again."

It was great to finally hear some positive news. Remo had been so full of doom and gloom after the bust. How ironic that now he practically had the keys to the city.

"I guess house arrest is no picnic," he said. "You look awful."

"Awful," I muttered. I was still processing everything he had told me. If this Sanchez-Castillo were trying to stamp out corruption, then surely he would be very interested in what Rivera, Delgado, and Hernandez were up to. On the other hand, speaking up could land me in prison. Remo was innocent, after all. Hernandez was holding onto an incriminating tape of mine. Sanchez-Castillo may well have been the one who gave the FBI permission to come to the island in the first place.

"Wait," I said, catching what Remo had said. "How did you know I was under house arrest?"

"Tony told me. He also told me he's found a new location for the office, and that the clerks are getting out any day now." I was so caught up in my own nightmare, it seemed strange that anything else was happening. "He's planning to reopen as soon as they're released."

"Thank God," I sighed. "I can't wait to get out of here."

Remo looked despondent. "So you're going home?"

"Home?" I asked, incredulous. Where did Remo think my home was? Italy, where I was born? New York, where I grew up? Or Canada, where I was a citizen?

Despite everything, I never considered leaving Santo Domingo. What would I do? Knock on my mother's door in Westchester with Justine in tow—divorced, penniless, unemployed, and bearing the scarlet letter of a criminal record?

"This is home," I told him. "My home and Justine's home. I'm not leaving Santo Domingo."

■

I SOON FOUND OUT that the situation was not quite as rosy as Tony believed. "Your friends are going to be deported," Hernandez told me flatly during one of his nocturnal visits. I wondered if he was telling the truth. I knew how much Hernandez relished inflicting emotional damage on me.

"When?"

"Tomorrow morning. With the FBI." I sensed he was telling the truth. Before Hernandez left that night, he gave me back the keys to my car.

■

I WOKE UP EARLY the following morning and peered over the balcony. No unmarked police car was waiting outside the entrance. I opened the front door and walked tentatively down the stairs, past the courtyard, breathing in the heavy, fragrant smell of the tropical shrubbery. Lopez, the day guard, wordlessly opened the gate. I peered outside. Nothing. Was I really free?

I walked the half-block to the *colmado* and bought a copy of *Listin Diario*, anticipating a tap on the shoulder from the secret police. But no one stopped me. I hurried back to the apartment and spread the paper out on the counter. The front page reported that a group of Americans had been taken into FBI custody the previous evening and were awaiting transportation to the United States. I went into the living room and picked up the phone. The dial tone was normal. I heard no more telltale clicking sounds or echoes in the background. For me, at least, the nightmare was finally over.

I called Tony's cell. "They deported everyone," I said simply.

"Rivera just told me," Tony sighed. "Not only that, the son of a bitch won't let me bring down any more Americans. He wants me to hire locals. Where the hell am I going find English-speaking locals?" I suggested that Tony talk to Remo, but he just continued complaining. "I need people who speak fluent English. Not Horacio English. Perfect Eng—"

"Tony! I want you to move back in," I interrupted, silencing him.

I had spent hours thinking about Tony these past few weeks. I'd thought about men in my past that I'd been interested in romantically. What if I never found another man I would love as passionately as I'd once loved Tony? Was I throwing away the best relationship I might ever have, simply because he didn't live up to my standards of perfection? I knew that Tony had never stopped loving me. I was the one who had given up on us. I had a tendency to give up on things as soon as they went the slightest bit wrong.

"Are you sure?"

"Positive."

That day, I took Justine to the beach. By the time I carried her upstairs that evening, she was fast asleep. As I walked past the kitchen, I spotted an English newspaper on the counter. With a surge of relief I realized that Tony was home. I crept to Justine's room and lay her gently down in bed. She was worn out from chasing waves and building sand castles. I covered her with a light cotton blanket, and closed the door softly behind me.

Back in the kitchen I opened the *San Francisco Chronicle*. On page two was the piece on the clerks' deportation.

Twenty-five US citizens accused of running a sports-betting ring in the Dominican Republic were handed over to federal authorities today. The operation was allegedly run by San Francisco resident Anthony LoBue, who faces charges of racketeering, money laundering and illegal gambling in connection with the operation, which raked in 100 million dollars a month from gamblers across the United States. The huge dragnet was the result of a long-running probe by federal agents and the US attorney's organized crime strike force, according to FBI Special Agent Jack Peterson. Eight months ago, authorities raided a pawnshop whose owner, David Feldman, is a suspect in what authorities have described as the biggest probe into illegal sports betting in Northern California. Federal agents tapped Feldman's phone, leading investigators to the offshore gambling operation. So far authorities have refused to return the one million in cash confiscated from his business.

I closed the paper and walked into the bedroom. Tony was in there, unpacking. "Who's David Feldman?" I asked.

"I missed you too," he said sarcastically. He came to give me a kiss, but I skillfully maneuvered him into a hug instead.

"Jesus, what did you do to your hair?" he asked, running his fingers through my shorn locks.

"It's practical. Who's David Feldman?"

"Owns a pawnshop in San Fran. Let's just say he's kind of a bank, for bookmakers."

"I thought Sacco did his laundering in L.A."

"He does. It's like I said all along, this bust had nothing to do with us. The feds were after LoBue, not Sacco. The whole investigation was San Francisco–based. It never even touched L.A. It was just bad luck. Feldman led the feds to LoBue, and somehow LoBue got us involved. My name came up—Ron's too—but as of now, we're both in the clear. As far as the feds are concerned, they got their man."

I could finally tell Tony about LoBue's warning. "I met Sonny LoBue in the holding cell. He wanted me to warn you. His exact words were, *tell Tony that Ron's going to fuck him.*"

Tony scowled. "That's ridiculous. LoBue's a thug. Ron doesn't even know the guy."

30

ECONOMIC HARD TIMES WERE hardly new to the Dominican people, but in 1991 life was particularly tough. Unemployment rose to over 30%. Inflation spiraled and jobs were in short supply. Even the upper classes were struggling to find work. It was an ideal time to hire local clerks.

Tony invited Remo over to discuss the possibility of sourcing staff from Atlántico's clientele. Over the past few months Remo had been forced to lay off a third of his staff. He informed us that even his wealthy customers were feeling the pinch. Customers were switching to beer or mineral water, or choosing to nurse a single cocktail all night.

Tony was still skeptical. "What makes you think that they would want to work for me? Why would a bunch of well-educated young professionals want to quit their careers to take bets over the phone?"

"You'll be paying them in dollars. The peso is becoming more and more worthless. Trust me, they'll jump at the chance to earn a salary in a stable currency."

"And they speak perfect English?" Tony asked skeptically.

"Perfect English," Remo confirmed. "They've been educated in America, they've lived in America, and they sound American."

Remo proposed what he believed was a suitable wage, and Tony upped it by a hundred dollars, settling on a starting salary of nine hundred U.S. a month. This was a substantial income in the D.R., but sixteen hundred less than the salary we had paid our American clerks. Bonuses would be handed out once a year, at Christmastime instead of the end of each season, and Tony would no longer have to cover living expenses. He calculated that once the business was running smoothly, our operating expenses would be lower despite police payoffs.

Soon the office was filled with new faces. Even Colonel Rivera's son would be starting as a clerk. His English wasn't perfect but—as Tony pointed out—he would have hired him even if he'd only spoken Chinese. Having the colonel's son on the payroll offered us an extra level of protection. Tony put him in the Baby Office, where he couldn't do too much harm. While Tony and Remo got busy recruiting new staff, I began looking for another place to live. Apartments for rent were plentiful, as middle-class families increasingly abandoned city life for the more affordable countryside. I still wanted to be close to the city, in a good area and not too far from where Justine would be starting preschool in the fall.

I made an appointment to view an apartment in a large residential complex. Señor Camino was eager to show me several three-bedroom apartments he had available. The first, he promised, was a gem. I followed him to a dimly lit entryway, where an optimistic architect had installed an elevator. Without exchanging a word we took the stairs to the top floor, unwilling to risk getting stuck during a sudden power outage.

Camino unlocked the door to a small, nondescript living area. It was lined with windows on one side, but it lacked a balcony. A spiral staircase separated the living area from the modest dining area. I followed Camino down the hallway to three unimpressive bedrooms and two adequate bathrooms. Afterwards he led me to the small open kitchen. It had shellacked pine cupboards, old appliances, and a built-in breakfast bar that was barely big enough to accommodate two stools. The doorway at the other end of the kitchen led to the maid's quarters. The hallway was lined with wrought-iron bars resembling a cage. A locked gate opened onto an outdoor metal-grid spiral staircase that was meant to act as the servants' entrance. I popped my head into the maid's room. There was barely space for a single bed, and the toilet was in the same cramped quarters. *I would never put Rosa or anyone else in there,* I thought.

"It's really not what I was looking for, I'm afraid," I told Señor Camino.

"You haven't seen the best part," he said, insisting I follow him.

I was totally unprepared for what was upstairs. Beyond a glass-walled room was a balcony that wrapped around three sides of the building. On one side was a built-in barbeque and on the other a small swimming pool, complete with wooden deck. Suddenly I wanted this apartment more than anything. My mind raced: I would put Rosa in the spare bedroom and use the maid's quarters for storage. I could sand and paint the cupboards and replace the kitchen appliances and all the doors. I pictured Justine frolicking in the pool and riding her tricycle outside on the huge terrace. It even had a second way out: the maid's entrance could serve as an emergency exit.

I was still missing my passport, though. As long as Hernandez had it, I couldn't leave the country, or even my apartment. I would have to produce my passport in order to complete the application process for my new place. Tony didn't have time to deal with my problem. I'd tried sending Domingo to the police station to collect it, but he'd returned with the number of Hernandez's direct line instead. I tried reporting it lost to the Canadian Embassy, only to be told that I would have to file a police report and that they'd launch a "thorough investigation" before releasing a new one. As I exhausted each possibility in turn, I became dimly aware that there was only one option left. I would have to face Hernandez again.

■

THE YOUNG POLICEWOMAN AT the main reception desk checked my name against a long list. Locating it, she summoned a uniformed guard, who led me down a long corridor to the familiar key-access elevator. I followed him to Hernandez's door, where I steeled myself against seeing him again.

The general greeted me as if I were an old friend, ordering coffee from the guard. "I don't want any," I said.

"Two cups," he told the guard. "Take a seat, Marisa."

Empty cardboard boxes lay on the floor, folders were stacked on his desk, his diplomas were missing from the wall and the alcohol was packed away. I started to wonder if Hernandez had been fired.

"I came for my passport," I said, struggling to keep the emotion out of my voice.

"You have time to share a farewell coffee with an old friend." It arrived moments later on a silver tray. I sat rigid and silent while it was poured into two fine porcelain cups.

"I will be leaving soon," Hernandez said as soon as the door to his office closed again. "I've been transferred to Mao, a small town northwest of Santiago. It's known for its spectacular sunsets, which are said to be as red as the soil there." He took a sip of his coffee. "It is a part of the country few tourists ever take the opportunity to visit. I was hoping you would collect your passport there."

At this I looked up into his cloudy, diseased eyes. He was toying with me again. He had no intention of giving me my passport. I was about to stand up when he reached for the top drawer of his desk. He placed my passport in front of him and opened it without breaking eye contact with me.

"Officers are routinely transferred in an effort to keep corruption down," he said. Hernandez took one of his business cards, flipped it over, and copied down my full name from the passport. When he was finished, he stamped the card and closed the passport.

"I will be in touch with my colleagues in Santo Domingo to ensure things are running smoothly with your new offices," he continued. "If you have a problem, you can contact me in Mao or through the main switchboard." He passed me the card. His name was embossed in black script under the blue, red, and green military coat of arms. Below in black letters was his title: "General P.N."

I turned the card over. On the back he had written: "*Marisa Lankester is a personal friend of the subscriber and of the Policia Nacional.*" Like the card that Sanchez-Castillo had given Remo, it offered a high level of protection. My first reaction was fury. Was this his way of apologizing for what he had done to me? I put it back on the table and slid it toward him.

Hernandez chuckled. "You're a clever girl. Put it in your wallet where it is safe and keep it to yourself. I rarely hand these out. I wouldn't make the mistake of turning down such a valuable gift."

I heard the menace behind his words. I took the card and tucked it into my wallet. He slid my passport over to me.

"Thank you," I mumbled.

"You look beautiful," he remarked. "You were getting too thin."

I drew in a sharp gasp. The words felt like a slap in the face. I wrenched the door open and charged past the guard, who hurried after me. Now my ordeal was really over. I would never have to see Hernandez again.

I stayed up late that night, making plans for the move. Tony was already in bed when I crept into the adjoining bathroom. I washed my face, brushed my teeth, tidied up. I tiptoed to bed and slipped in quietly next to him, hoping that he was already asleep. He reached for my hand.

"Good night," I said, squeezing it. I turned on my side.

Tony moved toward me in the dark and tugged at my night-gown. "I think you should take this off," he said huskily.

"I'm exhausted," I mumbled.

He kicked off the blanket and rose abruptly from the bed. "Why the hell did you ask me to move back in if you never want to have sex?" he spat, storming out of the bedroom.

I found him on the balcony, brooding on the rocking chair. I leaned against the doorway. "Tony . . . I'm sorry. I've been so wrapped up with finding an apartment and there's just so much going on now."

"When you asked me to move back in, I thought we were going to be a family again. But it's not like that. It feels like I'm just some guy who lives under the same roof with you."

I hung my head. Tony had been making a huge effort—not just with me, but also with Justine—and I was grateful. I thought I could push what happened with Hernandez out of my head, but I cringed every time Tony touched me. I craved being in his arms, where I felt safe and protected, but I wasn't ready to go any further. Tony understandably was. I had been feeding him one excuse after another—I had my period, or a headache; I was tired, or sick—anything to avoid having sex.

"I'm sorry," I said softly, reaching out to him.

He took my hand and led me back to the bedroom. When he made love to me that night, I felt almost as violated as I had with Hernandez.

I threw all of my energy into fixing up the new apartment. I painted Justine's room a soft lavender, replaced the old appli-ances, and sanded down the kitchen cupboards. I was still priming them long after Justine and Rosa had gone to bed, when Tony came home. He popped his head into the kitchen. "Close your eyes, I have a surprise for you."

I smelled a familiar aftershave over the industrial smell of paint. I opened my eyes, and there, grinning from ear to ear, was Car-mine. I threw my arms around his bony frame.

"How on earth did you get here? You were deported!"

"We have some pretty powerful friends in immigration these days," Tony grinned. "We can get anyone in and out without a paper trail."

"It's good to be back," Carmine said. "Man, I'm never going back to the States. Not after what the feds put me through."

"We've got another surprise." Tony and Carmine disappeared back outside. They returned holding a huge sign that said "TOMAJU" in slick navy-blue block letters.

"The name of the new office," Tony announced. "Like it?"

I shrugged. "It sounds Japanese." But a moment later I got it. I looked at Tony and laughed.

TOny, MArisa, JUstine: TOMAJU.

31

ALTHOUGH IT SEEMED LIKE a lifetime, only two months passed between the raid on Information Unlimited and the day Tomaju opened for business. On my first morning back at work, I drove Carmine to the office. He directed me to an unfamiliar part of town, where a *banca* seemed to occupy every block.

Carmine pointed to a pale-blue, two-story building with the Tomaju sign up on the second floor. My smile faded when I noticed the bright-red banner draped across the first-floor display window. It read: *Coming Soon—Commerciales Vargas.* "I don't believe it," I said, staring at the banner.

Whether I liked it or not, Tomaju was intrinsically linked to the Vargas clan. Conveniently for Horacio, Tony had rented the entire building, so he was able to give away this prime piece of commercial real estate to Horacio. Once again Tony needed a Dominican partner, a role Horacio was only too happy to fill. On paper, he was the president of the company. I had signed as vice-president, a position Tony would take over as soon as he was off probation.

Carmine showed me around the new space. In a small area up front customers could come in, place bets, and watch a game. The sparse, uninviting space featured a couple of tables, several chairs, and a small TV bolted to the wall. Clearly, Tony did not want to encourage the locals to hang around. Up on the wall was a small framed document—Tomaju's license from the Ministry of Sports. Gustavo's oversight had cost our clerks a month in jail and millions in lost revenue for us. As a result of this gross error, he'd received little more than a slap on the wrist and a notice of termination.

The young Dominican seated behind the counter acknowledged Carmine and depressed a button, and the door in the corner marked *Emplados Solamente* buzzed open. I followed Carmine down a long corridor, where a surveillance camera faced us. A second door clicked open and we stepped inside.

Security was paramount. Nobody except our clerks was allowed into the back area. Tony beckoned us into the enormous office, clearly nervous about how the first day would go. Standing next to him was a man I had never seen before. He was dressed head-to-toe in black, with several heavy gold chains around his neck. His hair was dyed jet-black and slicked down with a heavy layer of gel. He had an orange tan, and while his clothes and manner suggested he was aiming to look twenty-five, he was clearly several decades older.

"Marisa, this is Vincent," Tony said. "He'll be charting in the Baby Office."

"How you doin'?" he said in a thick East Coast accent. He held out a bejeweled and manicured hand. "Call me Vinnie." He and Carmine greeted each other like old friends before Tony and Vinnie disappeared into the Baby Office.

"Where do you know Elvis from?" I laughed.

"Staten Island," Carmine replied dryly.

This set off alarm bells. I knew that the East Coast was

mob-controlled and Vinnie practically screamed mafioso. "Really? did Ron have to get . . . permission?"

Carmine knew what I was getting at. "He don't need permission. Not out here."

"So Vinnie's people . . . they're going to be betting with us too?"

Carmine nodded. "He's going to earn a charter's salary, plus a commission on what his players bet."

I wondered what had happened to the "no more Americans" rule. Reading my mind, Carmine said, "I wouldn't worry about Vinnie. Under all that hair dye and bronzer is a sixty-five-year-old guy who's never stepped foot out of New York before. He won't last the month."

I wasn't so sure. I'd thought the same thing about Leslie when she first came down.

Carmine gave me a tour around our slick new offices. "Not bad," I said, ducking my head into the Baby Office, where Tony and Vinnie were huddled together. Tomaju looked like a serious company, now that we were located in a real office building instead of a converted villa. Carmine stayed behind in his office to prepare for the busy day ahead, while I settled into an empty cubicle in the Big Office. It was going to be just like the old days in L.A.

■

SOON THE OFFICE FILLED up with eager new recruits. I immediately felt out of place in my scruffy jeans and Tony's old football shirt. The fact that people recognized me from the Constanza commercial made me feel even more self-conscious of my sloppy appearance. Clearly, this wasn't going to be a shorts-and-sneakers operation anymore. The women were attractive and smartly dressed, and the men wore neat slacks and button-down shirts. Even Leslie arrived wearing a fitted skirt, blouse, and high heels. She came over and assured me that the new clerks were all extremely nice, but I still felt awkward and out of place.

The only other employee who looked as uncomfortable as I was came over and introduced himself. "Emery Rivera," he said, shyly offering me his hand. The colonel's son.

The two of us hung back, watching Vinnie work the room as if he were the host of a lavish cocktail party. All that was needed was a martini in his hand and some Sinatra on the stereo.

At twelve-forty-five, Tony told everyone to go to their prospective offices. As we took our seats he reminded everyone to record their plays and to call out maximum bets. Next door, I could faintly hear Carmine making the same announcement.

Leslie was in the cubicle next to me, and I leaned over. "Can you make me a brunette?" I whispered.

"What?"

"A brunette. I have to blend in more."

"The last thing you need to do is blend in more. You need to get out of your apartment and into the real world again. Look, Remo's organizing something for us at Atlántico, Friday night after work. I'll do your hair but you have to promise to come. No backing out at the last minute."

Tony called for silence and read out the opening line. I glanced around the room. Tomaju's staff included two lawyers, an architect, two engineers, a photographer, three dentists, a teacher, and four young society housewives. Together, I had no doubt that we made up the most educated, cultured, multilingual, and well-dressed group of bookmakers in history.

The second hand slowly approached the one. "We're up!" Tony's voice boomed through all four offices, and we scrambled to answer the phones.

■

LESLIE ARRIVED AT THE apartment the next morning with pots, brushes, powders, scissors, clips, and combs. As she prepared to start working on my hair, she handed me a copy of *Italian Vogue*. "This is the cut and color I'm going to give you," she said. Sitting in a pale-pink leather booth, holding a spoon provocatively to her lips, was a beautiful, auburn-haired Linda Evangelista.

As Leslie got to work, my excitement grew and grew. When she was finally done dying, cutting, and blow-drying my hair, she insisted upon doing my makeup. She shaped and darkened my eyebrows, layered my lashes with mascara, and painted my lips red. When she finished, she sat back and beamed with pride.

In the mirror the transformation was astonishing. This was exactly the psychological boost I'd needed. "I love it," I breathed, running my fingers through my hair. I would never again hear the familiar call of *"Rubia!"* or "Blondie!" again. Best of all, no one would ever associate me with the Constanza commercial.

That Friday night, I slipped into a dress and sandals. I fluffed my hair and left to collect Leslie on our way to Atlántico. I felt much less conspicuous walking into the club with my hair dark. I could pass for a light-skinned Dominican now. I followed Leslie to the table bordering the dance floor that Remo had reserved for us. Most of my new colleagues were already sipping cocktails, smoking cigarettes, and chatting. The atmosphere was light and playful as they exchanged impressions from their first week of bookmaking. One of the new clerks, a pretty girl called Gabriella, leaned in to me and purred, "You're so lucky. Your husband is so nice and so good-looking."

Soon most of the clerks were out on the floor dancing to "I'm Too Sexy" by Right Said Fred. Remo flopped down in an empty seat next to me. "I like your hair," he said.

"Thanks." I had to suppress a yawn. "I'm wiped. I don't think anyone else has been up since seven in the morning with a child."

Suddenly Remo straightened up. A tall, well-dressed man was making his way through the crowd, stopping along the way to greet and kiss several attractive women on the cheek. "What the hell's he doing here?" Remo muttered.

Leslie pushed her way past several clerks, eager to meet this mysterious gentleman. She tapped him on the arm, and when he turned to her, she tiptoed, smiled seductively, and kissed him once on each cheek.

I figured from Remo's reaction that this was Demetrio, his boss. I had heard a lot about him, but until tonight I'd never met him. Up close he seemed older than I'd imagined. Late thirties or early forties, I guessed. Deep lines were etched around his blue eyes and a few gray hairs were scattered in with the brown, but those were his only flaws. Our eyes locked as he approached.

"Remo. Why don't you introduce me to this beautiful lady?"

"Marisa," I said, shaking his hand.

"The Constanza girl," he smiled. Noting my surprise, he gave a self-effacing grin and said, "I'd recognize those eyes anywhere. Welcome to my club."

Remo was fluttering around us, very uncomfortable at the obvious electricity between us. "Her husband is one of my best friends," he chipped in. "Marisa was just stopping by . . . on the way home. To her family."

"Your services are required behind the main bar," Demetrio said casually, and Remo reluctantly left my side. "Can I get you a drink?" he offered.

The sound system was now blasting Mark Wahlberg's "Good Vibrations." Leslie was in her element, bouncing around on the dance floor with her friends and coworkers. She wouldn't notice if I slipped out now.

"No, thank you. I really should get home."

Demetrio offered to walk me to the gate, and I accepted. I followed as he wove his way through the crowd. As Remo hovered by the bar, his face betrayed a mixture of panic and shock as he watched us leave together. I rolled my eyes at him. *Really!*

Demetrio walked me past the elaborate doors and down the garden path toward the front gate. The sound of music faded away with every step. It was a beautiful evening. The stars were bright and clear, and the tropical flowers rustled gently in the breeze. I felt strangely at ease next to Demetrio, and he didn't spoil the moment by breaking the silence.

32

TOMAJU WAS SOON RUNNING like a well-oiled machine. Behind the scenes, however, it was a different story. Office life began to resemble a soap opera, and the main storyline was Gabriella's growing interest in Tony. It was no secret that she found him attractive. Her body language made it abundantly clear that she was his for the taking. Rather than being jealous or angry, I became quietly fascinated by her blatant attempts at seduction—the way her clothes became ever more provocative and her interchanges with Tony ever more laden with innuendo. While he was flattered by the attention, as the weeks went on, he did not act upon it.

While I was giving our relationship another chance, I was still emotionally damaged. Every time we had sex, I felt that he was stripping away my soul one piece at a time. Even his kisses, once so passionate and full of promise, now felt like an assault. I had not yet come to terms with what had happened with Hernandez. I barely wanted to admit it to myself. All I knew was that I needed to heal, and the only way for me to truly recover was to avoid sex until I was ready.

One afternoon I suggested to Gabriella that she ask Tony to teach her how to chart. Learning to chart would give her a legitimate reason to be at work early and stay late. I suppose I was giving her my blessing to start an affair with my ex-husband, and I wondered how long it would be before Tony acquiesced. We were divorced, after all.

I knew that they were sleeping together when Tony stopped being antagonistic toward me at home. The tension at home dissipated, and Tony and I settled into a superficial bliss. I thought of Gabriella as merely filling in sexually, and this arrangement took an enormous amount of pressure off of me. I had no intention of giving Tony up. We were a family again. Justine had her father back, and I felt safe, both financially and physically. I had no problem with what they were doing, as long as the relationship didn't develop any further.

Gabriella's affair with Tony was an open secret at the office, and it made her an outcast among her peers. Not only was she sleeping with the boss, she was charting part-time in the Baby Office. She became management. Management went out to dinner after work. Clerks partied at Atlántico. I aligned myself with the clerks and began joining them more and more often at the club. Atlántico might have seemed like an unlikely place to find peace of mind, yet neither my troubled relationship with Tony nor the ugly flashbacks of Hernandez surfaced there.

Demetrio began frequenting his club more and more. He would greet me by kissing me once on each cheek, lingering a bit longer than necessary, and glancing at me in a way that conveyed that it was just a matter of time before I became his next conquest.

"He likes you," Leslie winked, nudging my arm.

"But you like him," I replied.

"Liked. I'm seeing someone else."

I had to admit I enjoyed Demetrio's company, but I had no intention of taking things any further. As long as his sights were set on me, I was off-limits to everyone else in his club, and that suited me just fine. Atlántico was a haven where I could dance, hang out with my colleagues, and forget the rest of the world. Even Remo relaxed after a while. While still overprotective, he was comforted by the fact that I always left the club alone. In his curiously old-fashioned worldview this made me a "good girl." As for Leslie, he thought of her as a party girl, and once he confided his intense dislike of Gabriella.

"She's a gold-digger," he spat, "a home-wrecker."

That seemed to be the general consensus within our circle. Apparently everyone knew that I was being cheated on, and this brought me a great deal of undeserved sympathy. Remo was my closest friend, but I still couldn't tell him that I had pushed Gabriella into Tony's arms. If I told him that, then I'd have to tell him why.

■

ONE STEAMY DAY, I was drenched by a sudden tropical downpour as I sprinted from my car to Tomaju's front door. I did a double-take when the door opened and I found myself face-to-face with a beaming—and slightly sunburned—Ron Sacco.

"Ron!" I resisted the urge to hug him, since I was dripping wet. "What are you doing here?"

"Thought I'd better fly in to see how things are going."

Just then Gabriella came strolling out of Tony's office and headed toward us. I saw from the uncomfortable look that came over Ron's face that he knew about the affair. I felt my cheeks go red as I imagined how Tony had painted the situation. What had he said about me? That I was cold? Frigid? Adding to my discomfort, Gabriella sauntered over to us, looking very pretty and oozing confidence. I looked like a drowned rat standing next to her.

From the friendly banter between her and Ron I realized that they had already met. Ron must have already been in the country for a couple of days. I suddenly felt hurt and betrayed, and struggled to keep the smile frozen on my face. How ironic that the feelings of jealousy that had been completely absent when Tony and Gabriella started their affair should now come bubbling to the surface because of her closeness to Ron. I realized Gabriella was encroaching on my life, upon relationships I'd had for years.

Before he left for California, Ron organized a dinner for Tomaju at the V Centenario, the luxury hotel where he was staying. In the imposing dining room, he sat at the head of the table. Next to him were Tony and myself. Across from us were Carmine and Vinnie. Gabriella arrived next, wearing a little red dress, and immediately scanned the room for Tony. Of course, she had wanted to sit next to him, but this was out of the question. She had to settle for Carmine. The dining room filled up as the rest of the clerks took their places.

Suddenly a bright flash illuminated the table. The young Dominican girl holding the camera smiled at us, adjusting the lens to take another picture.

Vinnie burst to his feet. "What are you doing, lady?"

"She's a hotel photographer," Gabriella said. "They take pictures and post them in the lobby."

I could almost see the wheels turning as the Americans realized the potential repercussions of being caught on camera together. Tony was still on probation, and forbidden from leaving California or associating with any known bookmakers. Carmine was out on bail and due in court. Ron was still on probation and facing additional charges. And all of them were in the company of Vinnie, proving a concrete link between all three men and the mob.

Ron and Vinnie simultaneously lunged for the startled girl. "Give me the camera!" Ron snarled, as she took a step backward. Tony jumped up, warning Ron and Vinnie to keep it down. The entire restaurant had stopped to stare at the commotion. Tony took out his wallet, counted out three hundred dollars, and offered them to the photographer. She looked unsure before cautiously stepping forward to take the money. She fumbled with the back of the camera, popped out the roll of film, and handed it to Tony. He exposed the roll while the other diners looked on, aghast.

I hid behind the menu, mortified to be associated with such an undignified confrontation. When I finally allowed myself to peer over the menu again, the world had changed for me in a subtle but fundamental way. The photographer's bright flash had revealed the true nature of my companions. Tony, Ron, Carmine, and Vinnie were nothing more than career criminals. They would spend their entire lives rootless, hunted, always trying to stay one step ahead of the law.

It was a defining moment for me. Working in the D.R. only gave them a veneer of legitimacy. I didn't want to be associated with them any more than I had to. My gaze settled on Gabriella. She was smiling in Tony's direction, thrilled to be a part of his exciting world. Not so long ago that had been me, newly seduced by the allure of living outside of society's conventions.

All at once I felt weary and sad. I knew that all of those wonderful emotions I had once felt for Tony were gone forever. Our love had gone so horribly wrong. I didn't feel like the same girl anymore. I was no longer a member of their inner circle, no longer privy to their private discussions. Gabriella undoubtedly knew more about what was going on behind the scenes than I did.

∎

ON THE DAY AFTER Ron's big dinner, Tony had just finished reading the opening lines when Leslie jumped up and clamped her hand over her mouth. She sprinted to the bathroom, where the entire office could hear her retching violently into the toilet.

I dashed after her and held her hair out of her face as she continued to throw up. "Jesus, what did you eat last night?"

"It's not something I ate," she moaned, "it's something I did." She retched again, and I rubbed her back. I could hear the phones ringing and the clerks' muffled voices as they frantically recorded bets. What I had just heard was way more important than running lines.

"Are you . . . pregnant?" She nodded, shakily wiping her mouth.

"Who's the lucky guy?" I asked gently. Leslie hadn't been out for weeks, so I was stumped as to who it might be.

"You don't know him; no one does," she said, flushing the toilet. She stood up weakly and rinsed her mouth. "He's not rich. His name is Armando. He's . . . he's nothing like the guys I've been out with before. He's really kind. And down to earth. He's not arrogant at all!" Leslie dabbed her eyes. "He still lives at home, with his mom and his brother, and they're both really sweet. They're nice people, Marisa."

"Why didn't you tell me about him?"

"How could I? I—I knew what people would say! That he's poor, and he's only after me for my passport!"

I had never seen any man affect Leslie like this. "You're in *love* with him!"

"I—I know!" Leslie wailed, and burst into tears.

Not only did Armando possess all the qualities Leslie had described, he was also gorgeous. He proposed the moment she told him she was pregnant, and Leslie happily accepted. She began planning her dream wedding. She was determined to wear a fitted gown, which left us very little time to plan. The lavish ceremony took place six weeks later, in a magnificent colonial house. Leslie looked radiant in an ivory-silk empire dress that cleverly concealed her bump. Tony gave her away, walking her down the rose-petal-strewn marble staircase toward her handsome husband-to-be, who couldn't stop smiling. The entire office came, along with Leslie's mother and Colonel Rivera, who showed up wearing his full military uniform. His presence there spoke volumes: Tomaju continued to have his blessing.

That morning, the newspapers had reported that General Hernandez had retired, and at the reception I brought up the general's retirement with Remo. He laughed bitterly. "Hernandez didn't retire. Read between the lines. Who the hell retires at forty-nine? He was fired. He must have pissed off one of the higher-ups. You know how things work around here."

Rivera and Tony were leaning against the wall, drinking beers like a couple of old friends. Rivera had assured Tony that Hernandez's "retirement" would have no effect on Tomaju. Tony was making regular, generous payments to officers in the Police Department, the Secret Service, and immigration, and Hernandez would stay on the payroll regardless.

"I don't think you have anything to worry about," Remo remarked, nodding at the colonel. "The fact that he showed up, and in uniform, is a good sign. He's letting you know that everything is running smoothly."

■

BACK IN CALIFORNIA, LOCAL newspapers were reporting that Anthony LoBue had game-fixing charges tacked onto the extortion, racketeering, money-laundering, and illegal gambling charges already filed against him. It was alleged that he paid off referees and coaches to fix heavily wagered basketball and baseball games. He was also accused of fixing horse races in Toronto. The same article claimed that winnings from the operation were laundered at a San Francisco pawnshop owned by David Feldman.

Ron read the offending article aloud to us. "Now would you listen to this garbage?" he said. "'Ron Sacco of Los Angeles was identified as the leader of the sports-betting ring. He has not been charged in the case.'"

"That's fucked up," Tony commented.

I had been invited to this intimate gathering, and I was surprised and flattered. Apparently Ron wanted me to meet his new attorney, Donald Mooney, a short, baby-faced man in his late forties.

Mooney was the former head of the organized-crime task force in Los Angeles, and he had a reputation for going after criminals like a pit bull, prosecuting them to the limit. Yet Ron had made him an offer he couldn't refuse, and Mooney had astonished his colleagues by accepting. Ruthless, aggressive, and better connected than Harold Fisher, Mooney had no reservations about traveling to the Dominican Republic. It was just a matter of time before Ron was indicted, and he was paying Mooney to go to any lengths necessary to keep him out of jail.

Mooney picked up the thread. "No one is disputing that Ron is a bookmaker. But these allegations are completely ludicrous. If they convict him on these egregious charges, he'll serve twenty years at least."

"Everybody knows damn well that I never put a game on the boards if I suspected it was fixed. That's not how I operate."

We all knew this was true. Ron's enormous success was based on volume. He didn't care who won or lost, because he took ten percent either way. He had no reason to get involved in the complicated and risky business of game fixing.

"That's not all," Mooney said, leaning forward. "Someone in the D.R. is feeding information to the FBI."

"An informant?" This shocked me. A pensive silence settled over the table. "How do you know?"

Mooney shrugged. "The FBI knew that Ron was here."

"Doesn't everybody?" It was Ron's second trip to the country, and he'd hardly kept a low profile.

"Actually, no," Ron said, gazing at me intently. "The players have no idea that I'm coming here. Immigration has denied it. So have our friends at the police department."

Mooney cleared his throat. "The feds have an informant. There's no doubt about it." They were all staring at me. I realized with a sickening feeling that I was a suspect. The only reason I had been invited to this little party was so they could confront me.

I stood up and glared at Ron. "After everything I've done for you, you have the gall to accuse me of working with the feds?"

I threw my napkin on the table and stormed away. Ron scrambled to block my exit.

"Sweetheart! Wait, don't go!" He grabbed me by the shoulders and pleaded with me to stay. "This wasn't my idea. Or Tony's. It's just . . . look, everyone knows that the two of you are going through some difficulties right now. It seemed possible that you might be angry enough to do something about it."

"You've got motive," Mooney stated flatly.

"And you think I would get back at Tony by hurting Ron? That makes no sense."

"Someone at Tomaju is talking to the FBI."

"Well, it isn't me!" I insisted loudly.

"Babe, sit down," Tony said.

I hesitated, but still complied. As furious as I was, I wanted to know more. Mooney explained that he had tried to use his old connections to find out who the informant was, but no one was talking to him. "It's going to be harder for us to prove that Ron has nothing to do with LoBue's operation if the feds know that Ron's been out here."

"At least we have one bit of good news on the horizon," Ron announced. Tony and I looked at him expectantly. "I've been given an opportunity to defend myself."

"Ron's going to set the record straight," Mooney interjected. "He's going to address some of the more serious accusations against him. He's giving a sit-down interview to CBS."

"*What?*" Tony exclaimed.

"*60 Minutes* will be flying down here to interview him." Mooney carried on with the unconcerned air of a man giving a weather forecast. "I'll be with Ron throughout the interview to make sure—"

"Hold on," Tony said, his face darkening further. "*60 Minutes* is coming here? To talk to you?"

"But I thought you didn't want people to know that you're here," I said.

Mooney replied with the patronizing air of someone having to explain a simple problem to a slow child. "They're not going to reveal where the interview is taking place. That's one of my stipulations."

"Why here?" Tony demanded. "You could talk to them anywhere in the world. Why the fuck would you bring them to the D.R.?"

"They're not going to reveal the location of the interview,"

Ron reiterated, in a tone that made it clear that the conversation was over.

The atmosphere around the table grew thick with tension. Tony's jaw was clenched so tightly that I could see the veins bulging on his forehead. He took a sip of his beer and slammed the bottle on the table. I just wanted to get out of there and go home. I was already struggling with the imminent end of my relationship with Tony and the financial consequences it would have. I couldn't cope with the thought that an informant might be threatening my livelihood. I needed my job now more than ever—at least until I figured out another way to support myself.

Leslie returned from her two-week honeymoon in Italy visibly pregnant and glowing with happiness. "Married life suits you," I told her when she came over to show me the photos.

Some of her pictures reminded me of my childhood in Italy. I found myself mesmerized by one shot in particular. The image reminded me of my godmother's village outside Rome. I recalled making tortellini with her, and the candy store where she bought me black licorice. I remembered the sound of the bells from the church around the corner, and her neighbors' three black cats.

It was a part of Italy that I had long forgotten, and the memories this picture evoked were magical. "Can I make a copy of this?"

Leslie looked at me quizzically and smiled. "Of course you can!"

On my day off I drove to an art shop in Gazcue and carefully chose oil paints of the same rich colors as the photograph's, and the largest canvas I could find. I left loaded with supplies, and giddy with anticipation. The dining room became my studio, and the table my easel. I began that afternoon, penciling a rough sketch directly onto the canvas, and worked well into the night. I started again first thing in the morning and again as soon as I got home. There were no more sleepless nights. No more anxious fretting over the impending changes facing me. I forgot about Tomaju, about Tony and Gabriella, Ron, Hernandez, Horacio, and every other problem. Soon my nails were stained with color from the oil paints. Almost without thinking about it, I was an artist again.

33

On Sunday, December 13, 1992, Vinnie, Carmine, Tony, and I gathered around the television in the Big Office to watch Ron's interview on *60 Minutes*. Ron, now back in California, would have to wait another two hours to see the broadcast on the West Coast. Tony, convinced that the piece could only draw negative attention to the office, had sent the clerks home early. As far as he was concerned, the fewer the people who saw it, the better.

Steve Kroft, the presenter, appeared onscreen. *"If you had a couple of bucks riding on one of this afternoon's football games, you're part of what the federal government calls a fifty-billion-a-year illegal business. More than one billion of those dollars are bet with one man. You may win or lose . . .*

"But Ron Sacco always wins." A shot of Ron's face filled the screen. *"Sacco runs the biggest and most successful illegal bookmaking operation in history. His operation is nationwide and uses satellite communication, along with toll-free 800 numbers, for his clientele."*

Next up was a man identified as Jim Moody, the chief of the Organized Crime unit. He concurred that Ron was the top bookmaker in operation. *"A hundred million a month is an awful lot of money,"* he said.

Suddenly, Tony and I sat bolt upright as a pair of familiar faces filled the screen. It was the two undercover agents who had set up our second bust in L.A., Red and Duke. *"The FBI has been conducting a nationwide investigation of Ron Sacco and his associates, using these two men, Dan Hanks and Fred Valis, to infiltrate Sacco's world. For fifteen years they have worked as professional informants for federal law enforcement."* Hanks and Valis went on to describe their association with Sacco, talking about how they installed equipment for him while they were on the FBI's payroll.

Tony turned up the volume. *"Ron Sacco agreed to meet with us if we didn't reveal where the interview took place and allowed his attorney to be present. Sacco asked that we point out that he was not admitting any involvement in any illegal activity when he talked with us about the business of sports bookmaking."*

Kroft gave a brief rundown of betting terms. Then he broke down the process of making a bet. *"When you make a bet with Sacco's organization, you do it over the phone. The payoff is handled by a network of neighborhood agents. Valis and Hanks also acted as collectors and couriers of cash and checks between Sacco and his associates and those neighborhood agents. Dan Hanks says that in San Francisco he made deposits and withdrawals at what he called a 'special bank for the bookies,' a pawnshop in the middle of the city's high-crime Mission District. David Feldman, who admits to being a gambler, is the owner and operator of Mission Jewelry & Loan."*

At this Tony slammed his fist on the desk. All of his worst fears were being realized. "I warned him! But he wouldn't listen!" Carmine shushed him. Kroft was citing government sources that alleged that Feldman kept money on deposit in accounts for bookmakers associated with Sacco. *"Convinced that Feldman was playing a pivotal role in Ron Sacco and his associates' billion-dollar bookmaking operation, the FBI raided Feldman's pawnshop, seizing a million dollars."*

Next up was Jim Moody, claiming that the bookmaking business was controlled by the mob.

"Sources in the Justice Department say that's exactly how Ron Sacco's business is done—with organized crime approval, the approval of these men, New York's Gambino crime family and its recently jailed boss, John Gotti."

I glanced over at Vinnie, who blanched as the camera cut between Sacco and images of the Gambino crime family. "Aw, fuck me!" he said. The camera zoomed in on Ron. He looked like a deer in headlights, making a feeble attempt to dispute the claims. Jim Moody appeared on-screen again. *"In my opinion—and I've worked organized crime twenty-one years—you cannot operate a bookmaking operation without the Cosa Nostra."*

So far the program had insinuated links not only between Ron and Sonny LoBue, but also between him and the Gambino family. It was about to get worse. A shot of the street outside the office filled the screen. The camera panned around, pausing briefly on the Commerciales Vargas sign before traveling up to the second floor. I was horrified. They may as well have flashed our address and telephone number across the screen.

"And so Ron Sacco and company are currently under investigation by a federal grand jury in San Francisco for everything from bookmaking to trying to fix a college basketball game. To avoid the heat, the billion-dollar bookie came up with a new ploy. He moved his operations offshore, here, to the Caribbean island nation of the Dominican Republic, where gambling is legal."

"Jesus Christ!" Tony bellowed. He looked like someone had punched him in the gut.

"Sacco installed TV satellite dishes, and to keep touch with his clientele, he arranged for toll-free 800 numbers connected to AT&T in the United States; he is the largest telephone subscriber in the Dominican Republic. But if Sacco thought he was safe here in the Dominican Republic, he was wrong. The FBI put pressure on the Dominican government, and in January of 1992, Dominican authorities raided two villas and arrested scores of people said to be involved with Ron Sacco's 800-number bookmaking

operation. Weeks later, Ron Sacco was back in business at another location nearby, with the blessing of the Dominican authorities."

Kroft faced the camera. *"Sources in the Justice Department say that Sacco will be indicted later this summer."*

The program cut to a commercial break. Tony stood up, threw a chair across the room, and stormed to his phone, cursing along the way.

"Let's not panic," Carmine urged. "The feds can't get to us here. The Dominican Republic has no extradition treaty with the United States."

I looked down at my hands. Carmine had skipped his scheduled court appearance, and had no intention of ever returning to the States. He was now a fugitive.

Tony made a few calls and seemed visibly calmed by what he found out. He knew that the last time the feds asked Rivera abut Ron was back in August—over four months ago. Ron was supposed to have been indicted at the end of the summer, but it was already December and nothing had happened. Tony sat down next to us, looking very serious.

"Look, we know the feds can't touch us out here. They can't pull the same shit they did with Information Unlimited. If they tried it, Rivera would be the first to know." He sighed. "There's no denying it, though—Ron's in deep shit. Probably more so now, thanks to that tragic display."

"What about you?" I asked. We'd drifted apart, but I was sure he hadn't missed a probation meeting, or handed in a late report.

"I'm in the clear. So are you. No one's asking questions about either of us."

I took a deep breath. "That's good to know."

"The Dominicans are making a lot of money because of us," Tony said. "They're going to do everything in their power to protect their interests. I might not trust them a hundred percent, but I know Rivera would never put his kid in harm's way. As long as Emery keeps showing up for work, I know we're okay."

I wasn't sure if Tony was trying to convince himself or us.

Ron Sacco's disastrous interview with *60 Minutes* made him an overnight celebrity in America. Oddly, the law enforcement community didn't seem to react at all. It was business as usual at Tomaju—in fact, we were busier than ever. Ron's newfound notoriety resulted in an influx of new players, forcing Tony to hire four new clerks. One of the new clerks shared the president's surname. Officially, President Balaguer had never married or had children, but it was common knowledge that he had fathered three.

Tony left for his last probation meeting of the year, and was overjoyed when Ruth Gordon told him that he would not have to report to her again in person until the following May. Our home life continued much as it had before. Tony never broached the subject of moving out, although he often stayed away for days at a time. As for me, I stopped hanging out at Atlántico and stayed home painting instead. Life was humming along nicely, and by Christmas the horrors of Ron's *60 Minutes* interview were all but forgotten.

The office New Year's Eve party took place at the Chinese restaurant at the Jaragua. Overlooking the grand casino below, it was a festive place to ring in 1993. Vinnie was noticeably absent when we all sat down for dinner at ten.

Downstairs, a live band played while scantily clad dancers entertained the heaving crowd. It was a giant, festive party, packed with people determined to ring in the New Year by losing their money on poker and craps. Dessert was served just before midnight, when the first bottles of champagne were opened. The band started playing to announce the start of the official countdown. Hundreds of people were chanting along: *Ten! Nine! Eight* . . . climaxing with jubilant cheers of *"Happy New Year!"* and thunderous applause. Streamers, confetti, and balloons drifted down from the ceiling, covering everyone in sparkles and glitter.

The clerks exchanged knowing glances with each other. Four tables had been reserved at Atlántico, and everyone would be heading over there, despite Tony's warning about how busy we would be the following day. The Sugar Bowl was kicking off at the Superdome in New Orleans, and our players would be hitting the first betting day of the new year hard. We had all been instructed to get a good night's sleep, so the plan to head to Atlántico was a secret.

As the clerks began saying their goodbyes, Gabriella exchanged her seat for one closer to Tony. "I'm going to stick around a while, see if Vinnie shows up," Tony mumbled. I knew he had no intention of coming home tonight.

"I'll wait with you," Carmine said, in an effort to ease the awkward situation.

"Well, I'm going," I said, standing up. "Happy New Year."

Tony was already dialing the apartment, and Gabriella looked impatient for me to leave.

I walked to my car, relieved that 1992 was officially over. It had been the worst year of my life, but things were looking up. I had completed my first painting and had already started the sketch for my next piece: Untermyer Park on a wintry day, with the Hudson River below and the sheer cliffs on the other side. This time I would buy my art supplies in the States, where they were vastly cheaper.

Traffic was nonexistent as I headed toward home. I suddenly had the urge to stop by Atlántico. I cruised by, and as I approached the club someone pulled out of a parking spot directly in front of the entrance. Taking it as a sign, I parked my Daihatsu and headed inside. Passing the doorman, I had only taken a few steps when I spotted Demetrio by the garden bar. I was surprised by how happy I was to see him, but then my heart sank as I realized he was saying his goodbyes. Our eyes met and he came over to me.

"You're leaving already?" I made no attempt to hide the disappointment in my voice.

"It's too loud in there." Demetrio smiled. "And anyway, Remo has things under control."

"So," I asked, "where are you going?"

Demetrio smiled suggestively. "Someplace quieter, where I can welcome in the New Year . . . somewhere I can hear the waves while I enjoy a glass of wine."

■

DEMETRIO PARKED HIS CAR and pointed toward the restaurant.

"Neptuno," he said. "One of my favorite places on the island."

Neptuno was built with an enormous thatched roof that jutted out over a quaint seating area and a lower deck that stretched several meters out over the sea. Demetrio took my hand and led me inside. Lights installed underneath the deck illuminated the turquoise water below with a dreamy luminescence. He cocked his head to one side. "Can you hear it?" he asked, and I could: the gentle, rolling water lapping against the wooden beams. I couldn't help but be enchanted.

He chose a small candlelit table and ordered sautéed shrimp. "One of the perils of working on such a busy night," he said. "No chance to relax. Will you join me in a glass of wine?"

I shook my head. "No, thanks. I don't drink."

"I've noticed. But what I don't know is why you don't drink."

I shrugged. "I guess I just I like being in control. I've known too many people in my life who have to blame their regrettable behavior on being drunk or high."

Demetrio smiled playfully. "So all the mistakes you have made in your life took place when you were completely sober?"

"That's right."

"Drinking shouldn't be about getting drunk, Marisa. Wine is supposed to complement a meal." He ordered a bottle of pinot noir. When it arrived, he held his glass forward for me to try. I don't know if it was the spectacular setting or Demetrio's easy charm, but I felt giddy even without the wine. I could see why women all over the island had fallen for Demetrio's charms. I took a sip, then another, and another; and after a while I found myself staring at his lips and wondering what it would feel like to kiss him.

I wasn't used to the alcohol, and I began to feel relaxed and lightheaded. I found myself talking about my days at Ursuline, the strict all-girls Catholic high school I attended, and my sixteenth summer, when I wandered around Europe by myself. I told Demetrio that I was an artist, and he said he couldn't wait to see my work; he had a friend who owned a gallery and he offered to introduce me. I learned about his passion for sailing and surfing, and we compared cities and countries we had visited, trying to calculate if our paths might have crossed before.

He began feeding me shrimp drizzled in lemon, and passing me the wine glass at more frequent intervals. Thoroughly enjoying myself, I did not notice or care that the bottle was emptying. By now I was boldly flirting with him. We were also the only people left in the restaurant. He paid the bill, took my hand, and led me to the end of the dock. The moon was almost full and the stars were twinkling in the vast, clear sky.

"Remo tells me that you're married," I said.

We had reached the edge of the dock. We sat down, and I slipped off my sandals, dipping my feet in the warm water. He took off his shoes, rolled up his slacks and did the same. "Legally, that is true," he said. "My wife and I have not been together for years, however. Circumstances make it impossible for me to ask her for a divorce."

I tried to focus on what Demetrio was saying. He was opening up about his private life and I wanted to hear more, but I found my thoughts drifting to his beautiful hands, and how badly I wanted to feel them on my body. Some distant part of my brain piped up that he was married—but then again, he clearly wasn't having sex with his wife, just as I wasn't having sex with Tony. I tried to follow the train of his words, but my mind was fuzzy and unfocused. It was a perfect night, romantic and wonderful, and it felt so good to desire someone again.

Demetrio leaned back and rested on his elbows. I wanted to unbutton his shirt, but I felt woozy. I took off the jacket he had loaned me and passed it back to him. Maybe the shock of cool air against my skin might sober me up. Demetrio spread it out on the deck and reclined next to it. In the semi-darkness his deep blue eyes beckoned me to join him.

Instead I stood up, unzipped my dress and let it fall to the ground. I stood before him, naked except for a tiny black g-string. *Swimming will clear my head,* I thought as I dove into the sea. The water felt amazing on my skin—cool and incredibly sensual. As I surfaced, I looked behind me to see Demetrio's lean, muscular figure, stripped down to his underwear in the moonlight. He dove into the water with a splash and came up in front of me a few seconds later.

I looked into Demetrio's eyes and laughed. 1993 was starting out very well indeed. "You are full of surprises, Marisa," he said.

We faced each other, treading water. Our arms brushed each other's bodies as we tried to stay afloat. Kicking myself forward, I kissed him, long and soft, tasting the salt on his full lips. The kiss made my head spin. Or was it the wine? I swallowed water and started to splutter.

"Okay, you little alcoholic," Demetrio said, pulling me back to the dock. I was intensely aware of the feel of his arm wrapped around my torso, just under my breasts. "What did you have for dinner?" he asked.

I could only foggily recall picking at some chop suey at the Jaragua. "Lemon shrimp," I giggled, as everything seemed to go hazy.

Demetrio positioned my feet carefully on the ladder and pushed me upward. I flopped down on the dock as he came out of the water, looking like a wet Adonis. He was beautiful, I thought. His underwear clung to him, leaving little to the imagination. I was overwhelmed with desire. A lifetime had gone by since sex had seemed like a great idea.

"That's a lot of wine on an empty stomach, especially if you're not used to it," he said, using his jacket to towel me off.

Ignoring him, I tried to pull him down onto the deck.

"Oh no, you don't!" he laughed. "I'm taking you *home*."

"Don't want to go home," I slurred.

He brought his face close to mine. "I have no intention of causing a night you will regret," he grinned, helping me wriggle into my dress. "I want you fed, sober, and fully awake when I make love to you." I felt myself go weak in the knees.

The ride back was quiet. My stomach lurched with every pothole Demetrio dodged. "Where do you live? I can drop you off at home." I was sobering up now, and told him I had to pick up my car first. I couldn't leave it parked outside Atlántico. Everyone would assume I was having sex with someone, and I didn't want to get the reputation Remo was always warning me about.

"I need my car tomorrow," I said. I glanced at the digital clock on the car dashboard. It was 3:02 a.m. and I was already regretting what I'd done. I cringed, recalling the colorful adjectives the clerks used to describe Gabriella. I liked being known as a good girl.

"You're in no shape to drive, Marisa. I'll take you home in your car, and I'll have one of my employees follow us in mine."

People were still mulling around the gate to Atlántico when we pulled up. "It's right there." I pointed out my little car, wishing that I'd parked farther away.

Demetrio pulled over. "Back in a minute."

As he disappeared across the street, I staggered over to my car, fishing through my purse for the keys.

From behind me I heard Remo's distinctive voice. I fumbled with the keys, trying desperately to unlock my door. Remo was the last person I wanted to see in my current state. The keys slipped from my hand and landed on the pavement. "Shit!" I crouched down, groping around for them in the dark. I finally located them behind the front tire.

I stood up and gasped. Tony was towering over me, his face a mask of barely suppressed fury. He took in the wet hair and my slightly disheveled appearance. I was about to open my mouth to explain when I heard Demetrio returning.

"Let's go!" Demetrio said, cutting across the street.

Tony's gaze slowly fixed upon Demetrio and his thick, wet hair.

34

Tony swung at Demetrio.

I tried to stop him, to tell him that it wasn't what he thought, but it was too late. Tony's fist flashed toward Demetrio, who expertly deflected it and used the momentum to send my ex-husband tumbling to the ground. When Tony regained his composure, he leapt to his feet, eyeing his rival with an expression of pure rage.

Demetrio, on the other hand, looked incredibly poised. His stance suggested that he'd had martial-arts training. The men circled each other warily. People were streaming into the street, wanting to watch the action. From the corner of my eye, I saw a man pushing his way through the crowd: Demetrio's bodyguard. He pulled his gun from its holster, pointing the weapon at Tony.

"No!" I screamed.

Suddenly the guard hit the ground with a grunt. Remo had tackled him from behind and both men landed in a heap. I saw the gun skitter along the road and vanish under a car. Demetrio looked at Remo with a look of bewilderment.

Taking advantage of the split-second distraction, Tony swung again. This time he didn't miss. The blow landed squarely on Demetrio's jaw with a sickening thud. Demetrio stumbled backward. I tried to get between them, but Tony grabbed my wrist and wrenched me away. He set upon Demetrio again, determined to beat him senseless.

Remo pried Tony away. "Goddamn it, Tony, he's not worth it! You're going to wind up with a bullet in your head!"

Tony's eyes settled on me, standing off to the side, covering my mouth in horror. "Get in the fucking car!"

Terrified, I stumbled toward his Mitsubishi. Demetrio was getting unsteadily to his feet, aided by his security guard. He pointed at Remo and snarled, "You're fired!"

Remo had labored at Atlántico for years, helping transform it from a modest café into a playground for the island's elite. In one night of madness it was snatched away from him. Demetrio rubbed his jaw and wiped the blood trickling from the corner of his mouth. I wanted to go over to him, but I knew if I didn't get into the car there would only be more trouble.

The three of us flew out of the parking lot. Tony floored the accelerator, gripping the steering wheel with white knuckles, while Remo pleaded with him to slow down. How had such a perfect night gone so horribly wrong? Tony screeched to a halt outside of our place, and I followed him out.

He stormed up the steps. "At first I thought you were pushing me away because of my drinking. So I cut down, but nothing changes. Ron tells me it's hormones, and I got to be patient. So I'm waiting and waiting like a jackass, and now I find out you've been fucking someone else the whole time!" He wrenched open the door to the apartment, grabbed a suitcase, and started tossing clothes into it.

"That's not true!" I protested, following him as he stormed around the place grabbing his stuff. "You're wrong!"

There was no arguing with Tony once he had an idea fixed in his head. He dumped his suits and shoes into another bag, opened the safe, took out his gun, and started removing wads and wads of money.

"Hey, some of that's mine," I objected, but he pushed me away. I watched as he removed his passport and tucked it into his pocket. Then he took Justine's.

"You can't take that!" I protested.

Tony tensed up and charged towards me. "I saw how you looked at Demetrio," he hissed in my face. "You didn't give a shit about me back there. You only cared about what happened to him." He grabbed his bags and stormed toward the door. He paused. "By the way, you're fired. And this time, don't bother calling Ron. You no longer work for us." The door slammed, and his footsteps echoed down the stairs.

■

I WOKE UP HOURS later, feeling sick and disoriented. I sat up in bed and saw the state of the room—gaping drawers and clothes strewn everywhere—and the whole horrible fight came crashing back, along with a horrendous pounding headache. Would Demetrio ever want to see me again? I had told him I was divorced, and alluded to the fact that it had been ages since I had sex. I cringed to imagine what he must think of me now.

Suddenly I recalled Tony emptying the safe, and I stumbled out of bed towards it. The door to the safe was open. Except for a few thousand dollars and my ring, it was empty.

With a sick feeling in my gut, I began looking for my car keys. Instinct told me I needed to retrieve the Daihatsu as soon as possible. I frantically searched the apartment, to no avail. The last time I recalled having the keys was outside Atlántico. Hoping that I had dropped them during the early-morning fight, I showered and had Rosa call me a taxi.

The cab slowed down as the elaborate wrought-iron gates of Atlántico came into view. My car was gone. Tony had taken it. I stared out of the window, biting back tears, and gave the driver Remo's address.

■

"OPEN UP! IT'S ME!"

I kept on banging on the door until a bleary-eyed, unshaven Remo opened it a crack. I pushed in past him. I noted that his suit from last night was lying in a pile on the floor, caked with dirt. "Jesus," I said, trying to lighten the mood. "Where did you sleep— a building site?"

Remo still looked shell-shocked. "Three-and-a-half million men on this island," he said, "and you have to cheat on your husband with my boss."

"Ex-husband, remember? And what do you call what Tony's been doing with Gabriella?" I sat down and put my aching head in my hands. "I wish I *had* slept with Demetrio," I groaned. "You have no idea how badly I wanted to. I didn't, and I still have to deal with all of this."

Remo looked lost in thought. "I guess we're both out of a job," I ventured. The silence stretched. "Look," I said comfortingly, "at least *you* can go back to the States. I'm stuck here. Tony took Justine's passport. And anyway, I'm sure Demetrio will take you back."

"I just humiliated the man with the world's biggest ego in front of his adoring public," Remo said. "He won't take me back. Ever."

"You're being melodramatic. As soon as everybody finds out what really happened, life will go back to normal. You'll go back to Atlántico and I'll go back to Tomaju."

Remo turned very serious. "You can't go over there!" he said urgently. "Marisa, promise me you won't go near Tomaju!"

"Calm down!" I said. "Jesus, you think Tony's that angry with me?"

His eyes blazed. "Just promise, okay? He told them not to let you in."

Hearing a knock at the door, Remo took a sharp intake of breath. "Shhhh," he whispered. After another knock, a white envelope sailed underneath the door. Remo picked it up and tore it open. His face dropped as he read it. "Your boyfriend just evicted me," he said bitterly, slumping onto the couch. "On top of everything else, I'm now officially homeless."

"Demetrio is your landlord?"

"Was my landlord," he groaned. "I didn't have all my papers in order when I was looking for a place, so he let me rent this one. He owns a bunch on the island. Now I'm completely fucked."

The consequences of my impromptu dinner with Demetrio were exploding out of control. How could Demetrio be so vindictive as to evict Remo? He'd always seemed like such a gentleman. Were my instincts about him so wrong?

"Let me talk to him, Remo. Do you have your papers in order now?"

Remo winced. "Well . . . not exactly, no. I've never had the money to do it."

I raised an eyebrow. "That's the lamest excuse I've ever heard. I'll lend you money, okay? I still have some, so problem solved."

Far from being cheered, Remo looked like his entire world had come crashing down about him. I wanted to ask him what was wrong, but he seemed so desperately sad that all I could do was pity him.

"I think you need to get some sleep," I said gently. "Things'll seem better tomorrow, you'll see."

I left him there, dazed. Before I left I stopped and asked him something that had been bothering me since I'd woken up. "Why did Tony come looking for me last night, anyway?"

Remo sighed heavily. "He wasn't looking for you. He was looking for me. I guess you'd call his finding you with Demetrio an unexpected bonus."

■

I WAITED FOR A few days before I called Tony. He owed me money, I needed my car, and I needed to get back to work. Hoping that he would have calmed down enough to talk to me, I tried his cell phone. From his tone I knew I had underestimated the depth of his anger.

"What?"

I took a deep breath. "Can I have my car back, please? And the money you took?"

"Your car? You don't have a car. It's my car, I paid for it."

"But you bought it for me."

"And I gave to Horacio. And funnily enough, it was already registered to him." Furious, I decided to hang up before I said something to further inflame the situation. Before I could, Tony pressed on.

"By the way, *you* owe *me* money," he said. "Horacio just read me the terms of our divorce." My heart sank. "Apparently, I have joint custody of our daughter and I don't have to pay child support or alimony."

My blood ran cold. Those were the terms of my quickie divorce, but I'd never thought that Tony would someday use them against me. Surely he'd still help support his daughter?

"Also," he went on, "I want to remind you that the contract for the apartment is in your name, so I won't be paying rent anymore."

The full weight of what he was saying hit me all at once. Without a job, I wouldn't be able to support us, or pay Rosa's salary or Justine's exorbitant private-school fees.

"I didn't do anything!" I screamed.

"You can't make it here on your own. Let me know when I can have Justine."

With that, Tony hung up on me.

I stared at the phone in my hand, thunderstruck. Then a wave of fury started to build inside of me. Did Tony really think he could separate me from the person I loved more than anyone else? From my own daughter? I may have made a stupid mistake with our divorce papers, but I knew that one call from me to Ruth Gordon could put Tony in jail for years.

His next meeting with Ruth Gordon was scheduled for May. I

would just have to ride it out until then. I picked up the phone and called Veronica, the head of the modeling agency.

■

"DARRRLING!"

Veronica sashayed over to me as I stepped into the Agencia de Modelos, waving her cigarette holder by way of greeting. She stopped dead, as if noticing that I had lost a limb.

"What on earth did you do to your hair?" She tapped the ash from her pink Russian Sobranie cigarette into one of the several ashtrays she kept strategically placed around the room. "Come back and see me the moment you are blond again, so we can update your portfolio."

By this point Leslie had returned to California, where she would stay until she gave birth. I had no choice but to go to a salon to have my hair bleached. The Jaragua seemed like the logical place. I headed over, and insisted they squeeze me in. I sat down and told the stylist that I wanted my hair blond. She covered my hair with a thick, pungent paste, put a cap over it, and left me to read the latest issue of *Cosmo*.

After five minutes my scalp began to tingle. After ten it was seriously burning. I had never had to bleach my hair before, and had no idea it could be so painful. I called the girl over and asked her to rinse the mixture off. The cool water felt good against my scalp. Then she added shampoo, and I winced in pain. Something was wrong. The girl left me, mid-wash, and rushed off to fetch another woman, who took one look at my head and let out a horrified gasp. I sat forward, and burst into tears when I saw my reflection. My scalp was bright red. The roots of my hair were white, and the rest a light fluorescent green.

Stunned, I reached out to touch it, and a clump came off in my hand. There was a commotion in the salon as I wailed and asked how on earth this could have happened. The stylist tearfully confessed that she had never lightened Caucasian hair before. My scalp was raw and would need to heal before anything else could be done to my hair. In the meantime, the only solution was to cut what remained as short as possible.

When I walked into the apartment, the dumbstruck expression on Rosa's face sent me running to my room, where I cried harder than I ever had in my life. I looked in the mirror, taking in the beet-red face, blood-red scalp, and cropped snow-white fuzz. I sobbed miserably. I looked like a fucking chicken.

Then, from out of nowhere, a burst of laughter erupted out of me. The utter ludicrousness of the situation had suddenly become apparent. After everything I had endured in my life, after every-thing I had endured in the last year, did my hair really deserve this many tears? It was just hair. It would grow back. I had bigger problems to deal with.

■

"OPEN UP! IT'S ME!"

Two days later I was banging on Remo's door. I was deter-mined to drag my friend out of his slump. If I could manage to pull myself together after my disastrous start to the new year, then so could he. When he refused to open the door, I threat-ened to kick it down. Finally, he opened it a crack and I pushed myself inside.

I pulled open the curtains and he squinted against the morning light. He looked at me quizzically, then reached his hand out to touch the auburn wig I was wearing. "What's with the hair?" he muttered.

"I got it in Miami," I said.

"Why?"

I pulled off the wig and endured the horrified expression on his face. "The short version? The only capable hairdresser on the island is in America, having a baby." In addition to the auburn wig, I had three blond ones in different lengths and shades for modeling.

I wrinkled up my nose at the smell in his apartment. "Jesus, Remo, you have to pull yourself together!" Remo was unwashed and unshaven; empty food containers were piled up next to a stack of dirty dishes. I opened the blinds and window to let some fresh air in. "Are you still being evicted?" I asked.

"I have to be out in three days," he moaned.

I took a seat on the edge of the sofa. "Listen, Remo, you can stay with me. You can have the room upstairs."

"I don't think your husband would approve."

"Ex-husband. Anyway, he knows we're just friends, so that's not a problem. He also knows that you lost your job trying to protect him. He owes you. He should give you a job."

"I'm American. The police don't want Americans working there."

"Carmine and Vinnie work there. So why not you?" Remo's eyes were inexplicably welling with tears. "Look, if you're worried about the police, you could grade. Tony has four people working full-time through the night grading tickets. Nobody would even know you're there, and you wouldn't be taking bets. The pay's just as good."

A spark of interest appeared in his eyes. "I am used to working nights," he said.

Remo and I needed each other. If we pooled our resources, we could have a steady income and a place to live. I laid out the situation for him. Without getting help with the rent soon, I would lose the apartment. I could practically see the cogs turning in his brain.

"Come on, Remo. It'll be fun. Justine will be thrilled to have you there."

■

TWO DAYS LATER, REMO showed up with everything he owned in duffel bags. He refused to take the upstairs room, preferring instead to move into the empty maid's quarters. It was small and cramped, but private. That way he was completely separated from the rest of the apartment, and had his own private entrance. Rosa was the only one who had difficulty with the arrangement. She offered to swap with him, but he brushed away her overtures.

I soon learned why Remo had been so determined to have the tiny maid's quarters. A few days later, I opened the door dividing his area from the kitchen and found myself face-to-face with a tall, beautiful Haitian woman. She froze when she saw me, and Remo suddenly appeared behind her.

"Er—oh, hi! Marisa, this is Laurette." Laurette mumbled a quick goodbye, then disappeared down the metal staircase.

"Isn't she's the ladies'-room attendant at Atlántico?"

"That's right," Remo confirmed sheepishly, before hurriedly changing the subject. "Anyway, it's my first night grading. Any last words of advice?"

Just like me, Remo was entering the world of bookmaking without the slightest knowledge of sports or gambling. Even though he wasn't taking bets, he still had an awful lot to learn.

"Just try not to get discouraged," I told him. "It's going to feel overwhelming at first."

■

As REMO SETTLED INTO life at Tomaju, I got back into the routine of modeling. Veronica had been mortified at first when I showed her my ruined scalp, but soon saw the advantages of my new look. I was like a Barbie doll with interchangeable tresses, and my portfolio would reflect that. She was right—I was booked for jobs even before my pictures were developed.

One evening a week or so later, as Remo was preparing to leave for work, I heard the sound of a Harley-Davidson roaring toward the apartment. Remo sprinted to the window and blanched. He hadn't told Tony he had moved in with me, for fear of upsetting him, and now his worst fears were being realized. "It's Tony!" he said, his voice laden with panic. "He knows I'm here!"

"No, he doesn't," I assured him. "And even if he did, who cares? When did he get the bike?"

"He just had it flown in from Miami."

Below in the parking lot, Tony looked up, revved the engine and took off. The rumble of the motor hung in the air long after he had disappeared from view. I wondered what on earth had brought him out here.

Remo peeked over my shoulder. "Did you ever tell him about what Sonny LoBue said?"

"Yeah. He didn't seem bothered, though."

"You know Sacco's back, right? And it looks like he's planning on staying this time."

That could only mean one thing. "So they finally indicted him," I said.

This was bad news for Tony and Tomaju. Unlike Carmine, Ron was a high-profile fugitive, especially after *60 Minutes*. Even if the local police denied it, the feds would naturally assume he'd fled here. Ron, the founding father of the whole enterprise, was a huge bull's-eye on Tomaju's back as long as he was hiding out in the D.R.

"Remo, I don't think it's wise for you to keep working at the office while Ron's around. The FBI will be putting pressure on the Dominicans to hand him over."

"What about Tony?"

"As far as I know, he's still in the clear."

Remo nodded slowly. "What if Ron were caught? What would happen to Tomaju?"

I shrugged. "Well . . . nothing, I guess. Things would carry on as usual. His girlfriend Joanna would take over paying and collecting in the States." Remo looked deep in thought. I took some comfort in the fact that I would probably have quit Tomaju anyway, knowing that Ron was hiding out on the island. "Maybe it's time you tried to get your old job back. Maybe I should talk to Demetrio?"

I had not stopped thinking about Demetrio since that fateful night. My feelings for him had not changed at all. In fact, I was more determined than ever to have him. I knew I couldn't see him now, not with my hair in the state it was in. But pleading Remo's case would provide the perfect opportunity to talk to him.

"How long did you work for Sacco?" Remo asked.

"Hmm, it's been eight years." I shivered. It was strange to think that I had dedicated almost a decade of my life to Ron and his gambling empire.

"What do you know about him?" Remo pressed on. "I mean, really know about him."

"Okay, Remo," I said, sitting down and patting the sofa next to me. "You want to know about Ron? I'll tell you. But I want some information in exchange." Remo sat down, looking puzzled. "I'll tell you about Ron . . . if you tell me about Demetrio."

35

INXS's "Suicide Blonde" pumped from the sound system as a skinny, effeminate makeup artist worked on my face with a cigarette dangling from his lips. My latest modeling job was an unpaid appearance with twenty-two other models at a charity fashion show organized to raise funds for the Robert Reid Cabral Children's Hospital. Veronica had promised me that the exposure would be simply fabulous for my career.

Backstage, designers, hairdressers, and makeup artists flitted around, fussing over the models, trying desperately to get us all ready on time. Seemingly immune to the chaos, my makeup artist gave me strongly defined eyebrows using an angular brush and brown powder. When he'd finished, he added a second coat of mascara and painted my lips a deep red to complement the black crêpe evening gown I would be wearing. *"Hermosa!"* he said.

I slipped into the dress. Joaquin, the frazzled Puerto Rican designer responsible for this fussy creation, zipped me into it. As a stylist draped a heavy necklace around my throat, I reached for my blonde wig. Joaquin snatched it from me. "No wig!" he said. Before I could protest, he bustled me toward the stage.

I stepped out onto the runway with my impossibly short hair. Cameras erupted around me as I strode down the catwalk, my confidence growing with each step.

The following Sunday, images from the show were plastered all over the glossy pages of *Ritmo Social.* It was the first time I had been so prominently displayed in the local press. Even with my short hair and heavy makeup, I was instantly recognizable. That evening I again heard the sound of Tony's growling Harley as he circled the lot outside the house. After revving a few times, he roared off into the night. I peered through the blinds, watching his taillight disappear into the gloom.

He clearly wanted me to know he was coming around. I couldn't decide if he was trying to intimidate me or apologize to me. Maybe he'd come because he'd seen my picture in the paper.

I was too busy to worry about what Tony was thinking, as my modeling career was starting to take off. I was taking every job I could get, and working steadily. As with any freelance job, cash flow was a constant issue. I had already spent a small fortune on my wigs and art supplies. I would have to be extremely cautious with my money going forward. Even with Remo's help, my finances still looked grim.

When Veronica offered me a cash-in-hand job handing out awards onstage for an insurance company, I accepted without hesitation. It was hardly high-end work, but the lure of being paid as soon as the ceremony was over was too much to resist. The event was a dreadfully dull affair. My job was to look pretty while I handed out a series of awards to a bunch of charmless, drunk businessmen.

The event started over an hour late, so it was well past midnight when I finally presented the last prize with a phony smile on my face. Afterward, I tracked down the person responsible for organizing this dismal affair in the hotel's bar. He was a short, fat man with a comb-over. His eyes lit up when he saw me walking toward him.

"Why don't you stay for a drink?" he asked optimistically. "Or perhaps you'd like to stay for a more intimate celebration?"

I declined as politely I could, and left with my eight hundred pesos and as much dignity as I could scrape together. I felt like a prostitute when I climbed into my taxi at one in the morning, wearing high heels, heavy makeup, and a platinum-blond wig. Judging by the knowing looks the taxi driver was giving me, he had come to the same conclusion. I studiously stared out of the window, reprimanding myself for all my frivolous spending in the past. I should have been putting money in my bank account in Canada, I thought; I should have taken my finances more seriously. I was no better than Tony's mother Sophia, after all—and the realization stung. She too had once believed that Tony would always take care of her. I suspected it was just a matter of time before I would be forced to sell my diamond ring. I had intended for it to go to Justine one day, but that seemed less and less likely now.

When the taxi pulled up to my building I noticed that all the lights in my apartment were blazing. I rushed up the stairs to find Rosa, puffy-eyed, on the phone. She held out the receiver. Her expression fell somewhere between shock and pity. I snatched the phone and held it to my ear. It was Remo on the other line. He sounded exhausted. "There's been an accident . . . it's Tony. You'd better get down here. Quick."

"But what happened?"

"There's no time, Marisa! Hurry up. It doesn't look like he's going to make it."

■

ROSA CALLED FOR A taxi as I hurried into a pair of jeans and a T-shirt. I frantically tore off my wig and scrubbed my face clean. Rosa followed me into the bathroom. "Tony was here earlier," she said.

"Was he drunk?" I asked her.

"No, but different."

Before I could ask any more questions the cab was honking downstairs.

We pulled up outside Clinica Abreu, the top private hospital in Santo Domingo, with a screech of brakes. I passed the driver fifty pesos and sprinted for the emergency entrance, Remo's words echoing in my ears. *It doesn't look like he's going to make it.* Outside, doubled over, a man was vomiting into the bushes. As I approached he straightened up. It was Ron. He wiped his chin with a shaking hand. "It's bad," he mumbled. Then he doubled over and vomited again.

I pushed the doors open and gasped. Remo was rushing toward me, his clothes soaked in blood. "He's in bad shape," he said in a trembling voice. "He wasn't wearing a helmet or boots when it happened." From farther down the corridor I heard Tony's voice, strong and insistent, demanding a glass of water. It did not sound like the last words of a dying man. I shot Remo a puzzled look. He led me toward a green curtain and told me that the doctor was on his way.

I pulled the curtain back. Tony was lying flat on a trolley. His head whipped around to look at me. "Where were you?" he demanded.

His face was completely unharmed, without a scratch on it. As my eyes traveled down his body, though, I felt my stomach lurch. Now I knew why Ron had been sick outside.

The entire right side of Tony's body was a gory abstraction of torn flesh, a vivid wound that gaped open, exposing muscles and tendons. Jagged white things were sticking out of him from all angles, and I realized with a jolt that they were smashed bones, protruding from his flesh. He looked inside out. I couldn't believe he was still breathing. Compounding the horror, his body was swarming with fat, hungry flies, which settled on his exposed flesh to feed. In a dreamlike state I stepped forward to brush them away. Then I saw something that sickened me to my core. At first it looked as though his right foot was missing, but no . . . there it was. The foot was hanging off the edge of the trolley, connected to his leg by what looked like a single exposed tendon.

The smell of sickly sweet blood was overwhelming. "Where were you?" he demanded again, his voice cracking.

I took his face in my hands. "Shhhh—I was working. But I'm here now . . . "

"Please," he whispered, "tell the nurse to get me some water. I keep asking, but nobody will listen."

I didn't want Tony to see me cry, so I leaned closer until my cheek was touching his. Where was everyone? In America or Canada, a team of doctors would have been attending to him, trying to save his life. Here, he had been left on a trolley, on the edge of death, and no one was helping him.

"I know I fucked up," Tony said hoarsely. "Remo told me there was nothing between you and his boss. I'm sorry. I'm so sorry." He started to convulse, causing the jellied mass of his body to tremble.

Convinced he was dying, I kissed his forehead and whispered, "I love you." I wanted him to leave this world with some kind words. He responded with a sob.

Remo began talking to someone outside, and the curtains parted with a whoosh. I didn't pull away from Tony. His breaths were becoming shallow and irregular. A burst of Spanish profanities erupted behind me, followed by someone barking orders. "You must go now!" A man with dark hair and gold-rimmed, half-moon glasses appeared next to us. He looked oddly familiar. He introduced himself as Dr. Enrique.

Tony's eyes fluttered open again, but they were wild and unfocussed. With shocking speed and strength his good arm shot out and grabbed the doctor by the shirt. Tony yanked the startled man forward.

"Don't you dare cut off my leg!" he hissed. Then his hand went limp and he slumped into unconsciousness.

The doctor wheeled Tony away, yelling orders. I was left standing there, in total shock. I gazed uncomprehendingly at my hands, which were covered in blood. A pool was congealing on the floor where the trolley had stood. Remo was still holding Tony's gore-soaked cell phone. He slumped onto a metal folding chair with a groan of despair.

"Remo, what happened?" I asked.

"He drove into the back of a truck. The power was out; the truck didn't have any lights. He didn't see it until it was too late. I didn't know where to take him! Then I remembered Fernando— skinny kid, clerks in the Small Office. His father's a doctor and he told me to bring him here. Oh, God . . . " Remo held his head in his hands. "This is so bad."

A nurse came over and handed Remo a slip of paper. He looked at her, confused. "The patient needs a thousand cubic centimeters of blood immediately," she said. "You'll need four donors."

"What?"

The nurse coolly explained that in the Dominican Republic you could not receive blood without first donating it, due to chronic shortages. She wrote down the address of the Red Cross.

Remo grabbed me by the arm. "Come on, Ron's outside!"

Yet Ron was nowhere to be found.

"Where are we going to find two more donors?" I asked, as Remo desperately flagged down a taxi.

"You and I will donate," Remo said through gritted teeth, "and we'll buy the rest."

■

THE DRIVER KNEW THE way, but the journey was painfully slow. As he navigated the deep potholes that pitted these dark, unmarked streets, I brooded about Tony. With each passing second I sensed him slipping away. Remo was staring out of the window in a state of shock. When he spoke, it was almost to himself. "After Tony hit the truck, the driver got out. He took Tony's watch and gun, then left him in the street to die."

"How did you find him?"

"Somehow he managed to crawl to his cell phone and call the office. Thank God I was grading."

The taxi driver stopped the car and pointed at a one-story wooden structure with a weather-beaten *Cruz Roja* sign. A guard let us into the dim, musty-smelling building. Remo handed the slip of paper to the nurse, with the details of Tony's blood type and the amount we needed.

She frowned. "We only have the five-hundred-unit bags in stock."

"Fine," I said. We wouldn't need four donors after all. Remo and I could donate a thousand ccs between the two of us.

She pricked our fingers to determine our blood types, and then we followed her to a dingy back room. Inside was a row of metal cots. The nurse seemed in no particular hurry. When Remo asked if she could speed it up a little, he received a dirty look in response.

I laid down on a creaky bed. Nothing seemed clean or sterile. The floors and walls were caked with layers of grime, and the medical equipment looked old and outdated. The nurse snapped a rubber tourniquet around my arm, slapped my vein, and inserted the syringe. She then connected it to a long rubber tube that ran into a clear plastic bag propped on the side of the bed.

Next she hooked Remo up. I listened to her heavy, slow footsteps as they squeaked off down the corridor. I watched dully as the bag next to me began to fill, bit by agonizing bit. The process seemed to take an eternity. Tony's life depended upon how quickly we could get blood to him. What if we were too late?

The nurse finally returned and removed the needle from my arm, then from Remo's. She tied off the bags and meandered off to the admissions area with them. It seemed as if everything were happening in slow motion. I hurried after her and almost fell over when I suddenly became dizzy.

Remo caught my arm and smiled at me weakly. "Steady, we just gave a lot of blood."

A white box was waiting for us at the counter. "We only have five hundred units of type O negative available," the nurse informed us nonchalantly.

"The doctor told us to get a thousand," Remo said.

"I'll reserve the other five hundred units as soon as I have it."

"Señora, we just donated a thousand units. We need a thousand units back."

The nurse's face hardened. "O negative is the second-rarest blood type. This is all I have." She slid the cardboard box across the counter to Remo.

"Goddammit!" Remo pulled out his wallet and started counting out bills on the counter. "How much do you want for the blood?"

I grabbed the box. "Remo, she doesn't have any more O negative. Let's go."

By the time we returned to the hospital, it was four in the morning. We ran down the deserted corridors and banged on the OR doors. A surgical nurse took the cardboard box and the doors swung shut. Remo and I peered through the tiny window, watching them work on Tony. His eyes were taped shut and he had a plastic tube snaking out of his mouth. The equipment looked like it belonged to a previous century.

Remo and I slumped to the floor, shoulder to shoulder. I was an emotional mess. My mind started frantically turning the night's events over, trying to see how this horror could have been prevented.

Remo's eyes were welling with tears. "You, Tony, and Justine are the only things that make my life here bearable. You guys are my family. I don't know what I'd do if . . . if . . . "

Tony's cell phone started ringing, and Remo answered. I could hear Ron's voice on the other end, buzzing like a wasp. "You need to come back here and finish grading!"

Remo looked dumbstruck. "But we're still waiting for Tony to come out of the OR," he said.

"There's nothing you can do there. I need you here."

Remo put the phone down. In a disbelieving voice he said, "He hung up on me."

"You'd better go," I said. "Round up the rest of the graders and get them to the Red Cross as soon as they're finished."

■

THE HOSPITAL STARTED TO come alive again. The smell of coffee floated down the corridor and the echo of voices bounced off the walls. It was 1:10 in the afternoon when the doors to the OR finally swung open. I stood up as Dr. Enrique stepped out, ripping off his surgical mask.

"It's been an extremely difficult, complicated surgery. The foot was almost completely severed. There was only one blood supply feeding it."

"Can I see him?"

"No. He'll remain under sedation in the OR for as long as possible. We urgently need more blood. I can't do anything else for him now. His vital signs are too weak."

A hospital employee ushered me upstairs to the administration office. I filled out some paperwork and was told I'd have to provide a seventy-five-thousand-peso deposit. Tony was an expensive patient. His bill had to be paid whether he lived or died.

■

THE TAXI PULLED UP to the office and I hurried upstairs, hoping that someone might have the correct blood type. The phones were ringing, but as soon as the clerks saw me they rushed over.

"Tony's in the best possible hands," Fernando assured me. "My dad studied in France . . . he specialized in trauma. He's the best orthopedic surgeon on the island."

The rest of the clerks huddled around me for news. Remo was still there, his T-shirt stiff with blood. He had bad news: the graders had all been checked, and no one was a match. He'd also checked with every hospital in the country, and none of them had O negative.

"None of us are O negative," Gabriella added, as I fought back tears of frustration. Tony needed blood now.

"People! Pick up the phones!" Ron's voice bellowed as he

stormed into the room. An uneasy silence fell over the office as Ron made his priorities shockingly clear. He clapped his hands.

"Back to work!"

■

I FOLLOWED RON BACK to Tony's office. He was no longer the healthy, fresh-faced businessman I had met back in Los Angeles. Life had caught up with Ron all at once, and he looked tired and worn-down. His eyes had heavy bags under them, and a jittery, hunted look.

"The hospital is asking for a seventy-five-thousand-peso deposit," I said.

A look of annoyance clouded his face. "Doesn't Tony have medical insurance?"

"Medical insurance? There's no such thing here." I couldn't believe Ron was hesitating. "It's only six thousand dollars, Ron. Tony'll pay you back."

Ron stood up and closed the door. "I don't have a problem with the money," he said. Then he gave me a strange look. "But I do have a problem using the money to bail out someone who might be talking to the feds."

"Are you suggesting," I said carefully, "that Tony is the informant?"

"With all the information that's leaking out, you know whose name never comes up? Tony's. Don't you find that a little strange, given the fact that he runs this place? Wouldn't you be suspicious?"

I felt a mixture of fury and pity. There was an edge of paranoid desperation in his question. He was scared. He wasn't looking at a year in jail and a slap on the wrist anymore. Sacco would do hard time if he was captured. He'd placed the noose around his own neck by talking to the media, and he knew it.

Anyway, I had a pretty good idea of who the informant was.

"Tony's name doesn't come up because he's never missed a probation meeting. As far as the feds are concerned, Tony's in California hanging curtains for a living." I stood up. "If you won't lend him the money, then I need to find it somewhere else." I went to open the door.

"Wait . . . Marisa. The money'll be at the hospital later today, okay?" Ron's initial reaction was prompted by fear. His millions were no help to him now.

"Thank you," I said.

I returned to the OR, continuing my vigil. My hope receded with each passing minute. I knew that Tony was slipping away. How was I going to tell Justine that she had lost her father? The injustice of his fate ate at me. The accident hadn't killed him, but the lousy blood shortage could. While Tony lay dying in the operating room, I thought about the good times and the love we'd once shared. I had given up everything for this man. He had changed the entire direction of my life. I started to cry.

I heard footsteps running toward me. When Remo saw me crying, he blanched.

"Christ, am I too late?"

In his hand was a five-hundred-unit package of O negative blood.

■

I SOMEHOW EXPECTED TONY to be the only occupant of the intensive care unit, but four other patients were packed into the small, humid room. Tony looked terrible. His face was ghostly white, he had tubes sticking out of everywhere, and he was hooked up to a monitor that resembled a machine from a '60s sci-fi movie. His toes were caked in dried blood, and a metal device running from his shin to his ankle poked out over the bandages. His entire right side was bandaged, and with a shudder I noticed the vast difference in skin color between his two feet. The left looked relatively normal; the right was a pale shade of blue.

Dr. Enrique stated that the next twenty-four hours would be critical. If Tony survived, he would be facing an extensive series of grueling operations, including bone and skin grafts. He showed me on the X-rays that Tony's leg had shattered upon impact. Between the compound fractures and his half-severed foot, he had lost an estimated three inches of bone and a great deal of blood.

Blood loss would remain a critical issue in Tony's recovery. He would need more blood as soon as he was stable enough to undergo the next operation. "Plus," Dr. Enrique looked around and dropped his voice to a whisper, "there was a high level of cocaine in his bloodstream. Was he using the drug regularly?"

"I don't know."

I recalled all the times I had confronted Tony about his drug use, and all the times he had denied it.

"By law I am required to report my findings to the police. But under the circumstances, I will keep this information to myself."

Visiting hours in the ICU were limited, strictly reserved for immediate family members. Remo and I were determined that one of us would be present when Tony regained consciousness. I told the nurse that I was Tony's wife and that Remo was my brother. So, for a while at least, Remo finally got his wish. He became an official member of our family.

36

"Hey, Sister Ramirez, can I book you in for a sponge bath later?"

The nurses giggled and rolled their eyes. Tony was putting on a brave face, gamely flirting as he was wheeled past the nurses' station on his way to the elevator. I had to marvel at his tenacity. So far he was beating the odds. Not only had he survived the accident, but he'd also managed to avoid having his shattered leg amputated.

Following two difficult weeks in intensive care, he had been moved to a private suite on the clinic's fourth floor. There his recovery continued at a painfully slow pace. Although he was out of immediate danger, he was still weak. An endless regime of operations meant that he needed to go under general anesthesia at least three times a week. As soon as he regained his strength, he was scheduled for another physically demanding procedure. Four weeks after the accident, Tony could still barely manage to sit up in bed for a couple of hours.

Still, he tried to wisecrack with the orderly as he was pushed from the elevator to the OR, where Dr. Enrique and his surgical nurse were waiting. Today's procedure was a routine one. Tony's exposed bones, muscles, and tendons had to be cleaned, and any dead tissue removed. It would take less than an hour. This time, however, the procedure would be performed while Tony was fully conscious.

Because he had already undergone eleven serious operations within a matter of weeks, Dr. Enrique explained to us that Tony's system was flooded with dangerous levels of toxic drugs. Because of this, general anesthesia had to be reserved for the more serious procedures, like skin and bone grafting.

I gave Tony a reassuring smile as the orderlies lifted him onto the operating table. Tony's grin became a grimace as he prepared himself for the pain he knew was coming. Dr. Enrique began unwrapping the dressing on his thigh, while the nurse attended to his arm. She cleaned the meaty, ragged wounds incurred when the bone had ripped through the skin. Because he had suffered compound fractures, traditional casts had not been an option. With every slight movement of his fragile, unprotected limbs, Tony moaned in agony. I winced as I watched the procedure. I was almost as relieved as he was when the arm and thigh had been cleaned and tightly re-bandaged. Dr. Enrique told Tony that he would be able to support himself on crutches in another month or so.

Next, the nurse began removing the layers of gauze from the lower part of Tony's leg. I half expected him to cry out as the gauze came off and exposed his mutilated flesh, but he didn't make a sound. I was barely able to reconcile this bloody horror with any recognizable part of a human body.

A mass of exposed bone was framed by some skin and muscle. A metal brace ran along the outside of the lower part, from mid-shin to ankle, keeping the lifeless foot attached. The brace was anchored with screws, which had been drilled directly into the bone. I would be responsible for cleaning Tony's leg once he was discharged from the hospital, but until this moment I had no idea of how bad it really was. Sweat began to appear in beads on my forehead as the nurse scoured Tony's muscles and the twenty-odd centimeters of exposed bone with a stiff brush, until the entire lower leg was covered in bright red foam.

"Necrosis occurs when there is not enough blood to feed the tissue," Dr. Enrique explained as the bloody leg was patted dry. He produced a scalpel. "When large areas die, the flesh becomes gangrenous." I watched as he bent over the leg and began slicing off the edges of Tony's flesh where the skin had turned brown. Tony winced as the doctor shaved. "I cut until I draw blood. When I see blood, I know the tissue is alive."

Watching, I was gripped by a morbid fascination. When the doctor had finished, he manipulated the leg gently, turning it on its side. Then he began to clean the exposed, rubbery tendons, which did not cause Tony any discomfort. Nor did Tony react when Dr. Enrique inserted a long cotton swab into the exposed space between the bottom of Tony's leg and his foot, where it disappeared into the glutinous hole.

The nurse massaged a yellow salve onto the exposed bone and muscle, pushing the goop into the gaps between the metal screws and Tony's bone. Tony stared off into the distance, determinedly imagining he was somewhere else. His face relaxed once Dr. Enrique began the time-consuming process of re-dressing the wound, skillfully weaving a bandage around the screws to keep dirt from getting in.

Tony nodded when Dr. Enrique announced, "All done." His face was deathly pale, and I could only imagine how much pain he must be in. He didn't say a word as he was wheeled back past the nurses' station; all of the forced cheeriness had drained out of him. Back in his room, he was given a shot of morphine and he drifted off to sleep.

I leaned back on the sofa next to his bed, where I had been sleeping for the past several weeks. Tony was having a difficult time managing his pain, and Dr. Enrique was convinced that this was caused by his past drug use. Morphine took the edge off, but was reserved for post-op. Codeine and Demerol barely helped at all. The nights were the worst. He'd moan for hours and choke back sobs of despair. I spent many a long night trying to help reposition his leg.

Sometimes I hated Tony. I hated him for getting on his bike drunk and high. I hated him because we were both paying the price for his reckless stupidity, and there was no end in sight. My entire life was on hold so I could take care of my ex-husband. When I wasn't resenting Tony, I felt guilty for resenting him.

He would not be well enough to get around on his own for months. Dr. Enrique felt that he might well still lose his leg below the knee. That possibility, Tony refused even to acknowledge. With much effort, he was able to wiggle two of his toes, and he took this as a sign that he'd soon be up and walking around again, despite Enrique's advice to the contrary. Tony had no idea of the true extent of the injuries that lay under his bandages.

When the "No Visitors" sign was removed at the end of May, the office flooded in to see their boss. Tony put on his bravest face and optimistically assured the clerks that he'd be back at the office soon. The pressure for him to return to work was mounting. The office was struggling without him, and the snowballing hospital bills were eating away at his savings. The accident had already cost him sixty thousand dollars, a figure that ballooned with each successive operation. As much as Tony wanted to return to work, however, his body simply was not ready. Once the clerks said their goodbyes, he slumped back into his pillows, utterly drained.

Ron, the man Tony had described as having been a father to him, was not exactly brimming over with compassion. He was more upset by the disruption to Tomaju than by the suffering Tony was enduring.

"I can't afford to have him gone another month," he insisted. "If he's strong enough to sit up in a hospital bed, then he's strong enough to come back to work. Period."

Thankfully, Dr. Enrique refused to even discuss Tony's release from the hospital for another two weeks. In the meantime, the same auto-body shop that was repairing Tony's Harley was com-missioned to customize a wheelchair according to the doctor's specifications. Tony's Mitsubishi was exchanged for a pickup truck, so that the wheelchair could be stored in the truck bed. Then we set out to find him a first-floor apartment, so he could access it by wheelchair.

On May 27, six weeks after his accident and seven days after his thirty-sixth birthday, Tony was discharged from the hospital. He looked like he'd aged a decade. A half-hour later we wheeled him through the front door of his new fully furnished apartment on Avenida Anacona—and he promptly fainted.

His condition didn't miraculously get better. He was unable to get from the bed to his wheelchair without help. He couldn't get dressed or go to the bathroom unaided. I continued to nurse him through the long, pain-wracked nights.

"What's Horacio up to these days?" I'd ask sarcastically, heaving Tony to and from his wheelchair. "Out with Ron again, I suppose?"

Tony had no answer. His best friend, the man Tony had claimed would do anything for him, was nowhere to be found. Horacio was too busy worming his way into Ron's confidence; he had no time to nurse a cripple.

Tony reappeared at the office a week later. He made it through a grueling four-hour shift and helped himself to a few ice-cold Presidentes as a reward. That evening Ron and Horacio wheeled a blind-drunk Tony back to the apartment. I was furious. How could they be so irresponsible? Tony was slowly recovering, but the gaping hole at the base of his foot was still dangerously sus-ceptible to infection. "He's not supposed to have alcohol. He's on antibiotics."

"Ah, lighten up," Tony slurred. "And show some respect."

"A few beers won't kill him," Horacio said.

That was the final straw. "Okay," I spat. "Well, I'm done baby-sitting."

Tony grabbed me by the waist and tried to pull me onto his lap. "I'll give you something to sit on, baby!"

I broke free, snatched the keys to the truck, and stormed out, ignoring the laughter that followed me.

■

THE PHONE RANG WITHIN minutes of my getting home. As soon as I heard Horacio's voice on the other end, I slammed it down. He and Ron had let Tony get drunk, so they would have to deal with the consequences. After a night of taking care of him, they would realize just how helpless he really was. The phone rang again. I picked it up. It was Ron. I hung up again and left the receiver off the hook.

I was exhausted. Trying to juggle being a mother to Justine with the demands of taking care of her severely disabled father was exerting a heavy toll. I hadn't slept in my own bed in six long weeks. I wanted nothing more than to crawl under the covers and sleep.

But there was something I needed to do first. And now was the perfect time. Justine and Rosa were asleep. Remo was grading at Tomaju. I opened the kitchen door and crept down the open hallway. I paused outside Remo's door. Then, taking a deep breath, I slipped inside. I closed the metal blinds and turned on the light.

His room was spotless. Remo's single bed was neatly made. His button-down shirts and suits were pressed and hung on a horizontal pole affixed to the wall. On the dresser were several framed photos of him with Justine, Tony, and me, snapped during past holidays. I opened the top drawer of his dresser and found his underwear and socks in orderly piles. The drawer beneath it was full of perfectly folded T-shirts. Jeans and shorts occupied the third drawer. I smiled. Remo's tidiness bordered on anal. Then I pulled open the bottom drawer.

Bingo. He had made no effort to conceal the contents. Again, everything was neatly organized and stacked into piles—a hundred or so graded tickets, bound with a rubber band. There were balance sheets showing the daily totals, and several cassette tapes. In the process of a regular day all of these items would eventually have been destroyed. It wouldn't have been hard for Remo to take them unnoticed.

When I uncovered a large, unsealed Manila envelope, I picked it up and poured out the contents. Inside were photocopies of Tony's business cards, several notes in Ron's handwriting, and two of my old accounting books. There was also a very sophisticated recording device, unlike anything I had ever seen before. Next to it were several tapes in clear plastic covers, marked with a name that I easily recognized.

J. Peterson.

In a separate stack were copies of the phone bills that Remo had so generously offered to pay. Now I knew why he had done so. They itemized a series of lengthy, expensive phone calls to the 415 area code. The phone number matched the one listed on several pink FedEx receipts I found for documents mailed to J. Peterson at 450 Golden Gate Avenue. The sender was R. Grayson at the Hotel Lina in Santo Domingo. Resting against the side of the drawer was an empty Presidente beer bottle, stored in a Ziploc baggie marked "Sacco." At the very back was a thick Manila envelope stuffed with cash—most of it in pesos, some in dollars. Remo claimed he didn't have any money to get his papers in order, yet a glance at the envelope revealed that he'd stashed a hefty amount of cash away over the years.

Underneath the envelope were two FBI business cards, held together with a paper clip. One was worn and wrinkled and said, "Jack Peterson, Special Agent, Federal Bureau of Investigation." The address and phone number matched the FedEx receipts. The second card had the same elaborate gold seal, but this one was crisp and pristine. It belonged to "Ernesto Navarro, Supervisory Special Agent, Caribbean Liaison Officer." The address was listed as the Federal Building in Puerto Rico.

I had suspected for some time that Remo was the informant. As I rummaged through the evidence before me, I realized that the truth was even more complex. He was no mere informant. Remo actually appeared to be working for—or at least with—the FBI.

The only remaining item in the drawer was a U.S. passport. I picked it up, gripped by curiosity. I had long suspected that Remo was much younger than he claimed to be. I flipped the pages, and froze. A picture of Vinnie, not Remo, was staring back at me. My mind whirred. What on earth was Remo doing with Vinnie's passport?

The door opened behind me. I spun around, clutching the passport to my chest. Remo looked completely unperturbed to find me snooping through his things. He quickly scanned the room, taking in the open drawers, the scattered papers, and the passport in my hand. He casually reached over and plucked it from me.

"Vinnie's dead," he said simply.

37

THE SILENCE WAS SO deep and profound, I felt the entire world had stopped short.

"Dead? When—?"

Remo helped me to my feet. His soulful gray eyes bored right through me. "New Year's Eve," he said.

I recalled the evening well. All of us were waiting for Vinnie to show up at the Jaragua. That was six months ago . . .

"Tony came to Atlántico to get my help. That's when he saw you and Demetrio together. It was just lousy timing, Marisa."

"So after Tony drove me home—"

"Tony and I went to Vinnie and Carmine's apartment. The next thing I know, I'm looking down at a bathtub filled with black water . . . and Vinnie's under it."

I remembered that Carmine had cracked jokes about Vinnie's penchant for hair dye. I shuddered. "So what happened? Did he have . . . a heart attack?"

"Nobody knows. Carmine swears that he locked the door behind him when he left for the Jaragua. It was open when he came home. Nothing was out of place—except for Vinnie."

I recalled the look of terror on Vinnie's face when he saw the *60 Minutes* interview. Vinnie must have known the mob would figure out where he had gone, and why they had lost so many players. Vinnie wasn't scared of the FBI like the rest of us. He had bigger worries . . .

Suddenly I recalled something that put ice in the pit of my stomach. "Wait, I was at your apartment the next day! Your clothes—your shoes—they were covered in mud. You buried Vinnie!"

Remo shook his head. "No, Marisa, it wasn't like that. Vinnie was buried in a public cemetery that morning. That's why my clothes were dirty. Dominicans bury their dead straightaway, because of the heat. We needed a death certificate and it had to say that Vinnie was a Dominican national who'd died of natural causes. So Tony called Dr. Badillo."

"Of course he did." I wondered how much that had cost Tony.

"A few hours later, Tony and I stood by while they dug Vinnie's grave. You showed up at my apartment right after Tony dropped me off. I was still in shock, I guess."

"That's why you were so adamant about me not going to Tomaju."

"Of course!" Remo dropped his voice. "Tony was convinced that Vinnie had been whacked. He didn't want you anywhere near Tomaju. Even if he hadn't caught you with Demetrio."

I was stunned. Everything that had happened in the past six months took on a different significance in light of these revelations. And I realized that I didn't really know Remo at all. "I can't believe it," I said, shaking my head. "First I find out you're working for the FBI . . . and now I find out you helped cover up a murder."

Remo was affronted. "I don't work for the FBI."

I picked up a pink FedEx receipt and waved it at him. "You're sending the FBI evidence, for crissake!"

Remo snatched the slip from me and shoved it back into the drawer. "I'm trying to help Tony, okay? That's why you need to go back over to his apartment. Now."

"I'm not going back."

"Listen to me." Remo put his hand on my arm. "Ron's keys are in the glove compartment of the truck. He needs them. He tried to tell you, but you kept hanging up on him, so he sent me to get you. If you don't get back over there he's going to get suspicious. He's paranoid as hell right now, because he knows someone's talking to the feds."

"You're talking to the feds! You take the truck back!"

"Listen!" Remo hissed. "Tony missed his probation meeting because of the accident. The FBI knows he's here, which is great for Ron, because he's already told the district attorney that the business belongs to Tony. It doesn't help that he named it after the three of you. Unless somebody does something, Tony's going to be serving Sacco's twenty years for him."

I thought again of Sonny LoBue's warning. "Remo . . . that's what LoBue meant . . . "

"Of course it is. According to Peterson, LoBue and Ron are partners."

Everything made sense now. "That's why local phone records linked our offices. Sonny would have been calling the Big Office to get our lines. That's why he knew my nickname."

"Let's go!" Remo tried to usher me from the room, but I refused.

"I'm not getting involved," I protested. "This is all getting too—"

"I'm not asking you to get involved. I'm asking you to keep taking care of Tony. We need Ron to think that everything is okay. If he gets scared, he'll run. If he runs, Tony is fucked. He's a sitting duck right now."

I put my face in my hands as the true scope of our problems became apparent. "Tony pled guilty to three of Ron's felonies," I groaned.

"What?"

"Back in L.A. In '88. Tony told the court that the business belonged to him. In exchange, Ron paid our fines and legal fees."

"Do you see how easy it's going to be for Tony to take the fall?"

I grabbed my keys, telling myself that it wouldn't kill me to take care of Tony for a few more weeks. Remo ran downstairs to flag a taxi to the office, while I jumped in the truck to drive to Tony's apartment.

■

"IT'S ABOUT TIME," HORACIO sneered as I entered the apartment. He nudged Ron, who was napping on the couch. "Tony's asleep," he yawned, pulling himself up.

I handed Ron the keys without a word. The two of them walked toward the door, and then Ron paused.

"Listen, Marisa. Tony didn't tell me he was on antibiotics. If I'd known, I wouldn't have let him drink."

I was baffled. I sensed that Ron was being sincere, yet he was planning to betray Tony. Was he feeling torn now? Conflicted? "He'll be on antibiotics until after his skin graft," I said. "If his leg gets infected now, he could lose it."

"Come on," Horacio said, pulling Ron away. "Let's get out of here."

I collapsed on the couch as soon as they left. My life was unraveling. Ron, Tony, and Carmine were all fugitives. Vinnie was dead. It was only a matter of time before Tomaju was closed for good. What would I do then? I was thirty years old. How much longer would I be able to model?

Tony moaned in pain. I went to the bedroom and turned on the light. He was lying on the blankets, fully clothed, his face a mask of agony. The nights were still excruciating for him.

I opened the drawer with the medical supplies. Tony's hands were shaking as he fumbled with his zipper, trying to open his pants. I gently rolled him onto his hip, moving the leg as little as possible. I nudged his pants down and swabbed his buttocks with alcohol.

"I want my car back and Justine's passport," I said firmly.

Tony groaned his consent as I emptied the syringe.

∎

THE FOLLOWING AFTERNOON, I knocked loudly on Remo's door.

"What time is it?" he groaned.

"Time to talk."

Twenty minutes later, Remo was shaved and showered. We sat on the outside terrace.

"Okay, the truth," I said. "How old are you?"

He blushed a little. "Twenty-eight."

"I knew it!" I shook my head. "You're younger than me." It seemed so obvious now, looking at his smooth, unlined skin.

"Why did you keep Vinnie's passport?"

The question took him by surprise, and he didn't reply.

"And," I pressed on, "there's an envelope stuffed with cash in your room, yet you told me you couldn't afford to get your papers."

"Marisa," Remo said quietly, cutting me off. He struggled through a moment of last-minute indecision before he finally spoke again.

"I'm a fugitive."

I could scarcely believe it. Another fugitive? "What did you do?" I asked, genuinely perplexed.

"I made a mistake." He sighed and sat back in his chair. "It was a long time ago. I got caught."

"Doing what?"

"Trafficking drugs."

Nothing he could have said would have surprised me more. Remo—squeaky-clean, no-drinking, no-smoking, no-drugs Remo—a drug trafficker?

"When I was eighteen, I worked the door at a Jersey club," he said. "It was called Mingles. After I'd been there a while, the boss offered me a little work on the side. Every once in a while he'd ask me to fly down to Miami and pick up a bag for him." I raised an eyebrow.

"I guess I knew deep down it was probably money or drugs. But I figured so long as I didn't know for sure, then nothing bad could happen to me. All I really cared about was making enough money to get out of the projects. I didn't have anyone to look out for me. I had to rely on myself.

"It was a breeze, for a while. Then one day I get off the plane and three DEA agents are there waiting for me. They dragged me to a holding cell in the airport, and opened the bag in front of me."

"And?"

"It was stuffed with bags of white powder, all stamped and ready to go. They told me that because I had crossed state lines, and because of the amount I was carrying, I was looking at twenty years automatically. But they told me that my boss was the one they were really interested in. If I promised to help them get him, then they could work something out. Maybe even make the charges go away."

"So you agreed?"

"Hell yeah," Remo said, with a trace of wry humor. "Right after they described how popular I was going to be in prison with this pretty mouth of mine."

Remo took a deep breath and ran his fingers through his hair. "They gave me a form to sign, admitting my guilt and waiving my rights. They took my picture and turned me loose with the coke. I delivered the bag to my boss as if nothing had happened . . . but I felt right away that something wasn't right. I was scared. I went home, grabbed my stuff, and ran. That's how I ended up here."

"That's when you went to work for your uncle in Cabarete?"

"Yeah, except he's not my uncle. He's just some guy who came here to escape some trouble at home. My mom had helped him out once, so he owed me. He said I could work at his bar until things blew over. I thought I would be here for a year, tops. A few months after I arrived, I turned on the TV and there I am on *America's Most Wanted."* Remo shook his head sadly. "That's when I knew I was never going home again."

"You?" I said, barely believing my ears. "On *America's Most Wanted?"* I thought back to the raid on Information Unlimited. "That's why you were so freaked out when the office was busted."

Remo shuddered. "I thought those soldiers were there for *me.* Not until I saw all those handcuffs being dumped out on Carmine's desk did I realize they weren't. But then the FBI showed up. I knew that as soon as they fingerprinted me, it was all over. That's why I fought the guards at the station. I knew I was as good as dead if the feds got their hands on me."

"And after you were sedated, Demetrio bailed you out."

"Right, so I was never fingerprinted. Just before I was released, Agent Peterson actually came up to me and personally apologized for me getting caught up in the raid. He gave me his card and told me I should call him if I could think of anything that might help him in his investigation. I mean, I took it. I never intended to use it, though."

"So why did you?"

"Because of Ron. I never forgot LoBue's warning, so I picked up the phone, called Agent Peterson and told him that Ron Sacco was in the country. I actually thought I was doing Tony a favor."

"But Ron found out," I said. "Mooney knew someone had talked."

"Yeah. That was enough to put me off calling Peterson again. Then Sacco went back to the States, and I started grading at Tomaju. I thought everything was okay."

"Until Ron was indicted."

Remo nodded. "That's why I asked you what would happen if Ron went to jail. You said business would go on as usual, so I called Peterson again. He practically begged me for help. He knew that Ron was on the island, even if the local cops were denying it. I told Peterson that Ron was paying off the Dominicans and that I could prove it. That's when I realized I was in a perfect position to make a deal. I promised to help Peterson—if he promised to go to the DEA and convince them to drop the charges against me.

"It would have been perfect. Tony's in the clear, Ron's out of the picture, and I'm in the clear. It was going so well until Tony crashed his bike. As soon as Tony missed that probation meeting, Peterson started asking questions about him. Then Mooney went ahead and told the D.A. that Tony had taken over the business from Ron years ago. He's claiming that Tony's been running it out of Santo Domingo ever since."

"Jesus," I muttered.

"That's why I have that stuff in my room. I need to get my hands on anything that can prove the business belongs to Ron. I'm handing some of it over to the FBI next week."

My mouth went dry. "Peterson's coming here? Remo, I don't know if you should be involved with him. How can you trust a man who flat-out lied to the Dominican government and put all of us though hell?"

"It's not Peterson. He couldn't get permission from his superiors to come down. He arranged for me to meet with a guy called Ernesto Navarro. He's an FBI liaison officer from Puerto Rico. I've met him before. Seems like a good guy. He gave me the recording device. Peterson wanted me to get Ron's voice on tape."

"Did you?"

"Not yet. Ron's been so paranoid recently, and I haven't had a legitimate reason to call him."

I nodded, processing it all. "One last thing," I said. "Why keep the passport of a murdered man? That's pretty incriminating evidence to have in your possession."

"I came here in 1984. Back then all I needed to get on the island was a birth certificate. Now? You can't get off the island without a passport. That's why I took Vinnie's. It's my backup plan. If everything goes wrong, I figure I can get it doctored, use it to sneak back home. It's a long shot, but—"

His eyes were brimming with tears. "All I've dreamed about these last nine years is that one day I'll be able to go home again.

I know you love it here, but it was never home to me. I'll go crazy if I have to stay here."

Remo was my closest friend. I wanted to help him any way I could. "What can I do?" I asked softly.

"Well, are you on probation, or anything?"

"No."

"Are your papers in order?"

"Yes."

Remo looked cautiously hopeful. "Then I want you to come with me to meet Agent Navarro. I need you to tell him everything you know."

38

BEFORE OUR MEETING WITH Special Agent Ernesto Navarro I was sick with nervous anxiety. I wasn't sure what to expect, but after my horrible experiences with the FBI so far, I felt like I was walking into a lion's den. The reality was far less dramatic.

The agent seemed far more interested in his grilled-cheese sandwich than in the evidence Remo was presenting. The three of us took a corner table in the cafeteria at Clinica Abreu. The coast was clear: Ron was at Tomaju and Tony was currently undergoing another operation. Dr. Enrique was removing skin from Tony's thigh and using it to cover the exposed bone, muscles, and tendons of his lower leg.

Most of the time, the sight of three people huddled together speaking English over lunch would not have drawn much attention in the Dominican Republic. However, Navarro was black, so he was attracting quite a few curious stares. I shifted in my seat nervously as he dabbed grease off his chin.

"Sacco is a huge problem for Peterson," he said. "You know the way things work down here. The Dominicans aren't just going to allow Jack to barge into the country and take Sacco out on gambling charges alone."

"But it's not just gambling," Remo countered. He had a zealous gleam in his eye as he recited the list of laws Ron had broken. "There's racketeering . . . conspiracy . . . money laundering . . . not to mention extortion. Wouldn't that be enough?"

Navarro coolly raised his hand. He was in his mid-fifties, with graying temples, and carried an air of easy authority. "Now, let me finish. Peterson has no concrete proof that Sacco is even here. There's no record of Sacco entering the country."

Remo was visibly deflated. "But I sent all of that."

"I'm aware of the evidence you presented to Agent Peterson. But I'm telling you, it's not enough."

Remo retrieved a brown paper bag from the floor. He presented it eagerly to Navarro, who reluctantly put down his sandwich and peered inside. He pulled out the plastic bag containing Ron's empty Presidente bottle.

"And just what," Navarro asked, "is this?"

"Sacco's fingerprints."

Navarro burst out laughing. "I guess we'd better put you on the payroll," he said, wiping tears from his eyes. He handed the bottle back to Remo, who had turned beet-red.

Navarro recovered himself. "Look, I'm interested in this case because it involves corruption in the Dominican police force. As the FBI's liaison officer, I have to deal with these folks on a regular basis, and I need to know who I can trust."

He looked at me. "Remo tells me you know the names of several high-ranking Dominican officers on Sacco's payroll." I nodded. "Well then. I'd really appreciate you telling me who they are."

"I only know the names of the original group," I said before I began reeling off the list.

He interrupted me three names in. "Colonel Eduardo Rivera Munoz?"

"Yes."

Navarro shook his head with a tight smile. "That sneaky son of a bitch looked me straight in the eye yesterday and swore that Sacco wasn't in the country."

"Rivera used to come to the office every Friday night to collect for all of them." I reached into my wallet and produced General Hernandez's business card. I slid it across the table to Navarro. "This man was also directly involved."

Navarro studied Hernandez's card, flipping it over and reading the inscription on the back. When he looked up again, something passed between us—an instantaneous acknowledgment that he understood exactly what the general had put me through. I felt my cheeks redden.

"S-some of the officers were transferred," I stammered, "and new officers took their place."

"Hernandez was fired," Navarro said flatly. He glanced at the card again. "Can I keep this?"

I paused. Handing the FBI a business card that tied me to a corrupt general didn't seem like a smart idea. "I'd rather have it back."

Navarro returned it without question.

"You ever hear of Sanchez-Castillo?" Navarro studied my face, his eyes boring into me. Under the table Remo gave me a gentle kick. I knew very well who Sanchez-Castillo was. According to Remo, he was the fourth-most powerful man in the country, and an old classmate of Demetrio's. I shook my head.

"Sacco ever make payments to him?"

"Not that I'm aware of."

Navarro nodded slowly, looking relieved. "They tell me Sanchez-Castillo is waging a war on corruption down here. Refreshingly enough, he doesn't seem to have been compromised himself. At least not so far."

Navarro finished the last of his sandwich and waved the waitress over for coffee. "I understand you no longer work for Sacco," he said, dumping three packets of sugar into his steaming cup.

"That's right."

"Good." In a tone of voice that floated between patronizing and paternally concerned, he said, "Listen, you both seem like nice kids. So I'm going to give you the advice of someone who's been dealing with the Dominicans for thirty-two years. Do not do anything to endanger yourselves. It's not worth it."

He went on. "You know, Jack Peterson is a hell of a good guy. He took a lot of heat for that botched bust on Information Unlimited. The Dominican government was pissed off about it, and so was his own department." Navarro lowered his voice. "I happen to know that he faced a disciplinary hearing over that whole fiasco. Jack's determination to chase down Sacco is bordering on obsession. If you want my opinion, the Dominicans are never going to hand him over."

Neither Remo nor I said a word. Navarro leaned in close. "So he's not worth getting in trouble over, okay?"

"Okay," I agreed, feeling chastened.

"Great!" Agent Navarro stood up, pulled a few bills out of his wallet, and tossed them on the table. "That was good grilled cheese. And I appreciate the information about the local police." He winked at us. "You know how to get in touch with me," he said. And with that, he was gone.

The meeting had been a total failure. We both stared at the empty Presidente bottle on the table. "Do you have any idea how nervous I was to talk to him?" I asked Remo absently.

"What a waste of time!" Remo picked up the bottle, eyeing it as if it had somehow betrayed him.

"Am I right to assume that Navarro has no idea that you have Sanchez-Castillo's business card in your wallet?"

Remo didn't answer. Instead he set the bottle back on the table, got to his feet, and muttered, "Let's see how Tony is doing."

We abandoned Remo's prized piece of evidence and headed down the hallway toward the OR. Things were looking good for Ron and Tony, I mused. As long as they stayed in the Dominican Republic, apparently the feds couldn't touch them.

"Can I see that card?" Remo asked suddenly. "Where did you get it?"

"Forget it, Remo." I took the card out of my wallet and proceeded to tear it into a hundred pieces. It had served its purpose, and keeping it any longer seemed like a bad idea.

"Peterson will get Ron deported. I know it," Remo said.

I knew how badly he needed that to happen. If Peterson didn't get Ron, then Remo would never have his trafficking charges dropped. He would be a fugitive for the rest of his life.

■

AN HOUR LATER, DR. ENRIQUE emerged from the OR and announced that Tony's operation had been a complete success. X-rays confirmed that the breaks to his arm and femur were healing well, and he believed that Tony would soon be able to support himself on crutches. His ankle, however, continued to be a major cause for concern. Without the metal brace, Enrique told us, Tony's leg would collapse into his foot.

The compression bandages came off two weeks after the skin graft. Tony propped himself up on his elbows and—for the first time since the accident—announced that he was ready to see his leg.

His thigh bore perfectly symmetrical scars from the skin graft and another scar from the compound fracture, but otherwise looked normal. From the knee down, however, the limb was lumpy and grotesquely distorted. The skin covering it was a Frankenstein-like tapestry, a patchwork of different tones and colors.

"As you can see, I used both split-skin and full-skin grafts to cover the missing tissues," Dr. Enrique said proudly.

Tony blanched. For the first time he was confronting the true extent of his injuries.

"Are you okay?" I whispered.

Tony continued to stare at the twisted flesh below his knee. He pointed weakly at the metal brace. "Is that thing keeping my foot attached to my leg?"

"In a way, yes. It will have to stay in place for many more months."

During the car ride back to the office, Tony was unusually subdued. He was finally realizing that he would never be able to use his foot normally again. The bone graft would fill in the missing bone in his ankle, but it would be fused in a fixed position. He might never be able to walk on it.

As for me, my life had just gotten a lot easier: no more complicated, time-consuming cleanings. Once the bone graft was in place, the risk of infection would be greatly reduced. Tony was over the worst of his catastrophe. One day soon, he wouldn't need me at all.

He stared out of the window, seemingly a thousand miles away. He'd expected to make a full recovery, and now he was coming to terms with the harsh reality that he would be permanently disabled.

I parked in front of Tomaju. Tony slowly pulled himself out of the car. I felt an overwhelming rush of pity as he hobbled across the street on his new crutches and made his way painfully up the stairs. In just a few unhappy years I had witnessed Tony's transformation from a vibrant, attractive young adventurer to this broken, disillusioned, and handicapped man.

■

WHEN I RETURNED HOME, Remo was awake. "You're working tonight," I said to him. "Shouldn't you be sleeping?"

"Can't sleep," he said.

"Join the club." I flopped down on the sofa next to him. I couldn't remember the last time I'd had a good night's sleep. "It's the quiet that's the worst," I mused. "On the surface everything seems normal. It's the waiting, you know? I feel like I'm constantly on high alert for something to happen."

Remo sighed. "Maybe Navarro was right. Maybe nothing's going to happen."

"Maybe. But that's not all that's worrying me. Right now Tony's supporting me. But he's getting better, and at some point he's bound to ask me to move back in with him, or give him another chance. When I refuse, he's going to cut me off and take the car again. What do I do then?"

"He wouldn't do that."

I shot Remo a look. He was always the optimist when it came to Tony.

The phone rang. When I answered it, the hairs on the back of my neck stood up. I recognized the voice immediately as that of Agent Jack Peterson. "It's for you," I croaked, handing the phone to Remo. I watched intently as he listened, occasionally nodding or grunting in assent. This was the call he'd been anxiously awaiting. One way or another, it was going to change his life forever.

He replaced the receiver, his mouth open in shock. "The U.S. Attorney is going to approve the request to have Ron deported."

"Wow. I guess Navarro was wrong!"

"This is huge! Peterson says it's just a matter of weeks before the request will be formally granted."

"Then what?"

"I get a warning call before he comes down with his men. From that moment on I have to know Ron's exact whereabouts at all times."

I couldn't believe we were going to help the FBI to apprehend Ron Sacco. Remo was right. This *was* huge. The toughest part of the plan would be keeping Tony away from Ron when the feds arrived. I decided that I had to convince Dr. Enrique to schedule Tony's bone graft for an earlier date. If we could have Tony safely sequestered in the hospital when the FBI were arresting Ron, then Ron's lawyers could not deny that the business belonged to Sacco. It helped us to focus on the fact that getting Ron deported would help Tony; it quelled the nagging feelings of guilt we both had that Ron would likely go to jail for many years.

In theory, the plan was well laid. However, the sound of tires screeching in the parking lot the following afternoon was the first indication that things were about to go very wrong. When I got to the window Ron was in the parking lot, calling for me to throw down my car keys. Behind him, Tony was struggling to get out of the Toyota with his crutches.

I ran to Remo's room and shook him awake. "Get up! Something's happening!"

I grabbed the keys and dashed downstairs. "What's going on?"

"Get Justine!" Tony barked, pressing the keys to the Toyota into my hand. "Pack enough stuff for a few days!"

"But I don't understand!"

Ron was busy pulling stacks of documents out of the truck and carelessly shoving them into the trunk of the Daihatsu. "The police," he snarled, "were at Horacio's store, asking questions." I felt my stomach drop.

"Thank Christ they went to the old place," Tony said, "and not the one under Tomaju."

"Still, they went there looking for us." Ron slammed the trunk closed. "Luckily, someone had the sense to call and warn us."

My heart was pounding so loud I could barely hear myself ask, "Was the FBI there?"

"Nah," Ron said. "Locals, as far as we know."

"Come on! Get Justine and let's go. We're going to hide out for a few days, until we figure out what's going on."

Hide out? My face was splashed in every local magazine and my commercial still ran on all the local channels. Where would I hide? I couldn't. And I couldn't let Tony run off with Ron. Where would they hide out? They weren't exactly inconspicuous either.

Tony's cell rang. He listened intently, then hung up. "Rivera," he said. "He knows nothing about it. I believe him, too. He sent his kid to work today."

This news panicked Ron further. "We need to get out of here, now!"

"Go upstairs," Tony told me. "Get Justine."

"No," I said. I took a step backward. "Tony, don't get in that car. Stay here with me."

"Are you out of your mind?" Tony's voice cracked. "Get Justine and let's go! Just until we can figure out what's going on!"

My mind whirred. I had to stop him from getting in the car with Ron. "Tony, I'm begging you. Stay here with me. I'll hide you. I—I need to take care of your leg."

Tony's face darkened. "Do you want me to go to prison? Go upstairs, get Justine, and get in the fucking car!"

I shook my head. "I can't, Tony. I'm sorry."

Ron grabbed Tony's shoulder. "We're wasting time."

"Get in the car. Please!"

My eyes filled with tears. Tony stared at me in disbelief as I shook my head, turned, and walked away from him.

Remo had almost finished packing by the time I got upstairs. "Peterson double-crossed me!" he spat.

"No!" I grabbed Remo to stop him. "It's not the feds—it's local. Rivera said so."

"No way." Remo shook his arm free. "That bastard promised to warn me. He's trying to bust me as well."

"That doesn't make sense, Remo. He wouldn't risk losing track of Ron now. You have a deal. Call him."

But Remo could not be swayed. He zipped up the bag and slung it over his shoulder. He was facing years in prison and was petrified. Minutes after Tony and Ron left, Remo bolted downstairs with his duffel bag and vanished.

I knew that the police would be looking for Tony and Ron in a brand-new silver truck and that they would confiscate it once they found it—regardless of whether or not anyone was driving it. To keep this from happening, I brought the truck to the Toyota dealership and requested a service. I hoped that the truck would be safe there until I retrieved it. I took a taxi home. Once there, I tried to convince myself that I had nothing to worry about. I was divorced, the apartment was in my name, and I was no longer involved with the operation. I had all my proper permits, and had every right to be living in the Dominican Republic.

The evening passed without incident. Rosa made dinner and

we sat down to eat just as we would on any normal day. Afterward I played with Justine, bathed her, read to her, and put her to bed. Later, Rosa and I sat glued to the TV, flipping through the local channels for news. I tried Tony's cell phone several times, but it was out of range.

Later that night the phone rang. "Anything happening?" Remo sounded surprisingly calm.

"No," I said. "Nothing's on the news. How are you?"

"I talked to N," he said. "I'm still waiting to hear from P."

As serious as the situation was, I had to chuckle at Remo's cryptic way of speaking. "Where are you?"

There was a long pause. "The lost city," he answered.

"I'm on my way." I hung up before Remo could protest.

Atlántico was as busy as ever. My heart pounded in anticipation as I contemplated seeing Demetrio for the first time since that awful fight. I searched the sea of faces in the club, looking for him. Someone tapped me lightly on the shoulder and I came face-to-face with Remo's girlfriend, Laurette. She motioned for me to follow her, and we headed past the bathrooms toward an unmarked door, which she opened and closed again behind me. I found myself in a stairwell. I climbed upward with the muted echo of the music all around me.

In a quiet office, I found Remo sitting with his feet propped on a desk. "Where's Demetrio?" I asked him.

"Miami," Remo grunted. "Otherwise, I wouldn't be here."

My face fell. "When is he coming back?"

Remo shook his head disbelievingly. "I told you to forget about him, Marisa."

I pulled up a chair and sat down in a huff.

"You were right, this has nothing to do with the feds," Remo said heavily. "Navarro knew nothing about the bust. Apparently, this is just another shockwave from that *60 Minutes* interview. It pissed off a bunch of people in Washington, and they're threatening to cut off aid to the country if Ron isn't apprehended. Sanchez-Castillo finally got around to putting a task force together. He couldn't even tell his own men where they were going until the last minute, because Sacco has half the local police on the payroll."

I shook my head in disbelief. "And then they went charging over to the wrong place."

"Yeah. The only lead they had was that clip on *60 Minutes* showing the Commerciales Vargas sign. The police went to the old store, only to find out that there was no second story. By the time they figured out that there was a second store, everyone at Tomaju was long gone."

"So what happens now?"

Remo shrugged. "Navarro offered to assist the Dominicans with the investigation, but of course they want to handle it themselves. Marisa, do you have any idea where Ron and Tony might have gone?"

I had been pondering this all evening. "My best guess is the North Shore. They could blend in with the tourists in Puerto Plata."

"Tony isn't going to be blending in anywhere," Remo snorted. "Not with that metal thing sticking out of his leg."

The phone rang. As Remo went to answer it, I realized that the recording device I had found in his room was hooked up to the phone. He made a shushing motion before picking up the receiver. I listened as he cheerfully updated Peterson on everything that had happened. I heard Peterson on the other line, pleading, "Don't let Sacco slip through our fingers."

"Jack, I need you to tell the Dominicans that I'm working for you. Otherwise, I'm liable to get arrested myself."

"I can't do that."

Remo's face fell.

"Look, we never managed to get permission from the Dominican government to launch this investigation," Peterson went on. "They've made it very clear they don't want our help. I can't come down officially until the Dominicans ask me. I'm sorry, Remo. But I'm working on it. Ernesto Navarro is trying to get permission to go down as an observer."

The men said goodbye and Remo hung up the phone. "Why are you taping the FBI?" I asked him.

"You think I trust them? I've taped every conversation I ever had with Peterson. I have all his promises to drop the charges against me on record. Insurance, you know?"

It made sense. "Now what?"

"I'm going to Cabarete first thing in the morning. I'm getting out of here until this is resolved."

"What about the card from Sanchez-Castillo? Wouldn't that protect you?"

"Marisa, I was grading at Tomaju last night. It's all too close for comfort. I gotta leave town. Hey—" His face brightened. "Come with me. We can all go—you, me, Rosa, and Justine."

"I'm staying." I had no ties to Tony or Ron anymore. Running would make it look like I had something to hide. We tried Tony's cell one last time, but he still didn't pick up. I stood up to leave.

"Good luck, Marisa," Remo said, as I headed out of the office.

■

IT WAS WELL AFTER midnight by the time I climbed the stairs to my apartment. The adrenaline rush of the afternoon's drama had long since ebbed. I was overcome with exhaustion. I dragged my feet up the last flight of stairs and rounded the corner. Then I froze.

Outside of my door, fast asleep, was a plainclothes policeman. His body was slumped against the wall, his gun tucked into his belt. My heart began to pound. I backed up, taking a deep breath, and slipped off my shoes. The secret police had undoubtedly checked the apartment and knew I wasn't inside. This man was waiting for me to come home so he could drag me down to the police station for questioning. Another guard was probably stationed outside the maid's entrance.

I peeked around the corner again. He seemed to be in a pretty deep sleep. I realized that if I could just sneak past him and into the apartment, I'd be able to stay there with Justine and Rosa until the police captured Ron. I took a cautious step forward. Then another. And another.

I was standing right over him now, listening to his steady, even breathing. Never taking my eyes from his slumped form, I slid the key, bit by agonizing bit, into the lock. I turned it slowly, until I heard a gentle click.

The guard grunted and adjusted his position. The fingers of his left hand twitched slightly. I froze. I was so tantalizingly close to safety . . .

I began to turn the doorknob, watching his every move. Then I nudged the door open, inch by inch . . .

39

Two days later, I sat stewing in an interrogation room. Across from me, Major Gutierrez took off his glasses and rubbed his eyes. His uniform shirt was crumpled, and he was unshaven. Clearly, I wasn't the only one who was sleep-deprived. He replaced his glasses and sighed heavily.

Gutierrez was the current head of the Secret Service, and the reason I was back in custody. He had personally gone to my apartment and discovered me sound asleep in my bed. After recovering from the shock of finding me there, he promptly fired the two men who were supposed to be guarding my apartment, and personally escorted me back to the Palacio de la Policia Nacional for questioning. Unfortunately, I had little to add to what he already knew about Ron, Tony, and Tomaju.

Horacio had already told Gutierrez everything, right down to the fact that Tony had a metal bar on his leg. The only detail Horacio had not specified was the year and model of the car Ron and Tony might be driving. This made sense, as both cars were registered to him. Horacio didn't want the police to capture the fugitives in a vehicle he stood to inherit. The major had declared that I would not be released until Tony and Ron were caught, so I filled him in on that missing detail: Ron and Tony were driving a blue Daihatsu.

Gutierrez was clearly frustrated with how the investigation was going. Tony and Ron had been on the run for three days now, and his men were no closer to finding them. The major had aborted plans to interrogate our Dominican clerks the moment he discovered their family names. The last thing Gutierrez needed was to stir up the wrath of some of the islands' most powerful families and the premier legal teams they could afford to hire. Law enforcement in the Dominican Republic swung between two extremes: utter corruption and total incompetence.

The investigation cast its net wide. The Secret Service began trawling beaches, whorehouses, restaurants, and the Haitian border searching for a blue Daihatsu. Photographs of Ron and Tony were splashed across *Listin Diario* and *El Sieglo.* Amazingly, a cripple with a metal device protruding from his leg and his redhaired companion had vanished into thin air.

The major's glasses highlighted the bags under his eyes. I almost felt sorry for him. He was under enormous pressure to crack the case, and the strain on his face was showing. "Someone from the Canadian Embassy is here to see you," he said before leaving the room.

My spirits soared. Maybe I was getting out. A blue-eyed, blond-haired man in a suit entered the room and took a seat opposite me. "Bernard Simmons," he said curtly. "From the embassy."

I explained my situation, stumbling over the words in my hurry to plead my case. "I've been held here for two days without food. I haven't been charged with anything."

Simmons was indifferent to my plight. "Technically, they can hold you for a week before they are obligated to press charges, Ms. Lankester."

"A week? I'm a Canadian citizen! Can't you help me?"

"I am helping you. My job is to ensure that you're given the same rights as a Dominican prisoner. It seems that is the case. Do you wish me to contact a family member for you? Or an attorney?"

A family member? I thought about how my parents would react to the news that I was being detained in the Dominican Republic. No, thanks. "Mr. Simmons, the police haven't charged me because I haven't done anything wrong."

He shrugged. There was nothing more he could do. I resolved to wait it out. In another three days they would have to release me.

An hour after Simmons left, a stale slice of pizza and a glass of water were dumped on the desk in front of me. My stomach ached with hunger, but I didn't touch anything. I assumed the food had been sent at Simmons' request. Perhaps he had reminded the police of the consequences that would arise if a Canadian woman starved to death in their custody.

I decided I would protest my mistreatment by going on hunger strike. I sat back in my chair, crossed my arms, and stared defiantly into the two-way mirror. I felt protected, knowing that the Canadians were aware of my incarceration. The door opened, and an officer came in bearing a tray of sandwiches and coffee.

"Eat!" he said, placing it in front of me.

"No," I said firmly, sensing a distinct shift in power.

Major Gutierrez was summoned to deal with me. He looked less than pleased at being dragged away from his investigation to deal with my protest.

"You must eat something," he insisted.

"I'll eat when I go home, thank you."

"You are not going home," he growled.

"You have no right to keep me here. I haven't done anything wrong."

Gutierrez leaned forward and dropped his voice. "According to the documents we have seized, you are not only the *Ma* in Tomaju, but you are the vice-president of a company that was never licensed to take bets from overseas. You are the ex-wife of a man who has a warrant out for his arrest in the Unites States, and you are a former employee of Ron Sacco—a fugitive and the subject of a national manhunt. Ms. Lankester, you are up to your *neck* in this."

He let the full weight of his words sink in.

"I have every right to detain you," he said, straightening up again. "But since you are refusing to eat, I have no choice but to transfer you to the Palacio de Justicia."

My blood ran cold as I realized how badly my plan had backfired. The Palacio de Justicia. The medieval hellhole where I had witnessed the clerks stewing in their own filth. Where prisoners had to rely on family members for food and clothing.

"No, please . . . "

I reached out for the sandwich, but he whisked the tray away. "I will see to it that your maid is notified of the transfer," he said, before marching out of the room and closing the door behind him.

■

SEVERAL HOURS LATER, A guard unlocked the door to the large holding cell and shoved me inside. Most of the women were already curled up on the bare concrete floor, asleep. A few sat on metal chairs scattered around the cell, staring off into space. The room was lit by a single bulb, around which hundreds of flies were buzzing furiously. The stench of urine and feces was overpowering.

I took an empty spot by the bathroom wall at the far end of the cell. The smell was stronger here, but I was past caring. I laid on the floor and fell into a deep, dreamless sleep.

The guard roused us at seven the next morning by clanging his baton against the iron bars. I woke up with the sensation that something was cutting into my cheek. I sat up and touched my face gently. Something was stuck to my skin. I gingerly pulled it away—it was a huge, ragged, detached toenail that had once been painted a garish shade of purple. With a shudder of disgust

I threw it to the floor. I stood up stiffly and brushed myself off. I felt grimy all over. It was already sweltering in here, the atmosphere thick with the stench of unwashed bodies, piss, and despair. I felt nauseous and faint from hunger. I hoped that the major had really told Rosa I was in here; otherwise, I wouldn't eat.

Through the bars of the cell, heavily sweetened coffee was doled out to the prisoners in thimble-sized plastic cups. I needed to use the toilet and discovered that I had to squat over a hole in the floor, in the center of the doorless "bathroom." As the day went on and the temperature climbed, the stench grew more pungent with every passing hour. Thankfully, a guard came, taking half a dozen women with him. I watched them tramp down the hallway to a courtroom. That afternoon, a package arrived for me. Inside were sandwiches, drinking water, a clean T-shirt, underwear, and a copy of *Listin Diario. Thank you, Rosa.* I read the paper cover to cover. I found nothing about my detention, which made me extremely uneasy. If nobody knew I was here, how could anybody get me out?

Three stultifying days passed. Once I'd read the paper I had nothing else to do except observe the arrival of new prisoners, or watch the comings and goings of family members as they visited their daughters, sisters, nieces, aunts, mothers, and grandmothers. These desperate women's faces lit up as they received food, clothing, or the latest gossip. People often wandered along the corridor and stared at us, as if we were animals in a zoo. I kept to myself at the back of the cell. I had no idea how long I would be detained, and my hopes sank with every passing night I spent sleeping on the filthy concrete floor.

The evenings were quieter than the days. After dinner, we swept the cell and put any debris into a plastic bag. Women bathed by pouring bottles of water over themselves in the back of the cell. I would stand on a metal chair, on my tiptoes, to try to look out of the barred window. I could make out the top of a building a couple of blocks away. I realized, staring at the structure, that I was looking at the top two floors of Clinica Abreu. I knew the name of every nurse and doctor who had tended to

Tony's shattered body there. I was so close, yet so far away from all the people who had shown me so much kindness. I returned to the main part of the cell and laid down. Sleep didn't come easy—it never did. The lights had to be kept on twenty-four hours a day to keep the hungry rats at bay.

I dared not think about Justine. Crying wouldn't change the situation. It only made things worse. I soon learned it was better not to think too much about loved ones. In a place like that, thinking too much was a fast track to insanity.

A week passed, and still no charges were pressed against me. Yet I was given no indication that I would be released. Every morning, women were escorted from the cell to the courtroom on the other end of the building to be sentenced. Every morning, I listened for my name to be called, but it never was. I felt as though I had been left here to rot—I was simply forgotten. The press lost interest in Ron and Tony. News of the infamous fugitives had dwindled to a couple of lines buried in the back pages.

One day, a photograph of a Jeep for sale in the classified section of *Listin Diario* caught my eye. It was similar to Roger's Jeep, the one that General Hernandez had confiscated after the raid on Information Unlimited. I stared at the image of the Jeep, my mind racing.

What if Tony and Ron had gone to Hernandez for help? He was still on their payroll, after all. And what if he had agreed to exchange my Daihatsu for the red Jeep? Maybe the police hadn't found Tony and Ron because they were no longer driving the same car. It had to be the answer. Hernandez was no longer on the force, so Major Gutierrez wouldn't have bothered questioning him.

I scribbled down the make and model of the Cherokee, and asked the guard to take the information to Major Gutierrez. The guard simply looked at me and laughed. Fuming, I waited for another opportunity to communicate with the outside world. The next day I pleaded with the taxi driver who delivered my care package to take the note back to Rosa. He was reluctant at first, but finally relented.

Nothing seemed to come of my message in a bottle. I remained depressed, isolated, and shut off at the back of this stinking cell. Ron and Tony were determined to evade the law. Tony knew he might lose his leg unless he received proper treatment, yet he still hadn't turned himself in. What if the police never found them? Would I be locked up in here forever?

The next day, I received a note from Rosa in my care package. My heart soared as I read it. According to her, I was to be released very soon. That same day, *Listin Diario* reported that Sanchez-Castillo had been promoted to Chief of Police. Rosa's certainty about my upcoming release must be linked to this promotion. It seemed likely, especially if Remo was working behind the scenes on my behalf.

For the first time since I'd been locked up, I allowed myself to think about going home. I hugged my knees to my chest and imagined myself holding Justine again. I would squeeze her tightly, cover her sweet face in kisses, and cuddle her for hours on end. I thought about the long, hot bath I would take. I thought about being able to sleep in a real bed again.

I was so deep in thought that I didn't hear my name being called. Someone poked me in the ribs. I realized that I had been crying.

"Get up! You have visitors!"

I wiped my eyes and staggered to my feet. I could see the silhouettes of two men standing outside the bars at the front of the cell. As I came closer I realized they were agents Jack Peterson and Ernesto Navarro.

■

AT NINE-FIFTEEN THAT NIGHT, after my conversation with the FBI agents, I was too wound up to sleep. In ten hours and thirty minutes, I was scheduled to leave this filthy cell forever.

Unexpectedly, I heard someone whisper my name. I sat up. I heard it again. A familiar voice. Remo!

Most of the women were down for the night, so I had a clear view to the front of the cell. Remo was standing exactly were I'd seen Peterson and Navarro earlier in the day. I leapt up and jumped over the bodies of my sleeping cellmates.

Remo looked relaxed and healthy. His skin was tanned and glowing, his hair was streaked blond from the sun, and his big gray eyes twinkled. I reached out my hands and he squeezed them. Then his nose wrinkled. "Jesus, Marisa—you could use a shower!"

"I know, but thanks for pointing it out anyway."

"I'm sorry. Look, I have great news. You'll be able to take a shower tomorrow, because you're getting out."

"I know. Navarro and Peterson told me."

All the color drained out of Remo's face. He grabbed my arm and wrenched me toward him. "What do you mean? You spoke to them? When? Tell me!"

"Jesus!" I wrestled my arm free. "They were here today. They made a deal with me . . . I mean, I thought you knew."

Remo started pacing furiously outside the cell. "What kind of a deal?"

Suddenly I felt sick. Obviously something was very wrong, and somehow I was responsible. "They said that if I agreed to testify against Ron, they'd get me out of here."

Remo looked as though I'd slapped him. "That was *my* deal! That's the deal I made with Peterson!"

"I didn't know. How could I know?" I cried. "Look where I am, Remo! I've been here for thirteen days! How could I say no when they offered me a way out of this hell-hole?"

The guard angrily told us to keep our voices down.

"Don't you see?" Remo whispered urgently. "If they have you to testify, then they don't need me."

"But they told me that you'd be leaving the island with us. I thought you knew . . . "

Remo's face twisted as he realized the full scale of the FBI's betrayal. "Tell me exactly what they told you."

"They said I would go to court tomorrow morning, that it was just a formality. Afterward, they were taking me straight home to pick up Justine before we all flew to the States. They'd told me that they'd captured Ron and Tony, and we were all leaving together."

"They didn't capture anybody. We did!" Remo whispered. "We searched every beach on the North Shore, every hotel. Thanks to you and Rosa, we found the red Jeep."

"Who's we?"

"Sanchez-Castillo, Major Gutierrez and me. It's thanks to us that you're getting out tomorrow. None of this had anything to do with Peterson or Navarro. The Dominicans didn't want their help. Peterson couldn't even get permission to come down. The only reason Navarro is here is because they need him to escort Ron out of the country."

"What happened to Tony?" I asked.

"He's at Clinica Abreu under police protection. Dr. Enrique is taking care of him. Ron's under heavy guard at the police station. I was the one who called Navarro yesterday and told him that we'd found Sacco."

The FBI were not only planning on taking in Ron. They wanted Remo as well. All of Peterson's promises were empty. He'd used Remo to find Sacco, and as a reward Remo was going to be extradited to face drug-trafficking charges. "I'm so sorry, Remo."

"You want to hear the best part? Navarro is waiting for me at the Hotel Lina right now, supposedly to buy me dinner to celebrate. He's just waiting for me to walk in there so he and Peterson can slap the cuffs on me and have me flown out with Ron. Imagine that—Jack Peterson, the big fucking hero. He not only captures Ron Sacco, but also manages to bring in one of America's Most Wanted while he's at it." Remo shook his head, stunned at the depth of their treachery. "They'd have had me cuffed on the plane next to the man I helped capture. They lied to me. They both lied to me."

Remo was walking in circles now, his face filled with abject terror. He realized he was standing on the precipice of losing his freedom forever. "I have to get out of here," he said abruptly.

I called after him as he disappeared around the corner, but he did not stop.

I slid to the floor and began to cry. I'd unwittingly betrayed my best friend and allowed myself to get conned by two FBI agents. My heart felt as though it had been ripped out of my chest. I clung to the bars and sobbed bitterly, mortified by the utter injustice of it all.

I was still slumped against the bars hours later when I heard footsteps approaching. I looked up and saw Remo's silhouette.

The guard stepped toward him, saying that visiting hours were over. Remo simply flipped open his wallet. He held it up to the guard's face so he could see the card inside. The guard immediately stammered an apology. It was Sanchez-Castillo's new card. Under the name was the legend, *Chief of Police.*

Remo squatted down next to me. His entire demeanor had changed. He seemed hard and determined. "Marisa. Do you want to testify against Ron?"

"No," I snuffled.

"Do you want to go back to the States?"

I shook my head. "Remo, I have nothing to go back to."

He nodded grimly. "Okay," he said, his voice softening. He sat down on the floor beside me. "In that case, I have an idea."

40

POLICE CAPTURE AMERICAN FUGITIVE!

The story was front-page news in *Listin Diario* the following morning, just as Remo had predicted.

Ron Sacco, the mastermind of a billion-dollar, illegal gambling opera-tion, was apprehended in Puerto Plata by local police, along with his top associate.

Once Remo had known what he was looking for, finding the red Cherokee was relatively easy. Ron—either through arrogance or stupidity—had made no attempt whatsoever to hide it. It was parked right in front of the Paradise Beach resort, where he and Tony were hiding out. Once he'd spotted it, Remo immediately alerted the one person he knew would be more interested in apprehending Ron than in taking a bribe from him. For Sanchez-Castillo, arresting Ron Sacco was a pivotal moment. Not only did it put an end to an embarrassing political situation, but it also guaranteed his promotion to Chief of Police.

The capture of the world's most notorious bookmaker had gone off without violence or bloodshed. Ron believed right up until the end that his money would somehow save him.

"How much is it going to cost to fix this?" he reportedly asked Sanchez-Castillo when he and Tony were apprehended.

Dominican authorities described the capture as a major arrest in a foreign country, and speculated that Sacco would be returned to California to stand trial.

It was good to see the news in black and white. It finally felt real. I was also thankful that Tony had not been mentioned by name in the paper. He would remain under guard at Clinica Abreu until his leg was stable.

While Ron and Tony were safely in custody, though, I now found myself with a bigger problem. I was unwittingly at the center of an FBI double-cross that could send my closest friend to a federal penitentiary for twenty years. In the last few hours of my confinement my mind had been feverishly dissecting Remo's plan, testing it for holes. It was a huge gamble, but I knew I had no other choice.

A guard interrupted my thoughts by calling my name. It was showtime.

I stepped outside as the metal door clanged shut behind me. My heart began to pound in anticipation of what was to come. I attracted curious stares as I followed the guard down a crowded hallway past the main entrance and into a courtroom at the other end of the building.

I was told to take a seat in the center of the large room. My eyes darted around, taking in my surroundings. In front of me was a tall wooden platform with an imposing desk set upon it. I assumed that this was where the judge would sit. Running along the walls on either side of the room were the lawyers' podiums. Mine was the first case of the morning. The room was already filling up. In the public gallery I saw Peterson and Navarro sitting by the back wall.

According to Remo, Navarro would be armed, since he was here on official Bureau business, while Peterson—who had not received permission to enter the country—would be unarmed and on a tourist visa, just like everyone else. The men's clothing confirmed this. Navarro looked stiff and uncomfortable in a suit jacket. Peterson was casually dressed in a short-sleeve navy polo shirt and khaki pants.

I was not surprised that they looked so miserable. When Remo didn't show up for their "celebration dinner" last night, they realized that their plot to ensnare him had failed.

Perhaps Peterson had an inkling that Remo had taped their incriminating conversations. Maybe he suspected that all of those false promises he had made to Remo were on record. The fact was that while Remo was free, Peterson had a lot to fear. Remo had collected hard evidence that Peterson had been using a fugitive to gather information without permission from his superiors or the Dominican government. Should it ever come to light, that kind of illegal behavior could deal a damning blow to Peterson's career.

As for Navarro, he also had good reason to be displeased this morning. He was not going to be credited with helping to capture one of America's Most Wanted, as Peterson had promised him. Instead he would merely be escorting Ron Sacco out of the country.

Just before eight o'clock, the proceeding got under way. Several stern men in long black robes marched into the courtroom. A uniformed officer called for everyone to rise. A door at the front of the courtroom opened and a small, dark-skinned man in a black robe stepped inside. His purple cap identified him as the judge. He climbed the few steps to his desk and took his seat.

Despite the ridiculous purple hat, Judge Severino looked like a force to be reckoned with. His white hair was cropped tightly against his skull. His skin was paper-thin, his cheeks hollow. His eyes radiated intelligence as he called for the first case to be presented. I had heard Severino's name before. The women in the cell referred to him as "the hanging judge."

He regarded me with the kind of disdain that a strict parent reserves for a naughty child. He shook his head that someone like me had gotten myself so deeply involved in this mess. The lawyer

Remo had hired to represent me leaned over and reminded Judge Severino that the two men the police were really after were currently in custody.

The judge brushed him away. For a split second a mad urge came over me. I would tell him that the two FBI agents at the back of the room were planning on taking me out of the country against my wishes and under false pretenses. I bit my tongue. I knew that the FBI's influence was such that no one—not even Severino—would dare challenge their authority. He held my gaze without a glimmer of patience or compassion.

Remo had assured me that my case would be dismissed, since I had never been formally charged with a crime. Severino made a brief statement to the court, then handed down a caution and a fifty-peso fine. I struggled not to show any emotion as the verdict was announced. I had escaped with a fine and a slap on the wrist.

Court was adjourned, but I felt no relief. This had been the easy part. The next few minutes would prove pivotal. I walked as non-chalantly as possible to the back of the room. Peterson and Navarro descended upon me immediately and ushered me into the hallway outside. Peterson tried to assume an expression of joviality, but the strain was obvious under his phony smile. I was his star witness and he'd already let one of his quarry slip through his fingers.

"You must be relieved that's behind you, Marisa," Peterson said.

"Yes," I agreed, picking up my pace, "because I need to use the bathroom."

Peterson caught up with me and hooked his arm through mine. He wasn't going to let me go that easily. Instead he tried to swerve me toward the side exit, which was only meters away. "We'll have you home soon," he cooed. "You'll have plenty of time to freshen up before the flight leaves."

I stopped dead, looked him straight in the eye. "Jack, I just spent two weeks locked in a holding cell with twenty women, no running water, a hole in the floor for a toilet, and no privacy whatsoever. I'm not kidding when I say I have to use the bathroom."

I broke free of him and marched toward the ladies' room, my

breath coming in short, ragged huffs. *Please . . . please . . . please . . .*
To my dismay, Peterson followed me inside, his face filled with suspicion. Having already lost Remo, he wasn't going to take any chances. He needed me to testify against Ron, or at least provide a sworn affidavit. I waited anxiously as Peterson inspected the bathroom to make sure there was no other exit. It was a small room, with two stalls and a window too small and high to be used as an exit. When he was satisfied, he smiled apologetically and left me alone.

I knocked slightly on the left-most stall. With a click it was unlocked from the inside.

Rosa let me in.

We had no time to waste. Rosa pulled my T-shirt over my head as I kicked off my sneakers and rolled up my jeans. She placed a pair of sandals in front of me, and I jammed my feet into them while she wrestled a long cotton sundress over my head, making sure it completely concealed the jeans. Next came my auburn wig. I pulled it onto my head and smoothed it down hurriedly.

Rosa stuffed the discarded clothes into a plastic bag. She handed me a purse, whispered, "Good luck," then slipped out of the stall and left the bathroom.

I put on a pair of sunglasses and took a deep breath. My heart was pounding so loudly I could barely hear anything else. I felt faint, sick from adrenaline. I opened the door and calmly walked out, holding the purse with both my hands in an effort to conceal how much they were shaking.

Navarro and Peterson were valiantly helping Rosa to her feet after she had conveniently tripped next to them. I doubled back down the corridor, past the courtroom and toward the main entrance. The urge to run was overwhelming, but I walked slowly with my feet turned slightly inwards, just as Remo had instructed.

"A person's stride is unique," he had coached me. "So change your gait; walk differently. And for God's sake, don't look over your shoulder."

I kept advancing down the busy corridor, forging stiffly through a group of people milling around by the courtyard. The guard who had only an hour ago escorted me to the courtroom paid no attention to me as I walked past. My mouth was dry and my palms sweaty as I walked out of the main entrance and into the glorious early-morning sunshine. It felt exhilarating to be outside again after weeks cooped up in the prison's gloom. I could scarcely believe that the plan had gone so smoothly. I was only a short walk away from freedom now. All I had to do was stay calm as I waited for Remo to drive around the corner to collect me. In another few minutes we would be on our way to his "uncle's" place in Cabarete, on the north shore of the island.

My heart leapt as I recognized the vehicle Remo had described. With tinted windows, it appeared to be four different models of car haphazardly welded together. In other words, it looked like every other car in the country, except for the tiny telltale Dominican flag attached to the radio antenna.

I began descending the broad staircase from the courthouse entrance, trying to blend in with a group of women in front of me.

Just a little farther . . .

I heard the heart-stopping sound of running feet. For a moment everything seemed to freeze. I realized that Navarro and Peterson were looking for me already, much faster than I'd anticipated. They must have checked the bathroom and realized I'd escaped. We were now engaged in a frantic game of cat-and-mouse. I heard their approach as they pounded down the stairs, their footfalls getting closer and closer. I forced myself not to run. If I did, they'd pick me out from the crowd straightaway. It took every ounce of self-control I had, but I kept my steps slow and even.

They were closer now. Only a few feet away from me.

"Fuck!"

Peterson was standing right behind me, scanning the crowd for a short-haired blonde in blue jeans. I kept walking, steadily, casually. He was completely unaware that the brunette in the sundress was me.

"Goddammit!"

The rage in his voice was terrifying. I kept walking calmly toward the car, which was parked fifty meters away on the other side of the street. I heard Navarro next, yelling at Peterson to come check the other exit again. I allowed myself to breathe again when I heard their frantic steps heading back up the stairs.

We did it! I could scarcely believe we had pulled off the escape.

Just then I heard Justine's voice, as clear as a bell, calling out to me from the idling car.

"Mommy! Mommy!"

The door burst open and she bolted out of it, right into the street. Rosa jumped out and pulled her back inside, but it was too late. Dominican children don't call their mothers "Mommy."

I heard Navarro yell, *"She's over there!"*

I glanced behind me. Peterson and Navarro were hurtling down the steps toward me, pushing people out of the way and yelling at me to stop. With a kick of adrenaline I started to run for the car, but tripped over my sandals. I regained my footing and shook them off, sprinting barefoot across the warm tarmac to the car. I vaguely heard a screech of brakes and the furious honking of a horn as a taxi almost hit me. I kept on running, oblivious to the driver's furious curses. All I could hear were Peterson's footsteps as he bounded after me. He was gaining on me. I wasn't going to make it.

Suddenly Remo jumped out of the front seat.

"You have no legal hold over her!" he screamed at Peterson before he took off running in the opposite direction, sprinting alongside the row of vendors who were selling their wares on the busy sidewalk. Peterson shifted his focus from me, and took off in hot pursuit of Remo.

Navarro was a few paces behind me. I wrenched the door open and dove inside. I pushed the lock down moments before Navarro reached the car. He began wrenching at the door. Rosa screamed and from the corner of my eye, I saw him reaching into his holster for his gun. I twisted the key in the ignition. The engine turned over. I crushed the stick into first gear and floored the gas. We took off along Avenida Fabio Fiallo with a screech of rubber, leaving Navarro flailing in the street.

Justine squealed with happiness and reached forward to grab me around my neck. Rosa had to hold her back. We weren't out of the woods yet. Although we hadn't anticipated the plan going quite so wrong, thankfully Remo had the foresight to discuss a backup plan. I knew exactly where he would be heading.

"Hold on!"

I rounded the next corner at full speed, just as if I were driving in the Can-A-Mex rally again. I didn't slow down until we had entered the back parking lot at the Clinica Abreu. I pulled up in front of the emergency room entrance.

Please. Please be okay . . .

I prayed that Remo had managed to lose Peterson among the labyrinthine hallways and corridors of the clinic. Like me, Remo knew that hospital like the back of his hand. If he was able to out-pace Peterson even for a few seconds, he would have a significant advantage.

I kept my eyes glued to the building. I knew that with each passing second the likelihood that Remo had escaped was diminishing. My heart thumped in my chest and I gripped the steering wheel. I would not leave without Remo. I couldn't.

Come on . . .

With a crash the emergency room doors burst open and Remo came flying into the parking lot. His head swiveled from side to side as he searched for the car. I took off in his direction, pulled up and flung open the passenger door. As Remo dove inside, I saw Peterson sprinting out of the clinic. Remo slammed the door shut and I pulled away with a screech, leaving a trail of smoke and burning rubber behind.

"We did it!" I screamed. In the rearview mirror I caught one final glimpse of Special Agent Jack Peterson—his face a mask of utter disbelief—as we tore away, our euphoric cheers still hanging in the air.

I turned the corner and eased into the monolithic morning traffic. Our car instantly became anonymous as we joined the sea of similar vehicles on the appropriately named Avenida Independencia.

EPILOGUE

I REMAINED IN SANTO Domingo long after Ron and Tony were deported. My permanent residency came through, and I managed to land a coveted job with Kraft General Foods. With my life back on track, I planned to stay on the island. But as the 1996 elections approached, violence once again plagued the country. It was time for me to leave.

Ron Sacco received the longest-ever sentence secured by the United States for a bookmaking offense. Six of Sacco's former clerks testified against him, and Ron spent the next five-and-a-half years in prison. After his release he moved to Costa Rica, where he joined CRIS (Costa Rica International Sports), the company founded by several of his former employees in his absence. Hundreds of bookmaking operations followed, making Costa Rica the new center of online gaming in the Americas.

Tony served three years' house arrest in Red Bluff, California, before accepting an offer to manage another offshore gambling operation.

As for Remo, I heard rumors that he took over his "uncle's" business in Cabarete. That's where I like to think of him: on the beach, running a little restaurant under a thatched awning, happily creating dishes for the tourists. But sometimes, walking down a street in a city somewhere, I'll spot a face in a crowd that reminds me of him, and wonder if our paths might ever cross again.

GLOSSARY

Action   A bet of any kind.

Agent   A person responsible for paying and collecting for a group of players.

Beard   Someone who places a bet for someone else in order to conceal or protect the identity of the real bettor.

Bet   To risk money on the outcome of an event.

Book   An establishment that accepts bets on sporting events.

Bookmaker   Someone who accepts bets.

Buck   One hundred dollars.

Buy (Points)   When a player pays an additional price to receive half a point or more in his favor on a point spread game.

Cap   The maximum amount a player is permitted to lose.

Chalk   The favorite.

Chalk Player   Someone who usually plays the favored teams.

Circled Game   A game with reduced betting action because of injuries, bad weather, propositions, or halves of games. These games cannot be included in parlays or teasers.

Charter   The person who changes the point spreads on games based on how the players are betting.

Clerk   The person reading lines and taking bets from players.

Computer Group   The group of bettors, led by computer expert Ivan Mindlin, who came up with their own point spread and collectively bet millions on their picks. Also referred to as Ivy, as in Ivy League.

Cover   A point spread win.

Cut Off   When a player is no longer permitted to place bets with a bookmaker.

Dime   A thousand-dollar sports-betting wager.

Dog   The team perceived to be most likely to lose.

Dog Player   A player who usually bets on the underdog.

Dollar   One hundred dollars.

Edge   A person's advantage when it comes to sports betting.

Even Money   A bet whose odds are 1/1.

Exotic   A wager other than a straight bet or parlay; also referred to as a prop or proposition.

Favorite   The team expected to win an event.

Figure   The amount owed to or by a bookmaker.

Follower   A player who bet the same on games as the Computer Group.

Future   Odds that are posted in advance of a major sporting event including the Super Bowl, the World Series, the Stanley Cup, and the NBA Championship. This is called a Future bet.

Gamble   To risk money on the outcome of an event.

Grader   A person who determines which tickets won or lost.

Handicapper   Someone who predicts the outcome of a sporting event based on statistics.

Hot Game   A game that is drawing a lot of action on one side.

Hook   A half-point.

Juice   The bookmaker's commission on a losing bet, also known as "vigorish" or "vig."

Line   The current odds or point spread on a particular event.

Lock   A sure bet.

Master   The document used to keep track of a player's current balance.

Listed Pitchers   A baseball bet which will be placed only if both of the pitchers scheduled to start a game actually start. If they don't, the bet is cancelled.

Long Shot   A team or horse perceived to be unlikely to win.

Middle   To win both sides of the same contest in a sports-betting event. Betting on the underdog at one point spread and the favorite at a different point spread, and winning both sides.

Nickel   Five hundred dollars.

No Action   A wager in sports betting in which no money is lost nor won.

Odds   The likelihood of an outcome occurring, stated in numbers form.

Off the Board   A game that a bookmaker will not accept bets on.

One Dollar   A hundred dollars.

Opening Line   The earliest line posted for a particular sporting event.

Over   A bet that the combined point total of two teams will be above the specified total number of points predicted.

Parlay   A bet with two or more teams in which all teams must win or cover for the bettor to win and receive higher payouts.

Pick 'Em   When neither team is favored. Also called a "pick."

Player   A person placing a bet.

Point Spread   The predicted scoring differential between two opponents.

Price   The odds or point spread.

Push   When a game ends with no winner or loser.

Rip 'Em   The act of separating the original ticket from its carbon copy.

Round Robin   A series of three or more teams in 2-team parlays.

Run Down   To read the odds for the games on the schedule.

Run Numbers   When two graders compare answers on the result of the previous day's tickets.

Sharp   A knowledgeable or professional gambler.

Spread   The predicted scoring differential between two opponents as quoted by a sports book.

Straight Bet   A single bet on one team.

Straight-up   Winning a game without any regard to the point spread.

Taking the Points   Betting on the underdog, and its advantage in the point spread.

Teaser   A bet in which you combine the bets and adjust the point spread or total of each individual play.

Ticket   The slip of paper a sports-betting wager is written on.

Tie   A wager in which no money is lost nor won because the teams' scores were equal to the number of points in the given line.

Total   The combined number of runs, points, or goals scored by both teams during the game, including overtime.

Under   A wager in which the bettor guesses that the total points scored by two teams will be under a certain figure.

Underdog   The team perceived to be most likely to lose. Also known as the "dog."

Wager   To risk money on the outcome of an event.

Wise Guy   A knowledgeable bettor, handicapper, or professional bettor.

(Some of these definitions are from Doc's Sports Service.)

9 783906 196046